Toward
Free Trade
in the Americas

Toward
Free Trade
in the Americas

José Manuel Salazar-Xirinachs
Maryse Robert

Editors

ORGANIZATION OF AMERICAN STATES

BROOKINGS INSTITUTION PRESS
Washington, D.C.

Copyright © 2001
GENERAL SECRETARIAT/ORGANIZATION OF AMERICAN STATES

Library of Congress Cataloging-in-Publication data

Toward free trade in the Americas / José Manuel Salazar-Xirinachs and
    Maryse Robert, editors.
        p.   cm.
    Includes bibliographical references and index.
    ISBN 0-8157-0089-X
    1. Free trade—America. 2. America—Commerce. 3. America—Economic
integration. I. Salazar X., José Manuel (Salazar Xirinachs) II. Robert, Maryse.

HF1745.T69 2001
382'.71'097—dc21   2001000443

9 8 7 6 5 4 3 2 1

The paper used in this publication meets minimum requirements of the American National Standard for Information Sciences—Permanence of Paper for Printed Library Materials: ANSI Z39.48-1992.

Typeset in Adobe Garamond

Composition by Cynthia Stock
Silver Spring, Maryland

Printed by Phoenix Color
Hagerstown, Maryland

Contents

v

Part III. Trade Rules in the Americas

Part IV. The Road Ahead: The Free Trade Area of the Americas

Foreword

During the past five years, the Organization of American States (OAS) has been closely involved, through its Trade Unit, in trade policy and economic integration issues in the Western Hemisphere. An important part of the work of the Trade Unit is to provide technical and analytical support to the negotiations for the establishment of the Free Trade Area of the Americas (FTAA) and to develop technical cooperation activities for countries of the region. In performing this mission, and in reflecting on its own experience, the team of experts at the Trade Unit has in recent years produced a significant number of contributions to the analysis of trade issues, including several books and numerous studies.

This is the third volume produced by the Trade Unit and published jointly with the Brookings Institution Press. The first, *Trade Rules in the Making: Challenges in Regional and Multilateral Negotiations*, edited by Miguel Rodríguez, Patrick Low, and Barbara Kotschwar and published in 1999, contains a series of articles written by Trade Unit staff and other recognized experts on issues related to the consistency of regional agreements, in particular the FTAA, with the World Trade Organization.

The second volume, *Services Trade in the Western Hemisphere: Liberalization, Integration, and Reform*, edited by Sherry Stephenson, deputy director of the Trade Unit, and published in 2000, discusses the challenges of liberalizing, integrating, and reforming trade in services in the Western Hemisphere. Although much has been written about services trade negotiations at the multilateral level, this volume represents a pioneering effort by distinguished experts in the field to analyze the linkages between the multilateral, regional (FTAA), and subregional (MERCOSUR, the Caribbean, the Central American Common Market, the Andean Community, and the North American Free Trade Agreement) approaches to services trade liberalization.

The purpose of the present volume, edited by José Manuel Salazar-Xirinachs and Maryse Robert, respectively director and senior trade specialist at the Trade Unit, is to describe and analyze recent trends, current developments, and future prospects of trade agreements and integration efforts among countries of the Western Hemisphere at the turn of the century.

One of the most radical and positive changes in the Americas during the 1990s was the reorientation and revitalization of countries' trade policy. This volume describes and analyzes these changes, distinguishing three spheres in which the forms of interdependence between countries in the hemisphere have been redefined. The first sphere pertains to business activities, as reflected in trade and investment flows between countries of the Americas and with the rest of the world. The second sphere relates to the new web of trade agreements. These new agreements are not only broader in terms of the issues they cover and deeper in terms of their market access provisions, but also more effective in integrating markets, since they touch upon various forms of domestic regulation excluded from international commitments in the past. Finally, going beyond the strictly economic incentives for economic integration, a number of chapters in this book analyze the new political and collective security rationale that also drives the integration process, particularly within the framework of the inter-American system and the Summit of the Americas process.

It should be noted that the editors and authors of this book relied on a common methodology in describing recent trends and current developments of existing trade agreements and in analyzing the various functional areas of trade negotiations. This common structure makes this book especially useful as a basic reference tool. It not only provides an overview of integration processes in the Americas as of the year 2001, but also identifies areas of convergence and divergence among the various trade agreements and enumerates the main challenges faced for the entire spectrum of issues under consideration in trade negotiations, in particular the FTAA.

The General Secretariat of the Organization of American States takes great pleasure in presenting this book, which is being published simultaneously in English and Spanish. We trust it will prove useful for trade negotiators, entrepreneurs, members of the academic community, students, and more generally, the various sectors of society interested in the complex realities and challenges of trade policy and negotiations in the Americas at the turn of the century.

César Gaviria
Secretary General
Organization of American States

Acknowledgments

The publication of this book is very much the result of a team effort by the members of the OAS Trade Unit. Their commitment and enthusiasm for this volume, published simultaneously in English and Spanish, made the realization of this project possible. We are particularly indebted to all the contributors for taking the time from their busy schedule to bring us a comprehensive overview of the progress to date in moving toward free trade in the Americas.

Karsten Steinfatt deserves our deepest gratitude for his professionalism and dedication to this project. He edited numerous chapters of the book and coordinated with us the publication of this volume from beginning to end. We are also grateful to Sherry Stephenson, Theresa Wetter, and César Parga for reviewing several chapters and providing helpful comments, and to Francisco Coves, Ivonne Zúniga, and Sandra Burns for their invaluable assistance in all other aspects of this project.

Special thanks are due to Christopher Kelaher and Janet Walker of the Brookings Institution Press for their efforts and good humor in managing the editing process in a timely fashion. We would also like to express our gratitude to Marty Gottron for her very useful suggestions in copyediting and improving the manuscript, to Susan Woollen for coordinating the development of the cover, and to Rebecca Clark for promoting this book to a large market.

Finally, we would like to emphasize that neither the Organization of American States nor its member states are accountable for any errors, omissions, or statements made in this book. This responsibility lies with the editors and authors of this volume.

Toward
Free Trade
in the Americas

JOSÉ MANUEL SALAZAR-XIRINACHS
MARYSE ROBERT

1 | *Introduction*

Latin America and the Caribbean experienced nothing less than an economic revolution in the 1990s. The market-oriented reforms that these countries had begun to implement in the mid-1980s helped revitalize their economies, led to more sustainable growth, and reshaped the network of economic relations among them. As unilateral trade liberalization measures have become firmly entrenched and countries have achieved greater economic stability, a new framework within which to conduct regional trade and investment relations has gradually been established. Along with North America, Latin America and the Caribbean have negotiated modern free trade agreements that go beyond the elimination of tariffs and nontariff barriers in goods to include provisions on services, investment, intellectual property, government procurement, and dispute settlement; and they have entered into deeper and wider forms of integration at the subregional level. Both the North American Free Trade Agreement (NAFTA) and the Common Market of the South (MERCOSUR) were created in the 1990s, and the average tariff for Latin America and the Caribbean has been reduced from around 35 percent in the early 1990s to approximately 10 percent today.

Trade liberalization was further enhanced when the thirty-four democratically elected governments of the hemisphere met at the First Summit

1

of the Americas held in Miami in December 1994 and agreed to start working toward the creation of the Free Trade Area of the Americas (FTAA) in which barriers to trade and investment among the participating countries will be progressively eliminated. The decision to conclude negotiations no later than 2005 is a clear sign of a firm commitment to trade liberalization.

This book is about the changes in trade policies and regimes in the Americas during the 1990s. The objective of *Toward Free Trade in the Americas* is to take stock of the progress to date in advancing free trade in the region. The volume examines trade flows between countries within regional groupings and between members of different subregional arrangements, and it discusses the relative importance of trade in services in the Western Hemisphere and the substantial increase in foreign direct investment flows to the Americas. It describes the main characteristics of the trade arrangements signed between countries of the hemisphere and explores the development of trade rules in these arrangements, as well as the areas of convergence and divergence, and the main challenges faced in the FTAA negotiations. Finally, the book reports on the recent developments in the construction of the Free Trade Area of the Americas and concludes with a discussion on the noneconomic dimension of interdependence in the hemisphere. This book shows that interdependence among the countries of the Americas has increased in three related realms: business activities as reflected in trade and investment flows; legal commitments and regulatory frameworks necessary to implement a free trade regime; and what could be called strategic interdependence.

More specifically, the book is organized in four parts. Part one reviews the main trends in trade and investment flows in the Americas, in general and by subregion. Structural changes in trade and investment flows have been closely associated not only with trade liberalization and economic reforms, but also with a new phenomenon in the area of trade negotiations: the expansion of international positive rule-making and its incorporation into domestic legislation. Part two covers all the trade agreements signed between countries in the Americas. It describes their origin (history and membership) and institutional framework, provides a brief history of their main obligations, and discusses the latest developments as of December 2000, including a description of negotiations in progress. Trade agreements are grouped according to the following typology: customs unions (Central American Common Market; Andean Community; Caribbean Community and Common Market, or CARICOM; and MERCOSUR), free trade agreements (NAFTA and other free trade agreements), and nonreciprocal preferential trade agreements (Caribbean Basin Initiative, the Andean Trade Preference

Act, CARIBCAN, CARICOM-Colombia, and CARICOM-Venezuela) and partial-scope agreements (negotiated under the framework of the Latin American Integration Association, or ALADI, in Spanish) (table 1-1).

Part three examines the evolution, current situation, and main challenges in key disciplines covered by all the trade arrangements described in part two. The discipline areas include trade in goods and agriculture, which covers issues such as tariffs and nontariff barriers, rules of origin, and safeguard measures; standards and technical barriers to trade; services; investment; intellectual property rights; competition policy; government procurement; and dispute settlement. Each chapter in part three of this volume identifies the main challenges for hemispheric free trade in its respective issue area.

Two areas are worth highlighting here. In the area of services, more and more countries are recognizing the importance of an efficient service sector for growth and economic development. As a result no fewer than fourteen agreements negotiated in the 1990s between countries of the region have incorporated rules, disciplines, and mechanisms to advance toward liberalization of the services sectors. Even though the approach used to negotiate liberalization varies among some agreements, there are important commonalities in the normative content of these instruments. In addition, a majority of them have ambitious objectives that go well beyond the goals contemplated in the World Trade Organization's General Agreement on Trade in Services, either because they contain more strict disciplines or because they aim at a more extensive degree of liberalization.

The modern trade agreements negotiated in the 1990s have also incorporated investment disciplines with many common elements. Like traditional agreements in this field, they seek to strengthen the standards of protection to investments and investors and provide an effective dispute settlement mechanism between the investor and the state in which the investment is located. A growing number of the agreements signed in the 1990s go beyond this objective, however, and recognize a "right of establishment" for the investor. In so doing they incorporate a market access component that was not present in previous agreements. Together with the growing number of bilateral investment treaties in force in the region, these new agreements have formed an extensive normative network among countries in the Americas in an area where multilateral disciplines have yet to be negotiated.

In addition to services and investment, the other positive rule-making areas covered in individual chapters are trade in goods and agriculture, standards and technical barriers to trade, intellectual property rights,

Table 1-1. *Customs Unions and Free Trade Agreements in the Western Hemisphere*

Agreement	Signed	Entered into force
Customs unions		
Andean Community	May 26, 1969[a]	Oct. 16, 1969
CARICOM (Caribbean Community and Common Market)[b]	July 4, 1973	Aug. 1, 1973
CACM (Central American Common Market)	Dec. 13, 1960	June 4, 1961[c]
MERCOSUR (Common Market of the South)[d]	March 26, 1991	Jan. 1, 1995
Free trade agreements		
NAFTA (North American Free Trade Agreement)[e]	Dec. 17, 1992	Jan. 1, 1994
Costa Rica-Mexico	April 15, 1994	Jan. 1, 1995
Group of Three (Colombia, Mexico, Venezuela)	June 13, 1994[f]	Jan. 1, 1995
Bolivia-Mexico	Sept. 10, 1994	Jan. 1, 1995
Canada-Chile	Dec. 5, 1996	July 5, 1997
Mexico-Nicaragua	Dec. 18, 1997	July 1, 1998
Central America-Dominican Republic	April 16, 1998[g]	. . .
Chile-Mexico	April 17, 1998[h]	Aug. 1, 1999
CARICOM-Dominican Republic	Aug. 22, 1998[i]	. . .
Central America-Chile	Oct. 18, 1999[j]	. . .
Mexico-Northern Triangle (El Salvador, Guatemala, Honduras)	June 29, 2000	. . .
Andean Community-MERCOSUR	In negotiation	. . .
Central America-Panama	In negotiation	. . .
Chile-United States	In negotiation	. . .
Costa Rica-Canada	In negotiation	. . .
Mexico-Ecuador	In negotiation	. . .
Mexico-Panama	In negotiation	. . .
Mexico-Peru	In negotiation	. . .
Mexico-Trinidad and Tobago	In negotiation	. . .

a. With the signing of the Trujillo Protocol in 1996 and the Sucre Protocol in 1997, the five Andean countries—Bolivia, Colombia, Ecuador, Peru, and Venezuela—restructured and revitalized their regional integration efforts under the name Andean Community.

b. The members of the Caribbean Community are: Antigua and Barbuda, The Bahamas, Barbados, Belize, Dominica, Grenada, Guyana, Jamaica, St. Kitts and Nevis, St. Lucia, St. Vincent and the Grenadines, Suriname, Trinidad and Tobago, and Montserrat (an overseas territory of the United Kingdom). The Bahamas is a member of the Caribbean Community, though not the Common Market. Haiti will become the fifteenth member of CARICOM once it deposits its instruments of accession with the group's secretary general. The British Virgin Islands and the Turks and Caicos Islands count as associate members of CARICOM.

competition policy, government procurement, and dispute settlement. The detailed analyses in these chapters of each subject area paint a complete picture of the legal and rule-based dimension of interdependence in the Western Hemisphere.

Part four contains an overview of the progress achieved in the FTAA negotiations between April 1998, when these negotiations were launched at the Summit of the Americas in Santiago, and early 2001 as heads of state and government prepare to meet again in Quebec City in April 2001. It argues that even though the main benefits of the FTAA will not accrue to countries until this agreement comes into effect, the FTAA negotiating process has already generated a number of important benefits or positive externalities. Part four also argues that the challenge of the next four years will be to maintain the momentum driving the negotiations forward and to continue to narrow the various negotiating positions so that common ground is reached and a "clean" text is achieved in all areas. Equally important is the need to address the institutional issues required for the agreement to become operational. A major change of gear in the negotiations is envisaged the moment countries decide to initiate market access negotiations for both goods and services.

Part four also examines the different components of the complex new matrix of interdependence that characterizes international relations among the countries of the Americas. The new agenda of hemispheric cooperation

---

c. The agreement entered into force on this date for El Salvador, Guatemala, and Nicaragua; on April 27, 1962, for Honduras; and on September 23, 1963, for Costa Rica. With the signing of the Tegucigalpa Protocol in 1991 and the Guatemala Protocol in 1996, the countries of the Central American Common Market—El Salvador, Costa Rica, Guatemala, Honduras, and Nicaragua—restructured and revitalized their regional integration efforts.

d. The members are Argentina, Brazil, Paraguay, and Uruguay.

e. Before signing NAFTA, Canada and the United States had concluded the Canada-U.S. Free Trade Agreement, which entered into force on January 1, 1989.

f. Chapters III (national treatment and market access for goods), IV (automotive sector), V (Sec. A) (agricultural sector), VI (rules of origin), VIII (safeguards), IX (unfair practices in international trade), XVI (state enterprises), and XVIII (intellectual property) do not apply between Colombia and Venezuela. See Article 103 (1) of the agreement.

g. This agreement applies bilaterally between each Central American country and the Dominican Republic.

h. On September 22, 1991, Chile and Mexico had signed a free trade agreement within the framework of the Latin American Integration Association (ALADI).

i. A protocol to implement the agreement was signed on April 28, 2000.

j. This agreement applies bilaterally between each Central American country and Chile.

promoted by the Summit of the Americas process and by the inter-American system on issues that range from the protection of democracy and human rights to the fight against corruption and drug trafficking add an element of rationality and commitment, not only economic, but also political and strategic to economic integration processes in general and to the FTAA negotiations in particular. Thus these negotiations not only are different in some fundamental ways from the WTO process, but they also are advancing in a very different political context in terms of systemic interdependencies, cooperative initiatives among the eventual partners, and institutional instrumentalities. They are part of the broader strategic agenda of hemispheric cooperation as well as of the general legal architecture of the inter-American system. Among other points, it is argued that this strategic agenda provides opportunities for the creation of the Free Trade Area of the Americas, for buttressing its rationale, and for building support for it— opportunities that are not present in other trade forums.

PART I

Trade and Investment Flows: Hemispheric Trends

KARSTEN STEINFATT
PATRICIO CONTRERAS

2 | *Trade and Investment Flows in the Americas*

The picture of economic integration in the Western Hemisphere has changed dramatically in the last fifteen years. The wide-ranging and ambitious market-oriented reforms that most Latin American and Caribbean countries implemented in the 1980s have not only reinvigorated existing regional integration arrangements, but have also led to the creation of new integration schemes throughout the hemisphere. This transformed economic landscape has energized competition among private actors, triggering the movement of goods, services, and capital across the hemisphere's borders on a scale largely unseen in previous decades.

This chapter identifies and examines the principal trends in trade and investment flows characterizing the new landscape of economic integration in the Western Hemisphere. The first section analyzes the direction of merchandise trade both from a general, hemispheric perspective and from the perspectives of five regional integration schemes: the Andean Community, the Central American Common Market (CACM), the Caribbean

Karsten Steinfatt wrote the section on merchandise trade, and Patricio Contreras wrote the sections on trade in services and investment. Karsten Steinfatt wishes to thank Paola Andrea Fernández Otero for her able research assistance and Dr. Philomen Harrison of the CARICOM Secretariat for providing data on CARICOM trade flows.

9

Community and Common Market (CARICOM), the Common Market of the South (MERCOSUR), and the North American Free Trade Agreement (NAFTA). One of the most forceful points emerging from the analysis is that the concerted liberalization efforts undertaken by countries within these integration arrangements have been supportive of, and complementary to, both the unilateral and multilateral trade liberalization initiatives pursued by these countries during the 1980s and 1990s.

Although severe data limitations in the domain of services trade stand in the way of a detailed analysis, the second section seeks to provide an overview of the pattern of trade in services in the hemisphere and discusses the role this trade plays in different economies of the region. The third section shows how investment flows, largely unheard of a few years ago, are playing an increasingly significant role in hemispheric economic integration.

General Patterns of Merchandise Trade in the Hemisphere

Both as a producer of goods and as a market for the products of various other regions of the world, the Western Hemisphere is more than ever before a major player in the sphere of international commercial relations. In 1999 the region's total trade (imports and exports) in goods amounted to more than $2.8 trillion—one-quarter of total world trade.[1] The hemisphere absorbed 12 percent of the European Union's total exports and almost 30 percent of Asia's, while 16 percent of all goods exported by countries in the Americas found their way to markets in the European Union, and another 16 percent to markets in Asia.

This picture is partly the result of new trade policies implemented by the vast majority of countries in the hemisphere since the mid-1980s. Although the Americas witnessed a remarkable expansion of trade in the 1970s, that expansion took place behind high tariff walls erected around regional integration initiatives such as the Latin American Free Trade Association and the Andean Group. These initiatives fueled the growth of intraregional trade but did very little to expose domestic producers to the winds of international competition.

Toward the end of the 1970s and the beginning of the 1980s, demand for developing country exports slowed as a result of the second oil shock and the ensuing recession and inflation in the developed world. Domestic markets were not sufficiently large to compensate for slowed export de-

---

1. All monetary units in this book are given in U.S. dollars unless otherwise specified.

mand and to allow countries to deepen import-substitution industrialization strategies. Consequently many countries in Latin America and the Caribbean began to embark upon ambitious economic reform programs that sought to replace strategies of protected, state-assisted industrialization with outward-oriented, export-driven approaches to development. As these reforms gathered pace, trade flows in the Western Hemisphere began a period of steady and vigorous growth. Between 1987 and 1999, total trade in the hemisphere expanded by 170 percent. The growth of trade in Latin America and the Caribbean was even more dramatic, increasing by more than 250 percent during the same period, a testament to the depth of the liberalization efforts undertaken by the vast majority of countries in the region.

Trade growth in Latin America and the Caribbean decelerated in the late 1990s. Total trade in 1998 grew by a meager 3 percent, and declined by more than 2.5 percent in 1999. This short-term trend should not be construed as a shift away from the region's efforts to build more open markets. Rather, the slower growth of imports and exports needs to be viewed against the backdrop of adverse economic circumstances prevailing around the world, most notably falling commodity prices, a global financial crisis, and a decline in demand for Latin American and Caribbean imports in a majority of advanced economies. Finally, natural disasters, particularly Hurricane Mitch, also affected the capacity of some countries in the region to sustain the high rates of trade growth they had been experiencing. Notwithstanding this adverse economic climate, not all countries were affected to the same degree. Member countries of MERCOSUR and the Andean Community experienced the most drastic falls in exports, whereas countries with closer trade ties to the buoyant U.S. economy—Mexico and Central America, for example—were able to weather some or all of the unfavorable conditions.

Looking at the data for the entire decade, not just the last two or three years, sheds further light on the central and growing role played by trade and economic interdependence in the region. Between 1990 and 1999, imports to Latin America and the Caribbean grew, on average, almost three times as fast as did imports to Africa or the Middle East and almost twice as fast as did imports to Asia. During the same period, Latin America and the Caribbean's export growth averaged 8 percent a year, the second highest among all regions of the world.

The growing importance of trade for the Western Hemisphere has been accompanied by a higher degree of economic integration among the countries of the region, as evidenced by the steady increase in the level of intraregional trade since 1987. Today, almost 60 percent of the region's total exports are destined for the countries of the Western Hemisphere, roughly six times more than the level of intraregional trade among the Arab countries and almost twice the level among the East Asian economies. The only region in the world with a level of intraregional trade comparable to that of the Western Hemisphere is the European Union.

To a large extent, the high level of trade among countries of the hemisphere is driven by trade among the three NAFTA partners, Canada, Mexico, and the United States; that trade accounted for almost three-quarters of total intrahemispheric trade in 1999. Countries in Latin America and the Caribbean have increasingly become major export destinations for each other's products, however. Between 1987 and 1998 intraregional exports in Latin America and the Caribbean as a share of total exports have increased by one-third, to 20 percent from around 15 percent, only slightly lower than the corresponding share of exports among China, Indonesia, Japan, Malaysia, the Philippines, the Republic of Korea, and Thailand taken as a group. This indicates a very significant degree of economic interdependence between Latin American countries.

A more disaggregated view of the region's trade patterns sheds light on the structure of trade among the countries of the Western Hemisphere. As table 2-1 shows, of the twenty-seven countries of the Americas for which 1999 data are available, nineteen have their primary export market in the hemisphere. The United States is the largest single export destination for sixteen countries, Brazil for two, and Canada and Argentina for one each. For the seven remaining countries, the largest export market is the European Union, followed by the United States.

During the 1990s exports of Latin American and Caribbean countries to each other grew more rapidly than these countries' exports to the rest of the world. Whereas intraregional exports expanded, on average, by 14 percent each year between 1990 and 1999, extraregional exports grew by 10 percent each year. Meanwhile, imports to the region, both from other countries in the region and from the rest of the world, increased sharply, by an annual average of 14 percent each. As Devlin and Ffrench-Davis observed, exchange rate behavior was a major variable explaining both the import boom and the heterogeneity in the growth rates of intra- and extraregional exports in Latin America and the Caribbean.[2] Specifically, during the 1980s

2. Devlin and Ffrench-Davis (1998, p. 5).

Table 2-1. *Trade Relations of Western Hemisphere Countries, 1999*

Exporting country	Primary market	Secondary market
Barbados, Canada, Colombia, Costa Rica, Ecuador, Guatemala, Haiti, Honduras, Jamaica, Mexico, Peru, Trinidad and Tobago, Venezuela	United States	European Union
Bahamas, Brazil, Chile, Dominican Republic, Guyana, Panama, Suriname	European Union	United States
Argentina, Uruguay	Brazil	European Union
Paraguay	Argentina	Brazil
United States	Canada	European Union
El Salvador	United States	Guatemala
Nicaragua	United States	Honduras
Bolivia	United States	Peru

Source: OAS Trade Unit, based on data in IMF (various years).

the currencies of several countries in the Americas appreciated in real terms as a result of capital account liberalization and inflows of foreign capital. Stronger currencies translated into higher imports and lower exports. At the same time, stronger currencies within the region meant that extraregional exports tailed off more than did intraregional ones.

In this context it should be noted that the import boom in Latin America and the Caribbean during the 1990s, reflected in the region's high average growth rates for extraregional imports, suggests that economic integration within the hemisphere has complemented and supported countries' efforts to integrate into the world economy. Put differently, countries in the Americas have been pursuing a multilayered approach to trade policy reform, consisting not only of regional integration initiatives but also of liberalization efforts at the unilateral and multilateral levels. After fifteen years of steady progress in liberalizing their trade regimes and revitalizing trade flows, countries in the Americas constitute an example of the synergies and complementarities existing among unilateral, regional, and multilateral approaches to trade liberalization.

Merchandise Trade Patterns by Region

As already noted, countries in the Americas have been pursuing trade liberalization through a variety of channels. Prominent among these are the myriad of regional trade arrangements, including free trade agreements and other economic integration schemes such as customs unions. During the last decade the web of trade agreements has extended further than ever before and is fast reshaping the landscape of economic integration in the hemisphere.

Andean Community

During the 1970s trade among Bolivia, Colombia, Ecuador, Peru, and Venezuela, and between each one of them and the rest of the world, expanded significantly.[3] Intra- and extraregional trade increased at annual average rates in excess of 20 percent. This upward trend was reversed temporarily in the wake of the debt crisis of 1982, but Andean trade flows picked up again in the late 1980s and early 1990s, when the five countries undertook a series of initiatives to revitalize economic integration, most notably the creation of a free trade area in 1993.

As a result of these initiatives, the annual growth rate for exports from the Andean countries to each other was higher than that for Andean exports to the rest of the world during the first five years of the 1990s (figure 2-1a). In fact, all Andean countries except Peru experienced a double-digit average growth rate for intra-Andean exports for the entire decade and only an average single-digit growth rate for extra-Andean exports. Specifically, Peru's 9 percent average growth rate for exports to its Andean partners contrasts sharply with Venezuela's 20 percent and Colombia's 23 percent. At the same time, Peru's exports to the rest of the world increased, on average, by 11 percent a year between 1990 and 1997, while those of Colombia and Venezuela increased by 7 and 3 percent, respectively. One possible explanation for the divergence in export growth rates between Peru and its Andean partners might relate to the different liberalization schedules adopted by each country following calls by Andean leaders to accelerate economic integration in the region in 1990. Tariffs between Colombia and Venezuela were eliminated as early as 1992, whereas Peru, which adopted a more gradual approach to regional trade liberalization, was not scheduled to liberalize the entirety of its tariff lines vis-à-vis Andean countries until 2005.[4]

---

3. The data in this chapter cover the five members of the Andean Community—Bolivia, Colombia, Ecuador, Peru, and Venezuela. As explained in chapter 3 of this volume, the Andean Community, initially known as the Andean Pact (later called the Andean Group), counted Chile as a member until 1976. Venezuela, which was not a founding member, joined in 1973.

4. Inter-American Development Bank (1999, p. 8).

Figure 2-1. *Trends in Andean Community Trade, 1990–99*

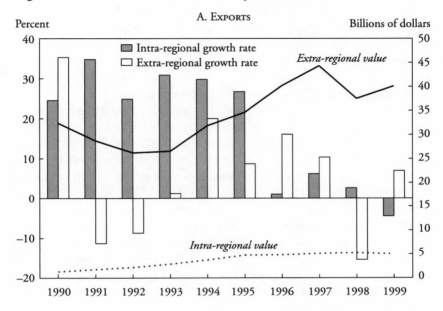

A. Exports

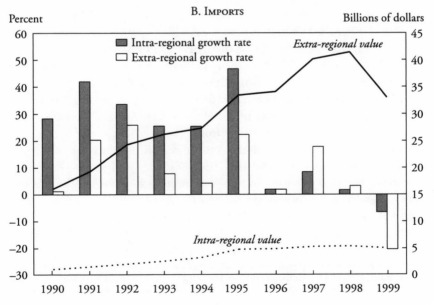

B. Imports

Source: OAS Trade Unit, based on data in IMF (various years).

In addition, Peru, more than any other Andean country, has significant trade links with Asia; between 1990 and 1997, roughly one-fourth of Peru's total exports were destined for that region.[5] It is also noteworthy that exports from Bolivia, Ecuador, and Venezuela to the Andean region grew extremely rapidly before the creation of the Andean free trade zone in 1993, perhaps as a result of higher investment in the context of economic reform measures introduced in these countries during the late 1980s.

For Colombia and Venezuela, which account for the bulk of intra-Andean exports, the importance of the Andean Community as an export market rose significantly during the first part of the 1990s. Despite wide fluctuations since then, the numbers for both countries in 1999 were roughly equal to their 1993 and 1994 levels: 14 percent of Colombian and 10 percent of Venezuelan exports were destined for the Andean region. The data also reveal how the tariff elimination program between Colombia and Venezuela, completed in early 1992, reinforced both countries' position as each other's principal trading partner within the Andean Community. In the meantime, the remaining members have seen an increase in the importance of the community as an export market, although not all rely on their Andean partners as markets for exports to the same extent. In 1999, for example, Peru and Ecuador sold between 7 and 9 percent of their total exports to the region, whereas Bolivia's intra-Andean share exceeded 35 percent.

Since 1990 the five members of the Andean Community have become more integrated not only among themselves, but also with the rest of the hemisphere, as evidenced by the rising share of hemispheric exports in their total trade. In 1999, 76 percent of the community's exports went to another country in the hemisphere, compared with 66 percent in 1990. Nearly two-thirds of Andean exports to the Western Hemisphere were bound to the NAFTA area, in particular the United States.

Andean imports from both the Andean region and the rest of the world grew vigorously between 1990 and 1999, as shown in figure 2-1b, and the difference between the growth rates for intra- and extra-Andean imports was somewhat less pronounced than in the case of exports. Intra-Andean imports increased by an average of 20 percent a year, while imports from the rest of the world increased by 9 percent. The coupling in many Andean countries of unilateral liberalization efforts with initiatives to open to regional trade may partly explain the smaller difference registered between

5. This may also explain the decline in the rate of growth of Peruvian extraregional exports after 1997, the year in which the Asian financial crisis broke out.

intra- and extraregional imports than between intra- and extraregional exports.

Countries in the Andean region now import a larger share of products from their partners in the community than they did in 1990. The increase has been particularly pronounced in Colombia and Ecuador. In Venezuela and to a lesser extent Ecuador, the increase was attributable to an increase in imports from Colombia, whereas Colombia's increase was attributable to Venezuelan imports. The surge in Bolivia's share of intraregional imports resulted mainly from higher imports from Peru. After increasing dramatically in 1991, Peru's share of intra-Andean imports, the bulk of which originate in Colombia and Venezuela, fluctuated widely and was roughly the same in 1999 as it was in 1991.

Traditionally, the Andean countries have relied extensively on the Western Hemisphere for imports, buying 60 to 65 percent of their total from the Americas. Although this figure did not change much during the 1990s, the increasing share of intra-Andean imports led to a steady decline in the share from NAFTA, from 72 percent in 1985 to 60 percent in 1999.

CARICOM

During the 1990s total trade for the countries of the Caribbean Community and Common Market (CARICOM) increased by more than one-third, from $9 billion to more than $12 billion.[6] This increase has been driven mostly by an expansion of CARICOM's imports, which grew at an annual average rate of 7 percent between 1990 and 1998. Two countries, Jamaica and Trinidad and Tobago, account for almost 80 percent of the region's total exports and about 60 percent of its imports.

As in most other regions of the hemisphere, trade among CARICOM countries increased at significantly faster rates than trade between CARICOM and the rest of the world. This asymmetry is largely a result of the uneven performance of intraregional exports, which grew at an average annual rate of 9 percent between 1990 and 1998, and extraregional exports, which on average remained almost flat throughout the period. In contrast, imports, both from CARICOM countries and from the rest of

6. The data in this section cover Antigua and Barbuda, Barbados, Belize, Dominica, Grenada, Guyana, Jamaica, Montserrat, St. Kitts and Nevis, St. Lucia, St. Vincent and the Grenadines, Trinidad and Tobago, and after June 1995, Suriname. Data for Antigua and Barbuda, Belize, Guyana, Montserrat, and St. Vincent and the Grenadines were not available for certain years.

the world, grew at roughly the same average annual rate of 7 percent between 1990 and 1998 (figure 2-2). As a result, the importance of the CARICOM market has increased for products originating in the region. In 1998 intra-CARICOM exports accounted for more than one-fifth of the group's total exports.

The United States remains the largest market for CARICOM exports, absorbing 35 percent of the region's total sales abroad. But the importance of that market has decreased significantly since 1975, when almost two-thirds of CARICOM's exports were destined for the United States. Meanwhile, the commercial links between the Caribbean and Latin America have intensified, following CARICOM's signing of trade liberalization agreements with Colombia, the Dominican Republic, and Venezuela. Between 1990 and 1998 CARICOM exports to the Andean Community and to Mexico grew at an annual average rate of 13 percent, while sales to the members of the Central American Common Market grew at an annual average of more than 20 percent. Latin America still remains a relatively minor trade partner for CARICOM, however, as only 10 percent of total CARICOM imports and 5 percent of exports originate in, or are bound for, Latin America.

Central American Common Market

During the two decades that followed the creation of the Central American Common Market in 1961, trade among the five CACM member countries and between them and the rest of the world increased steadily.[7] Between 1970 and 1980, for example, the group's total exports jumped from $1.1 billion to $4.8 billion, while imports increased from $1.2 billion to almost $6 billion. The upward trend was suddenly reversed in the early 1980s, due to economic factors and to escalating armed conflicts in the region. By 1989 imports had barely returned to precrisis levels, while exports were still $650 million below their level in 1980.

The 1990s, especially the latter half, witnessed a strong expansion of exports from Central America (figure 2-3a). Between 1990 and 1999 total exports from the region increased at an annual average rate of 17 percent, reflecting a vigorous expansion of both extra- and intraregional exports. Furthermore, and in contrast to the other regions of the Americas, during the 1990s exports from the Central American countries to the rest of the

---

7. The five members of CACM are Costa Rica, El Salvador, Guatemala, Honduras, and Nicaragua.

Figure 2-2. *Trends in CARICOM Trade, 1991–98*

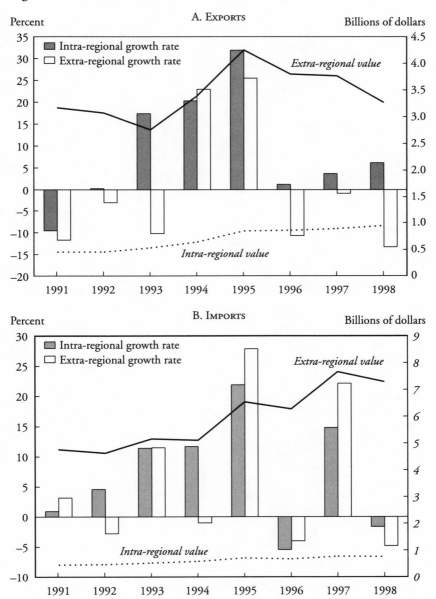

Source: OAS Trade Unit, based on data provided by the Statistics Division of the CARICOM Secretariat.

Figure 2-3. *Trends in CACM Trade, 1990–99*

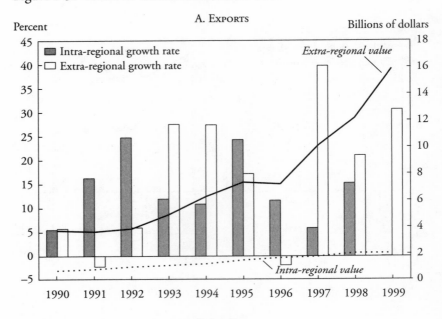

A. Exports

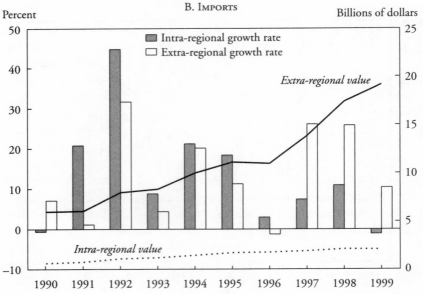

B. Imports

Source: OAS Trade Unit, based on data in IMF (various years).

world grew at a faster rate than their exports to each other. Extraregional exports grew at an average of 18 percent a year, compared with 13 percent for intraregional exports. Of the five CACM members, only Nicaragua and Honduras registered growth rates for intraregional exports significantly greater than those for extraregional ones.

Because of the higher growth of extraregional exports, exports among the Central American republics, as a percentage of total trade, are lower— 11 percent in 1999, compared with 26 percent in 1970 and 23 percent in 1980. For El Salvador, Guatemala, and Nicaragua, the CACM has been a relatively important market, absorbing between 15 percent and 30 percent of these countries' total exports during the 1990s. In contrast, Honduras and Costa Rica have sold less than 10 percent of their total exports to their CACM partners since 1990.

The United States is the largest market for exports from the CACM. In 1999 more than 55 percent of Central American exports were destined for the United States, compared with 40 percent in 1990. The importance of the other two members of NAFTA as export markets for the Central American countries has historically been minimal, as have been commercial links with the countries of the Andean Community, CARICOM, and MERCOSUR. Recently, however, Mexico has been growing in importance as a trading partner with Costa Rica.

As figure 2-3b shows, imports to Central American countries from each other and from the rest of the world have grown at similar average annual rates of about 14 percent during the 1990s. For most countries in the region, the difference between the growth rate of imports from Central America and that of imports from the rest of the world was relatively insignificant, only between one and five percentage points. A notable exception was Nicaragua, whose annual average growth rate for imports from Central America exceeded that for imports from the rest of the world by seventeen percentage points. This finding strongly suggests that countries in the area opened to world trade at the same time as they were seeking to revitalize their common market. In this regard, unilateral liberalization efforts by the five countries as well as their entry into the World Trade Organization are likely to have played a key role in boosting imports.

Central American countries differ widely in the extent to which they rely on the members of the CACM as sources of imports. In 1999, Costa Rica and Honduras bought around 5 percent of their total imports from other Central American countries; Guatemala, 9 percent; El Salvador, 14 percent; and Nicaragua, 27 percent. North America, in particular the United

States, is Central America's principal supplier of imported merchandise in the Western Hemisphere. In 1999 products originating in the United States accounted for almost 44 percent of the region's total imports. Mexico plays a relatively more important role as an import source than as an export destination for the region: during the 1990s Central American countries acquired 5 to 7 percent of their total imports from Mexico. In contrast the importance of the Andean Community as a source of imports for Central America has declined sharply: whereas in 1990 Andean products accounted for 9 percent of Central America's total imports, a decade later their share had fallen below 5 percent.

MERCOSUR

Total trade in the MERCOSUR area has expanded significantly in the past fifteen years. From $34.8 billion in 1985, total exports by Argentina, Brazil, Paraguay, and Uruguay rose to almost $75 billion in 1999. The growth of imports has been even larger, rising from less than $20 billion in 1985 to more than $80 billion in 1999. Underlying these figures are substantial efforts by the four MERCOSUR countries to liberalize their trade regimes.

Before 1991, the year in which MERCOSUR formally came into being, exports among the four members were growing slightly faster than the group's exports to the rest of the world. Between 1985 and 1990, for example, intraregional exports increased at an average annual rate of 17 percent, only two percentage points more than the annual average growth rate of extraregional imports.

The divergence between intra- and extra-MERCOSUR exports widened after the signing in 1991 of the Treaty of Asunción, which triggered a transitional program of gradual, linear, and automatic tariff reductions aimed at establishing a free trade area among the MERCOSUR countries by December 1995 (figure 2-4a). Accordingly, between 1992 and 1995, intragroup exports expanded by an annual average rate of 25 percent, compared with 8 percent for extraregional exports. Argentina's exports to other members of the group grew the fastest, averaging more than 40 percent a year. Paraguay's were also impressive, at 30 percent a year. Uruguay's exports to MERCOSUR countries grew at an average annual rate of 22 percent; Brazil's, at 15 percent.

Together, Brazil and Argentina account for more than 80 percent of total exports from MERCOSUR countries to each other. Furthermore, the

Figure 2-4. *Trends in MERCOSUR Trade, 1990–99*

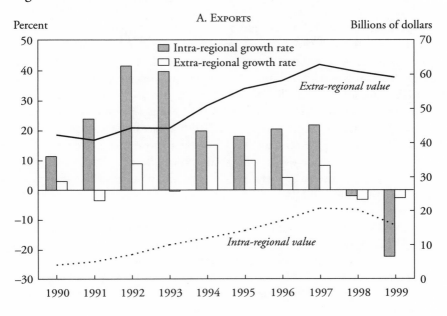

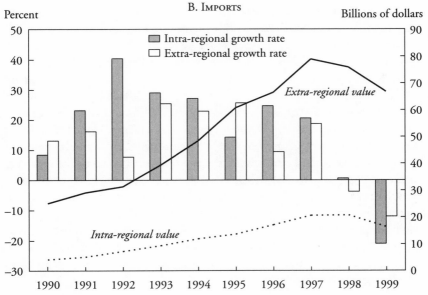

Source: OAS Trade Unit, based on data in IMF (various years).

share of MERCOSUR-bound exports from Argentina, Paraguay, and Uruguay in these countries' total sales of goods abroad has increased sharply since 1988. In 1999, for example, it ranged from 30 percent in Argentina, to 47 percent in Uruguay, and 61 percent in Paraguay. Brazil has traditionally been the principal market for these three countries. In 1999, however, Argentina overtook Brazil as the main destination within MERCOSUR for Paraguayan exports. In contrast to Argentina, Paraguay, and Uruguay, Brazil's exports to other MERCOSUR partners as a proportion of its total exports lingered around 4 percent until 1990, increasing significantly thereafter to almost 15 percent in 1999. In this context, Argentina absorbed only about 2 percent of Brazil's total exports before 1991; since then Argentina has consolidated its position as the main buyer of Brazilian products in the MERCOSUR area, accounting for 11 percent of total Brazilian exports.

NAFTA remains the principal market for MERCOSUR products in the Western Hemisphere. Although the three NAFTA countries now consume a smaller share of MERCOSUR's exports than they did even ten years ago, the trade links between the MERCOSUR and NAFTA countries remain strong. That is especially true for Brazil and the United States: nearly $25 of every $100 Brazil trades is traded with the United States.[8] Chile, which in 1996 concluded an Economic Complementation Agreement with MERCOSUR, has steadily increased its imports of MERCOSUR merchandise since 1985. The share of the Andean Community in MERCOSUR's total exports has lingered around 10 percent since 1985.

The divergence between the rates of growth of intra- and extra-MERCOSUR imports was less pronounced than it was for exports during much of the 1990s (figure 2-4b). Between 1990 and 1999 intraregional imports grew at an average annual rate of 18 percent, compared with 12 percent annual average growth for extraregional imports. As in other regions of the Western Hemisphere, the asymmetrical behavior between exports and imports in MERCOSUR can be explained by the members' simultaneous efforts to implement regional integration initiatives and unilateral trade liberalization programs and the domestic and external obstacles facing export expansion. Fluctuations in real exchange rates probably also played a role. Moreover, even before 1991 intraregional imports were already growing at a faster rate than extraregional ones, perhaps because of

8. The corresponding figure for Brazil's trade with countries of the European Union and Asia (including Japan) is $30 and $12, respectively.

the economic integration initiative undertaken by Argentina and Brazil, including the removal of all barriers to bilateral trade.

Import data reflect the high degree of interdependence among MERCOSUR member countries. In 1999 one-fifth of total imports came from each other, double the amount recorded in 1985. To a large extent, the growing importance of Brazil as a consumer of MERCOSUR products drove this increase; 14 percent of Brazil's imports came from its MERCOSUR partners in 1999, compared with just 5 percent in 1985. Brazil is also the principal source of imports for Argentina and Paraguay. In 1998 Argentina surpassed Brazil as Uruguay's main source of imports in MERCOSUR.

Although products imported from other regions of the hemisphere now represent a smaller share of MERCOSUR's total imports, Chile's share has increased slightly since 1985, from 4 to 6 percent. Around half of MERCOSUR's total imports from the hemisphere originate in North America.

NAFTA

The process of economic integration between Canada, Mexico, and the United States began long before the North American Free Trade Agreement entered into force on January 1, 1994. Following the Latin American debt crisis of 1982, Mexico embarked upon a series of wide-ranging economic reforms that resulted in more openness and greater trade, particularly with its northern neighbor. Meanwhile, Canada and the United States further deepened their economic ties through a free trade agreement signed in 1988.

The data are consistent with this story: in the years preceding NAFTA, trade among Canada, Mexico, and the United States grew, on average, at a faster rate than trade between this group and the rest of the world (figure 2-5). Specifically, intraregional exports expanded by an average rate of 10 percent between 1989 and 1993, double the average rate of growth for extraregional exports. In their aggregate form, these figures largely reflect developments in the United States and conceal the burgeoning exports from the two smaller countries to the United States in the years before 1994. Mexico's intraregional exports expanded by an annual average rate of more than 30 percent between 1989 and 1993, while its exports to the rest of the world grew at an average of 3 percent. Canada's exports to the rest of the world actually declined during this period by an average of 7 percent a

Figure 2-5. *Trends in NAFTA Trade, 1990–99*

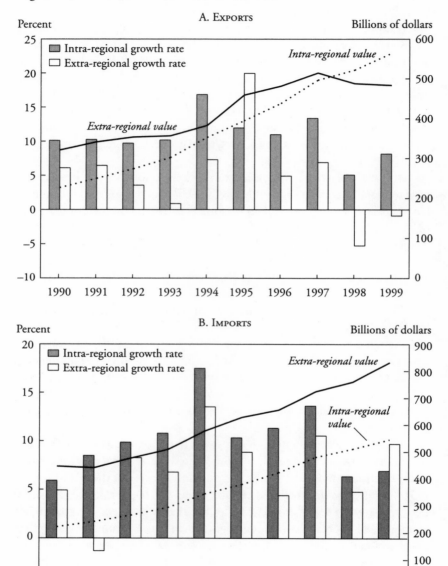

Source: OAS Trade Unit, based on data in IMF (various years).

year, while its intraregional exports grew at an average annual rate of 8 percent. The significant elimination of tariffs under NAFTA reinforced the expansion of trade flows among the members of the group. Between 1994 and 1999, intra-NAFTA exports continued to grow at an average annual rate of 10 percent. Moreover, in 1998 intra-NAFTA exports overtook exports to the rest of the world in absolute terms. Intraregional exports expanded fastest in Mexico (15 percent), followed by Canada and the United States (9 percent each).

The NAFTA area has become one of the most closely integrated areas in the world, as evidenced by the high level of trade among its three members. In 1999 intra-NAFTA exports accounted for more than half of the group's total exports, compared with 42 percent in 1986. One notable development is the sharp increase of Mexican products in the flow of intraregional exports. Since 1985 Mexican exporters, like those from Canada, have increased their dependence on the U.S. market. In 1999, both countries directed almost 90 percent of their exports to the United States. At the same time, the importance of the Mexican market to U.S. exporters has increased almost every year since 1987. A large proportion of this trade is in intermediate products, as production systems in the trading area become increasingly integrated. An exception to this trend occurred during the 1995 Mexican peso crisis, when U.S. exports to Mexico fell 9 percent. By 1996, however, U.S. exports to Mexico had fully recovered. In part, the quick recovery resulted from Mexico's initiative to exempt its NAFTA partners from a temporary tariff increase on five hundred items (or 5 percent of total tariff lines) following the crisis.[9] Meanwhile, the importance of the Canadian market for U.S. exporters has remained more or less constant over the last fifteen years.

Outside of North America, the principal markets for NAFTA products in the Western Hemisphere are Central America and the Caribbean, which since 1990 have taken in, on average, between 4 and 5 percent of NAFTA's total hemispheric exports annually. After registering an upward trend during the early and mid-1990s, MERCOSUR's share in NAFTA's product sales to the hemisphere declined somewhat in 1999 (partly because of Brazil's economic problems) to slightly more than 3 percent. Accordingly, MERCOSUR lost its position as the principal buyer of North American products in the hemisphere, a position that it had occupied since 1994. Another group that has seen its relative position as a buyer of NAFTA

9. Devlin and Ffrench-Davis (1998, p. 7).

products decline somewhat since 1987 is the Andean Community. From absorbing more than 4 percent of hemispheric exports from Canada, Mexico, and the United States in 1987, the Andean Community's share fell to 2 percent.

As in the case of exports, intra- and extra-NAFTA imports have grown at different rates since 1989. The divergence was particularly conspicuous between 1989 and 1993, when imports among the three NAFTA countries increased by an average annual rate of almost 9 percent, double the rate of extraregional imports. The strong pace of intraregional import growth during that period might reflect the role played by the Canada-United States Free Trade Agreement that entered into force in 1989. For the four years before that, the growth rate of extraregional imports exceeded that of intraregional ones in both Canada and the United States. Imports into Mexico from the NAFTA area grew at a higher annual average rate than imports from the rest of the world throughout the 1987–93 period, although both extra- and intraregional imports expanded at average annual rates in excess of 20 percent. That growth probably resulted from unilateral liberalization efforts, coupled with Mexico's liberalization commitments under the General Agreement on Tariffs and Trade, which it joined in 1986.

In 1999 imports originating in the NAFTA area accounted for about 30 percent of total imports to the United States, 70 percent of total imports to Canada, and 75 percent of total imports to Mexico. For most of the 1990s, the United States has increased its consumption of goods produced in the NAFTA area. This development reflects the increasing presence of Mexican imports in the United States from 1986 onward.

In 1987 MERCOSUR and the Andean Community each accounted for 6 percent of NAFTA's total imports from the Western Hemisphere. The shares of these two regional groupings have declined somewhat since then, to less than 3 percent in the case of MERCOSUR and 4 percent in the case of the Andean Community. In contrast, other countries and regions in the Americas, in particular Central America and the Caribbean, have maintained a relatively constant share in the hemispheric imports of the three NAFTA countries.

Services Trade in the Americas

Trade in services in the Western Hemisphere grew in relative importance during the 1990s, although considerable differences remain among countries. Significant growth in world trade in services unaccompanied by a similar development in Latin America and the Caribbean and a major gap between the expansion of services and merchandise markets in the region suggest that the levels of integration and liberalization of the services market in the region remain rather low. The potential contribution of a more efficient services sector to output and employment highlights the need to reinforce the integration and liberalization process implemented in the hemisphere during the 1990s. More open and integrated services markets should enhance competition and foreign investment and thus allow the economies in the region to reap the full benefits of a more efficient services provision.[10]

World trade in goods and services continued to expand in the 1990s, reaching nearly $7 trillion by the end of the decade. Services exports represented almost one-fifth of that total in 1999, or $1.3 trillion. The Western Hemisphere accounted for 25 percent of the total world trade in services in 1999, up from 23 percent in 1990 and slightly higher than Asia's share.[11] Exports of services in the Western Hemisphere expanded, on average, 1.12 times faster than merchandise exports during the 1990s, giving the region the second fastest growth rate in services exports after Asia (table 2-2).[12] Asia, however, experienced a marked drop in services exports in 1998 and 1999.[13] As a region, the European Union, with four of the five largest ex-

---

10. The United Nations estimates that 48 percent of total foreign direct investment in Latin America and the Caribbean was in the services sector in 1997.

11. The only source of information on trade in services available on a global basis is the International Monetary Fund's balance of payments statistics, reported by governments and reproduced in the *IMF Balance of Payments Yearbooks*. The World Trade Organization (WTO) also uses the IMF statistics for services trade in its *Annual Report*. Several problems affecting the comparability and reliability of data on trade in services arise when relying on balance of payments statistics. In addition, data based on these statistics often underestimate services trade. Figures are provided for cross-border trade of "commercial services," composed of shipping, tourism, and remittances, while excluding other forms of supply such as sales through foreign affiliates and movement of natural persons. In addition, services transactions resulting from foreign direct investment are not included. In many cases data are stated in net, rather than gross, values (exports minus imports).

12. Aggregated regional data considered in this study are based on estimates provided by the WTO secretariat. Comparisons among the different trading regions suffer in accuracy from the large number of countries not reporting data. Beginning in 1997 aggregated statistics for Caribbean and Central American countries (CARICOM and the CACM) are based on only subsamples of the universe of countries in those regions. Figures are not available for these regions and for the Andean Community for 1999. In Latin America twenty-five countries did not report data in 1999, and nine did not report in 1998.

13. Still, a majority of the largest services exporters among developing countries are in Asia, including, in order of importance, Hong Kong China, the People's Republic of China, Republic of Korea, Singapore, Chinese Taipei, Thailand, India, and Malaysia.

Table 2-2. *Exports of Goods and Services, 1999*

Region	Value (billions of dollars) 1990	1999	Annual average change (percent) 1990–99	Share of world total (percent) 1990	1999
Commercial services					
World	782	1,339	7.5	100	100
Western Hemisphere	180	338	8.1	23.0	25.2
North America	151	284	8.2	19.2	21.2
Latin America	30	54	7.5	3.8	4.0
European Union	370	566	6.9	47.3	42.2
Africa	19	28	6.9	2.4	2.1
Asia	131	267	9.0	16.8	19.9
Goods					
World	3,439	5,611	6.3	100	100
Western Hemisphere	667	1,226	7.2	19.4	21.9
North America	522	934	6.8	15.2	16.6
Latin America	145	293	8.4	4.2	5.2
European Union	1,509	2,176	6.2	43.9	38.8
Africa	103	113	3.5	3.0	2.0
Asia	792	1,543	8.0	23.0	27.5

Source: OAS Trade Unit estimates, based on WTO figures.

porters of services in the world—the United Kingdom, France, Germany, and Italy, continues to dominate world services exports with a share of over 40 percent.

Within the Western Hemisphere, considerable differences exist among countries with respect to the relative importance of services trade. During the 1990s the United States accounted for almost three-quarters of total services exports. High levels of investment and consumption and lower U.S. import prices—resulting from the sharp real appreciation of the dollar and moderate to null increases in prices for internationally traded services—have enabled the United States to maintain growth rates of both exports and imports of services well above world averages since 1996.[14]

14. The limited information available for services trade points to a moderate decrease in the dollar prices of international commercial services through 1998. Price data (from the WTO secretariat) for U.S. services trade show that price increases in the 1990s tended to be much smaller for transportation services than for travel and other commercial services.

Services exports from Latin America and the Caribbean have been less dynamic than those of the United States. The value of these exports grew from $29.7 billion in 1990 to $53.5 billion in 1999, a rate equal to the world's annual average growth rate for the 1990s. As a percentage of gross domestic product (GDP), exports of services from Latin America and the Caribbean remained almost stagnant, in contrast to Canada and the United States, whose combined ratio of export services to GDP rose from 2.5 percent in 1990 to 3.0 percent in 1999.

Merchandise trade and services trade have performed quite differently in the Western Hemisphere in the 1990s. As shown in table 2-2, services trade has proven more dynamic than merchandise trade in North America, while the opposite is true for Latin America and Caribbean. The difference may be attributable to the high degree of liberalization in the services sector in the United States and Canada, as shown by the concentration of merger and acquisitions activity in this sector during the 1990s.[15] In Latin America and the Caribbean, the still rather closed nature of services markets presumably has prevented this sector from paralleling the dynamism of the highly liberalized merchandise sector.[16]

A measure commonly used to gauge the degree of specialization in services export in a region or country is the ratio of services exports to merchandise exports. According to this measure, the Western Hemisphere ranks with Africa and the European Union, whose ratios range between 25 and 28 percent, and well above Asia's 17 percent.

The degree of specialization in services exports varies substantially among countries in the Western Hemisphere. Ordered by their ratio of services exports to merchandise exports, three groups of countries can be identified: the "highly specialized" group for which the ratio of services exports to merchandise exports is greater than or equal to 1; the "moderately specialized" group whose ratio ranges between 80 and 25 percent; and the "least specialized" group of countries with ratios of less than 25 percent.

Table 2-3 presents countries in the Western Hemisphere ranked according to this measure for 1998. Interesting facts arise from the table. The

15. Merger and acquisition sales in the U.S. services sector grew from 40 percent in 1990 to more than 70 in 1999; see UNCTAD (2000).

16. It is interesting to note that the goods and services sectors in Mexico responded quite differently to the NAFTA. In contrast to the boost in merchandise exports experienced by Mexico after joining NAFTA, no such reaction occurred in exports of services as shown by the drop in Mexico's ratio of services exports to GDP since 1995. This situation could also reflect the fact that it was easier for Mexican producers of goods to adapt their production structure more quickly than Mexican producers of services.

Table 2-3. *Degree of Specialization in Services Exports in the
Western Hemisphere, 1990 and 1998*

Country	Ratio of services exports to merchandise exports		Services exports as percentage of GDP	
	1990	1998	1990	1998
Highly specialized				
Grenada	233.3	500.00[a]	28.50	35.6[a]
Barbados	300.0	391.73	36.63	51.1[a]
St. Lucia	117.3	349.35[a]	37.51	47.3[a]
Dominican Republic	147.8	304.53	15.31	15.6[a]
St. Vincent and the Grenadines	49.4	200.00[a]	20.72	33.4
Panama	266.8	199.36	17.07	17.0
Jamaica	86.0	131.63	23.03	26.1
Dominica	60.0	114.29	19.84	25.0
Haiti	26.9	101.71	1.44	3.5
Moderately specialized				
Belize	76.9	79.22	20.61	19.5
Bahamas	139.5	78.25	47.17	41.6
Uruguay	27.2	49.91	5.50	6.9[a]
Paraguay	42.1	45.94	7.67	5.5[a]
United States	33.6	35.16	2.38	2.9
Peru	22.1	28.82	2.18	2.6
Chile	21.3	27.17	5.89	5.2
Nicaragua	10.3	26.35	3.37	5.3
Trinidad and Tobago	15.5	25.35	6.35	9.3
Least specialized				
Costa Rica	40.3	23.86	10.21	12.8
Honduras	14.6	22.92	3.96	6.8
Guatemala	26.9	22.50	4.09	3.0[a]
El Salvador	51.7	21.93	6.27	2.3
Bolivia	14.4	21.58	2.73	2.8
Colombia	22.9	18.42	3.84	2.2[a]
Ecuador	18.7	18.01	4.75	3.8
Argentina	18.3	17.00	1.60	1.3
Canada	14.4	14.10	3.20	5.1
Brazil	11.8	13.86	0.80	0.9
Mexico	17.7	10.16	2.75	3.0
Venezuela	6.4	7.54	2.31	1.2

Source: OAS Trade Unit estimates, based on WTO figures.
a. Figure for 1996.

larger economies in the hemisphere, with the exception of Chile and the United States, show a rather low degree of specialization in exports of services.[17] With the exception of Nicaragua and Panama, Central American economies show the least level of specialization. The most highly specialized exporters of services are the smaller economies of the Caribbean, where, except for Belize, services exports have gained in importance as a percentage of GDP during the decade of the 1990s. In the rest of the hemisphere, this upward trend has been recorded only by three of the larger economies (Canada, Mexico, and the United States) and three Central American economies (Costa Rica, Honduras, and Nicaragua).

On the whole, the limited data available would suggest that while services trade is both very important and growing in importance for many countries in the Western Hemisphere, much potential still exists for increasing the contribution of such trade to the region through greater market liberalization, appropriate regulatory reform, and enhanced hemispheric integration. For both the smaller and larger countries of the region, more open services markets imply higher levels of efficiency not only within and across the services sector, but also across a wide range of complementary economic activities. Further liberalization and integration are therefore key factors in allowing these countries to reap the full benefits associated with economic globalization.[18]

Foreign Direct Investment in the Americas

The surge of foreign direct investment (FDI) into the Western Hemisphere in the 1990s constitutes a concrete manifestation of the ambitious and wide-ranging economic reform programs undertaken by most countries in the region since the mid-1980s. Countries' continued ability to attract FDI during periods of economic turbulence points toward the pivotal role that structural reforms have played in ensuring that the region can bridge the usual shortage of internal funding that afflicts emerging economies and in placing the Americas on a firm path toward sustained economic growth and development.

Foreign direct investment in the Western Hemisphere soared in the 1990s, as Latin America and the Caribbean joined Canada and the United States as attractive long-term investment choices (figure 2-6). FDI in the

17. This result for Chile would seem to be in line with its significant investments in services industries abroad in recent years.
18. See, for instance, World Bank (1998).

Figure 2-6. *FDI Inflows to the Western Hemisphere*[a]

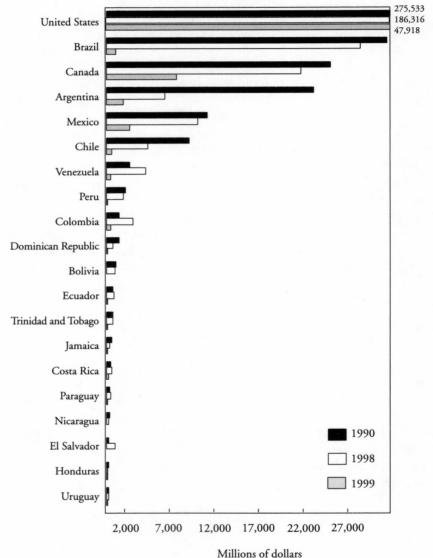

A. FDI Inflows, Top 20 Countries

Millions of dollars

B. FDI INFLOWS AS PERCENTAGE OF GROSS FIXED CAPITAL FORMATION

Source: OAS Trade Unit based on UNCTAD data.
a. OAS member states account for 99 percent (96.6 percent on average for the period 1990–99) of FDI flows to the Western Hemisphere.

region expanded from $64.7 billion in 1990 to $391 billion in 1999, an eight-fold increase in Latin America and the Caribbean and a four-fold increase in Canada and the United States. As a percentage of GDP, inward of FDI stock to Latin America and the Caribbean reached 19.5 percent in 1998, an increase of nine percentage points over 1990. The equivalent figure for Canada and the United States equaled 10.5 percent, two percentage points more than in 1990.[19]

Somewhat surprisingly, these developments took place in the midst of rolling crises affecting Mexico in 1994 and East Asia, Russia, and Brazil between mid-1997 and early 1999. The economic turbulence during this period led to a continuous reallocation of capital flows, reflected in periodic adjustments in portfolio investment and cutbacks in bank lending. Notwithstanding the adverse economic climate, the upward trend of FDI inflows to the region remained. The United States became the number one recipient of FDI in the world, after continuous growth since 1993. Meanwhile, Latin America and the Caribbean saw its share of FDI inflows to developing economies reach a record high—39.5 percent in 1998, from 26 percent in 1990—despite ongoing structural reforms in emerging Europe and buoyant economic growth in Asia (before 1998) (figure 2-7). In 1999, as foreign investors withdrew from the troubled economies of Southeast Asia and Russia, FDI across the Western Hemisphere continued to grow. As a result of this upward trend, FDI has become the single largest component of long-term capital in the hemisphere, exceeding the share of the FDI component in emerging economies in Asia and Europe.

Before the Asian and Brazilian crises, every trading group in the Western Hemisphere except NAFTA increased its stake in total FDI flows to the region (table 2-4). Only in 1998 did the Andean Community, CARICOM, and MERCOSUR see a reduction in their respective shares, as contagion effects hit both growth and medium-term prospects in these areas, and NAFTA became relatively more attractive to investors in response to strong U.S. markets. Remarkably, Brazil, despite its own economic crisis, was able to maintain increasing inflows of FDI—thereby stabilizing its share within the hemisphere—by means of revitalizing its privatization process. Argentina adopted a similar policy, which boosted its share of FDI within the hemisphere from 2.4 percent in 1998 to nearly 6 percent in 1999.

19. UNCTAD (2000). FDI stock is the value of the share of the FDI enterprise's capital and reserves (including retained profits) attributable to the parent enterprise, plus the net indebtedness of affiliates of the parent enterprise. The 1998 figure is the latest one reported.

Figure 2-7. *FDI Inflows to Developing Countries, by Region*

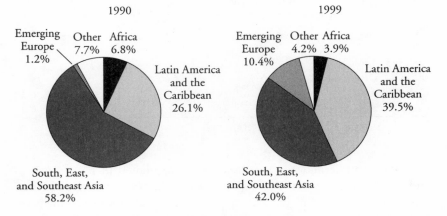

Source: OAS Trade Unit calculations, based on UNCTAD data.

The enhanced FDI in the Western Hemisphere results in part from continued growth in international flows of investment during the 1990s and, more important, from the increased confidence of international investors in the region's long-term prospects. Two factors were instrumental in triggering this optimistic assessment: first, the outstanding performance of the U.S. economy; and second, the profound structural reforms and more prudent macroeconomic policies implemented in Latin America and the Caribbean throughout the 1990s.

The strength of the U.S. economy, exemplified by nine years of continuous economic growth, is explained not only by strong fundamentals, but also by efficient labor and financial markets, a favorable business environment, high quality infrastructure, and leading technological innovation. In Latin America and the Caribbean, structural reforms came about as a response to the severe macroeconomic crises of the 1980s and were aimed at restoring fiscal and monetary discipline and at increasing the role of market mechanisms to improve resource allocation. The main reforms focused on privatization of public companies, liberalization of foreign trade and financial markets, flexibility in labor markets, and improvements in governance. At the same time, inflation reduction became the main focus of fiscal and monetary policy, while exchange rate policies were designed to reduce the high levels of volatility seen in the previous decade.

Table 2-4. *Share of FDI Inflows, OAS Member States by Region,*
Selected Years

Region	1990	1997	1998	1999
NAFTA	91.7	71.5	79.3	80.3
Andean Community	1.8	7.9	4.0	2.0
MERCOSUR	4.6	15.3	12.9	14.2
CARICOM	0.6	0.9	0.5	0.4
CACM	0.1	0.2	0.7	0.2

Source: OAS Trade Unit, based on UNCTAD data.

Of the numerous structural reforms implemented in Latin America
and the Caribbean, privatizations had perhaps the largest positive effect on
foreign investment. Mergers and acquisitions (M&As) were the main vehicle through which such investment took place (box 2-1). In fact, the
value of cross-border M&A sales of privatized firms between 1990 and
1999 totaled $89.6 billion (adjusted for inflation).[20] Moreover, during 1998
and 1999, Argentina, Brazil, and Chile were three of the top five world
sellers, with the first two leading the ranking in 1999. The recent boost in
the privatization process, illustrated by the sale of the telecommunications
company Telebras in Brazil and the petroleum company YPF in Argentina,
meant that sales in Latin America reconcentrated in capital-intensive industries. Notwithstanding, the acquisition of privately owned firms by foreign investors has also proved to be an important source of foreign
investment, particularly in the second half of the decade. The telecommunications, chemical and banking industries have accounted for an important share of these acquisitions.

The integration process in the Western Hemisphere—launched in the
context of structural reforms—has been another crucial determinant of
FDI in the region. Underpinned by changes in domestic laws on investment as well as the enactment of bilateral investment treaties between countries, the integration process has facilitated the expansion of U.S. firms and
the internationalization of Latin American companies, boosting intra-

20. Calculation by the Organization of American States based on data from the United Nations
Conference on Trade and Development (UNCTAD). Note that it is not possible to determine precisely the share of cross-border mergers and acquisitions in FDI inflows because the mode of financing—local or international capital markets—is not reported by most countries. In addition, because
mergers and acquisitions can be phased over several years, ratios of cross-border mergers and acquisitions to total FDI flows can be higher than one.

Box 2-1. *Mergers and Acquisitions in the Western Hemisphere*

Cross-border mergers and acquisitions (M&As)—defined as more than a 1 percent equity share by foreign firms—have been the main vehicle of foreign direct investment worldwide. In the Western Hemisphere the value of cross-border M&As rose from $72 billion in 1990 to $295 billion in 1999. M&As as a share of gross domestic product grew from 0.5 percent in 1991 to 2.6 percent in 1999.

From 1995 until 1997 this sharp increase was explained by the dynamic behavior of M&A activity across the hemisphere. M&A investment grew by 50 percent in the United States and by 40 percent in Canada during this period. Rapidly rising M&A sales by Latin American and Caribbean countries led to a nineteen percentage point reduction in the North American share (a ten percentage point reduction in the U.S. share). This trend was reversed in 1998, when rapid growth in the U.S. market caused M&A activity there to soar. In that year M&A sales in the United States reached a record high of $210 billion, after a 160 percent increase. Although this growth slowed in 1999, the United States remained the single most important target country for mergers and acquisitions, with a 79 percent share of the hemisphere's M&A investment and a 40 percent share of the world's M&A investment. The bulk of this investment had belonged to Japanese firms in the first half of the 1990s. European firms took the lead in the second half, after taking over or merging with U.S. enterprises in the automobile, pharmaceutical, oil and chemical, financial services, and telecommunications industries.

In addition to a good performance within the Western Hemisphere, the Latin American and Caribbean region also dominated cross-border M&A sales by developing countries during the 1990s. The region maintained a 60 percent average stake, attaining a 79 percent peak in 1998.

regional investment (table 2-5). In fact, foreign direct investment by Latin American firms, directed mainly toward the region, adds up to the total investments made by U.S. firms and constitutes the main source of FDI in Latin America and the Caribbean.[21] The main drivers of this process have been Argentine and Brazilian companies that have extended their activities within the MERCOSUR region, large Chilean services companies that have

21. In 1998 the United Nations estimated intraregional investment at approximately $8 billion.

Table 2-5. *FDI Outflows, Selected Years*
Millions of U.S. dollars

Region	1991	1998	1999	1991–98 % change
World	198,143	687,111	799,928	246.8
Developed countries	189,782	651,873	731,765	243.5
Developing countries	8,324	33,045	65,638	297.0
Africa	962	648	935	−32.6
Latin America and the Caribbean	667	9,405	27,325	1,310.0
Developing Europe	0	125	109	...
Asia	7,819	22,818	37,239	191.8
The Pacific	-4	49	30	1,325.0
Central and Eastern Europe	37	2,193	2,526	5,827.0

Source: OAS Trade Unit, based on UNCTAD data.

expanded into neighboring countries through participation in privatization projects, the integration of Colombian and Venezuelan markets through FDI, and investments by Mexican companies in Central and South America.[22] Of the nineteen largest privatization deals in the world involving foreign buyers between 1987 and 1999, U.S. transnationals acquired seven, while Argentine, Canadian, and Mexican transnationals acquired one each.[23]

Finally, the consolidation of the democratization process in the region, attained after the last two nondemocratically elected governments (Chile and Paraguay) left office in the late 1980s and early 1990s, was also welcomed by international investors as contributing to the stability of the Western Hemisphere.

The reform packages introduced by most countries in the Americas since the mid-1980s have thus led to a significant widening of the investor base of the economies of the hemisphere. By liberalizing capital flows, including FDI, and allowing financial integration these reforms not only facilitated the flow of international capital, but also better insulated the region against both international and regional economic difficulties.

22. UNCTAD (1999).
23. Although not significant at the hemispheric level, many Central American and Caribbean countries have also recorded increasing levels of investment in neighboring countries during the 1990s.

References

Devlin, Robert, and Ricardo Ffrench-Davis. 1998. "Towards an Evaluation of Regional Integration in Latin America in the 1990s." *INTAL ITD Working Paper 2.* Institute for the Integration of Latin America and the Caribbean and the Inter-American Development Bank, Integration and Regional Programs Department, Washington, D.C. (December).

Inter-American Development Bank. 1999. "Integration and Trade in the Americas." *Periodic Note.* Washington, D.C. (December).

IMF (International Monetary Fund). Various years. *Direction of Trade Statistics.* Washington, D.C.

UNCTAD (United Nations Conference on Trade and Development). 1999. *World Investment Report 1999.* Geneva.

———. 2000. *World Investment Report 2000.* Geneva.

World Bank. 1998. "Making Services an Engine of Growth." Development Research Group, Washington, D.C.

PART II

Regional Trade Arrangements

JOSÉ MANUEL SALAZAR-XIRINACHS
THERESA WETTER
KARSTEN STEINFATT
DANIELA IVASCANU

3 | *Customs Unions*

According to traditional analyses of the stages of economic integration, a customs union involves not only the removal of tariff and nontariff barriers to trade for imports from the union's members, but also the equalization of tariffs among members on imports from nonmembers. A customs union usually entails a higher degree of integration than a free trade area, in which members abolish tariffs and quotas on imports from each other but maintain their tariffs and quotas against nonmembers. At the same time, a customs union represents a lower degree of integration than a common market, which incorporates, in addition to the elements of a customs union, measures to allow free movement of factors of production among its members. Four of the Western Hemisphere's regional integration agreements could be classified as customs unions, even though their ultimate goal is to achieve a deeper level of integration. Of the four arrangements, three—the Central American Common Market (CACM), the Andean Community, and the Caribbean

The sections on the Central American Common Market, the Andean Community, CARICOM, and MERCOSUR were written by José Manuel Salazar-Xirinachs, Theresa Wetter, Karsten Steinfatt, and Daniela Ivascanu, respectively. Contributions were received from Maryse Robert, José Tavares, Barbara Kotschwar, Gisela Vergara, Jorge Mario Martínez, Alicia Reid, and Denise Goolsarran. Theresa Wetter wishes to thank Nicolás Lloreda for his comments and suggestions.

Community and Common Market (CARICOM)—have existed since the 1960s or early 1970s. Their nature and structure, however, have changed dramatically as integration efforts in these areas were reinvigorated in the early 1990s. The newest of the customs unions in the Americas is the Common Market of the South, or MERCOSUR, which came into being in 1991.

This chapter consists of four sections, one for each of the regional arrangements identified as customs unions. After providing a brief overview of the origin and membership of these integration schemes, each section highlights their main institutional features, as well as their achievements in the area of trade policy. As the analysis makes clear, the four agreements have made considerable progress in eliminating barriers to trade and establishing common external tariffs. Each section ends with a discussion of the principal developments in each agreement's external trade relations during recent years.

The Central American Common Market

The five countries of the Central American Isthmus attempted to establish a federal republic after gaining their independence from Spain in 1821, but the precariousness of their economic and infrastructural ties— an inheritance from the colonial period—helped to doom the project. The idea of integration nonetheless endured, mostly as a political ideal, giving rise to various partial projects for regional linkage. One of the latest was the creation of the Organization of Central American States (ODECA, for its Spanish acronym) in 1951, composed of the ministers for foreign affairs of Costa Rica, El Salvador, Guatemala, Honduras, and Nicaragua.

It was the United Nations Economic Commission for Latin America and the Caribbean (ECLAC) that put forward a totally novel idea for promoting Central American unity in contrast to the previous, mostly political, approaches. When the Organization of Central American States was established, a decision was made to move toward regional economic integration, although a framework for achieving that goal was not formulated. During the 1950s all five Central American countries negotiated bilateral trade agreements covering a limited number of products with at least one of their neighbors. At the same time the governments of Central America, with ECLAC's support, spent considerable energy and resources developing a workable approach to economic integration. This activity led initially to the signing of the Multilateral Agreement on Free Trade and Central American Economic Integration in June 1958; this agreement provided for regional free trade in numerous products and called for complete free trade within ten years. In September 1959 the five countries signed two additional agreements: the Agreement on Economic Integration Industries; and the Central American Agreement on the Equalization of Import Duties and Charges. The latter identified a number of products to which a common external tariff would be applied within five years. In February 1960 El Salvador, Guatemala, and Honduras signed the Treaty of Economic Association (also known as the Tripartite Treaty), which established, as a goal, free trade among the three countries for all products, albeit with a list of exceptions. Finally, in late 1960 the General Treaty on Central American Economic Integration (the General Treaty) was signed, superseding the previous agreements and providing the basic framework for economic integration efforts to date. In the 1990s economic integration efforts in the region underwent a major restructuring and reactivation, when the Central American Integration System was created by the Tegucigalpa Protocol and the General Treaty was amended by the Guatemala Protocol.

The General Treaty was signed on December 13, 1960, by Guatemala, El Salvador, Honduras, and Nicaragua. Costa Rica acceded on July 23, 1962.[1] The main objective of the General Treaty was the creation of a common market and a customs union within a period of not more than five years.[2]

The first decade of the Central American Common Market was marked by significant accomplishments. The regionwide market made impressive progress in promoting growth and import-substitution industrialization. The region attracted relatively large flows of foreign direct investment, which contributed to much of the growth and industrialization achieved during the CACM's first ten to fifteen years. The five countries also took significant steps to modernize their national and regional infrastructures as well as to develop industrial and managerial skills.[3] By 1966 tariffs had been eliminated on 94 percent of the products included in the tariff program. Intra-CACM exports grew by 900 percent to reach $300 million in 1970. Intraregional trade as a share of total trade for the five member countries grew from 5 percent in 1960 to 26 percent in 1970.

1. The General Treaty entered into force on June 4, 1961, for El Salvador, Guatemala, and Nicaragua; on April 27, 1962, for Honduras, and on September 23, 1963, for Costa Rica.
2. See Articles I and II of the General Treaty on Central American Economic Integration. A small number of commodities were excluded. Several protocols to the General Treaty have been signed by member countries and ratified by all or some of them.
3. Lizano and Salazar-Xirinachs (1999, p. 111).

However, political problems affected what by the late 1960s seemed like an economic success story. Honduras left the CACM in 1970, amid a short-lived war triggered by large migrations from El Salvador, and did not rejoin until 1995, when it ratified the Tegucigalpa Protocol. In addition, because the combined market of 25 million people was comparatively small, the new import-substitution strategy for driving economic growth showed clear signs of exhaustion by the mid-1970s. The flows of foreign direct investment declined substantially, and it became clear that despite the newly built industrial base, the growth dynamics of the region remained critically dependent on a few primary commodities. The slower growth and increased economic volatility in the 1970s, partly induced by external shocks, exacerbated the perception among some members of the CACM that the benefits of integration were unevenly distributed.

Attempts at reactivating the CACM were made during the 1970s but without great success. Most of the countries in the region responded to the slower economic dynamism of the 1970s by replacing the lost foreign direct investment with a major investment drive led by the public sector and supported by external borrowing. Debt-financed growth was short-lived, however, and led to a major debt crisis for all Central American countries in the early 1980s.

The foreign debt problems not only brought growth to a complete standstill in the early 1980s, but also caused major payment difficulties between CACM members, which affected businesses and contributed to a reduction of intraregional trade from $1.2 billion in 1980 to $450 million in 1986. The political turmoil and armed conflicts that engulfed the region during most of the 1980s also seriously affected national production and intraregional exports.

As political tensions dissipated and democratic government was restored in the late 1980s (including free elections in all five countries during 1989–90), attention turned increasingly to issues of economic development, reconstruction, and reform. A shift toward economic openness, export promotion, and market-friendly policies had been taking place in some countries since the mid-1980s. And the Caribbean Basin Initiative had been generating a new export dynamic and contributing to an increase in private investment in Central America.[4] Moreover, the governments brought to power in the 1989–90 round of elections were like-minded in their strong commitment to economic reform.

4. For a description of the Caribbean Basin Economic Recovery Act, see chapter 5 in this volume.

Particularly significant for the CACM was the June 1990 presidential summit convened in Antigua, Guatemala, in which a major plan was approved to reactivate and restructure the economic integration in the isthmus under new principles. The plan included several concrete steps to reactivate intraregional trade, strengthen institutions of economic integration, and reestablish at increasingly lower levels the common external tariff that had in practice ceased to exist after the late 1970s. Most important, it called for the return of Honduras as a full member of the CACM. Successive presidential and ministerial meetings in the early 1990s led to a well-organized regional agenda with three major areas of discussion: a strengthening of the legal and institutional framework of the "new" integration process; a priority program for reactivating the process of economic integration; and functional cooperation and sectoral issues.

As a result of work in the first area, the legal framework for regional integration was refurbished with two new protocols. The Tegucigalpa Protocol to the Charter of the Organization of Central American States (ODECA), signed in December 1991 by the presidents of Costa Rica, El Salvador, Guatemala, Honduras, and Nicaragua, created the Central American Integration System (SICA), which defines a new legal and institutional structure for regional integration broadly conceived. It establishes executive, parliamentary, and judicial functions at the regional level, creates ministerial commissions for functional areas of cooperation, and defines technical secretariats for support functions. It was ratified by the congresses of all countries, including Panama, which participated in its creation. Belize deposited the instrument of accession to the Tegucigalpa Protocol and to ODECA on December 4, 2000. The five CACM countries also signed, in October 1993, the Guatemala Protocol to the General Treaty, updating and amending the 1960 General Treaty of Economic Integration. Panama, which is an observer to the CACM process, signed the Guatemala Protocol but has not yet ratified it.[5]

The priority program for reactivating the integration process developed under the supervision of the ministers of economy and trade included the full reestablishment of free trade among the five CACM members by dismantling barriers to intraregional trade and reestablishing a unified common external tariff; coordination of external negotiations; joint actions to reduce the debt burden and to coordinate macroeconomic policy; strength-

5. The Guatemala Protocol entered into force on August 17, 1995. Article 60 of the Guatemala Protocol provides for the accession or association of any country from the Central American region.

ening of regional economic integration institutions; and coordination of external cooperation.[6]

The efforts during the 1990s to promote exports and to reactivate the CACM under new foundations can be considered successful when judged by the quantum leap in exports: total exports of the five countries grew from $4.3 billion in 1990 to $9.1 billion in 1995 and $16.6 billion in 1999. And intraregional trade recovered from a low of $450 million in 1986 to more than $2.5 billion in 1999. Central American business communities have also been very actively engaged in partnership and in undertaking major investments in neighboring countries. Measured against some of the proposed objectives, however, progress can be deemed more modest.[7]

The five countries were actively engaged in external trade negotiations. By the end of the decade they all had entered modern free trade agreements with Mexico. They also jointly negotiated a free trade agreement with the Dominican Republic (1998) and with Chile (1999). Despite some setbacks in 1999, the economic integration process was gaining new strength in 2000, as El Salvador and Guatemala were advancing in the creation of a customs union, which Honduras and Nicaragua decided to join in August 2000. At the time of this writing, the five Central American countries and Panama are engaged in negotiating a free trade agreement.

The Agreement Today: Legal and Institutional Framework

Central American integration remains legally and institutionally complex, despite the efforts initiated at a summit meeting held in Panama in July 1997 to streamline the numerous institutions of the process.[8] Various institutions with multiple purposes and diverse historic origins have been at the core of the integration process since the 1960s. New institutions were created in the 1980s, partly as a response to the myriad of social and political needs that became more acute during this period of social and economic turmoil. During the 1990s institutional reform and modernization received a lot of attention and occupied much of the time of ministerial and summit meetings.

The Tegucigalpa Protocol constitutes the highest-level legal norm and sets out the main objectives for regional cooperation in the political, eco-

6. Lizano and Salazar-Xirinachs (1999, p. 122).
7. Granados (1999).
8. BID-CEPAL (1998).

nomic, and social spheres. Institutionally, SICA encompasses all existing entities including those in charge of executive functions (the summit meetings, ministerial commissions, and other technical secretariats), judicial functions (the Central American Court of Justice), and legislative functions (the Central American Parliament). In terms of scope, SICA comprises the political, economic, social, cultural, and environmental subsystems of the integration process. SICA codified the responsibilities of presidents and foreign ministers. Located in San Salvador, SICA's main objective as a secretariat is to coordinate and execute the mandates from the Central American summits and decisions from the Council of Ministers of Foreign Affairs.

The Guatemala Protocol created the institutional framework for the economic integration subsystem of SICA. The protocol redefines the objectives and principles of economic integration, conceptualizes a series of progressive stages for integration, and calls on members to establish a customs union. It also commits countries to move toward the coordination and convergence of their macroeconomic policies, as well as of their external trade negotiations, and to cooperate on infrastructure and other sectoral matters. In contrast to the founding treaty, the Guatemala Protocol does not establish specific deadlines for achieving its goals; however, it keeps one central characteristic of the earlier integration scheme—the commitment of governments to go beyond a free trade agreement to establish a customs union with a common external tariff. Rather than including specific binding commitments in its text or annexes, the protocol envisages the integration process as advancing gradually based on complementary or "derived" legal instruments.

The Council of Ministers for Economic Integration, which consists of the ministers for the economy and presidents of the central banks of the member states, is responsible for the coordination, harmonization, and convergence of the members' economic policies. Other bodies of the economic integration subsystem are the Intersectoral Council of Ministers for Economic Integration, the Sectoral Council of Economic Integration, and the Executive Committee for Economic Integration. The technical administrative bodies include the Central American Economic Integration Secretariat (SIECA), the Secretariat of the Central American Agricultural Council, the Secretariat of the Central American Monetary Council, and the Secretariat of Central American Tourism Integration. The institutions of the economic integration subsystem are made up of the Central American Bank for Economic Integration, the Central American Institute for

Public Administration, and the Central American Institute for Industrial Technology and Research.

The Agreement Today: Coverage

The principal framework of the Central American integration process, the Guatemala Protocol, does not follow the model of modern free trade agreements, but it does call on the members to bring the free trade area of the CACM into full operation through the gradual elimination of tariff and nontariff barriers, the granting of national treatment to intraregional trade, and the adoption of a regional legal framework covering rules of origin, safeguards, unfair trade practices, intellectual property, services, sanitary measures, and standards and technical regulations. The protocol also calls on members to update subsidy and antidumping measures, reestablish a common external tariff system, and instill macroeconomic policy coordination.

The Convention on the Central American Tariff and Customs Regime signed in 1985 now includes the Central American Import Tariff, the Central American Legislation on the Customs Value of Goods, and the Central American Uniform Customs Code (CAUCA) and its regulations (RECAUCA). There have been three amendments to the convention. The customs code, which first entered into force in 1965 for all countries except Honduras (where it was adopted in 1992), has also been amended.[9]

Regulations have been adopted setting out the Central American legal frameworks on origin of goods (1995), unfair business practices (1995), safeguards (1996), standardization measures, metrology, and authorization procedures (1999), sanitary and phytosanitary measures and procedures (1999), and dispute resolution (2000).

The regulations on unfair trade practices superseded the provisions established in the General Treaty. They were adopted to develop the regulatory framework for the application of Article VI of the General Agreement on Tariffs and Trade, agreed to in 1994, and the World Trade Organization's Agreement on Subsidies and Countervailing Duties. The commitments agreed upon did not advance beyond what was agreed at the multilateral level.

The General Treaty establishes consultation mechanisms; expert groups; and conciliation, mediation, and arbitration processes. Negotiations for the creation of a dispute settlement mechanism concluded in 1999, and its

9. SIECA (2000a, p. 2).

regulatory framework was approved by the Council of Ministers for Economic Integration in 2000. The agreement establishes a procedure for the prevention or settlement of disputes related to the interpretation or application of regional agreements. Under the framework, countries agreed to try first to settle the dispute among themselves, then to arbitration, and finally to turn to the council as the mechanism of last resort.

Rules on services and investment and on government procurement are currently being discussed.[10] The General Treaty refers only to construction services and implies that regional enterprises will be granted national treatment. Each member country has taken steps to liberalize various areas of trade in services. The Guatemala Protocol calls for the harmonization of national laws in sectors such as banking, insurance, and capital markets.[11] Moreover, the protocol calls for the harmonization of national legislation to implement the 1962 Central American Convention on the Exercise of Post-Secondary Professions and the Recognition of Post-Secondary Studies. This instrument has been ratified and is currently in force in all CACM countries, with the exception of Nicaragua.

THE FREE TRADE AREA. As mentioned earlier, the CACM was successful from the very beginning in eliminating most tariffs on goods. The General Treaty established free trade for all products originating in the common market countries, with a few exceptions listed in Annex A of the treaty. Over the years the list of excluded products has been shortened, and today tariffs apply only to roasted coffee, alcoholic beverages, and petroleum products. No timetable has been agreed upon for removing the remaining tariffs. The ministers of economy and trade have the mandate to review this list on a yearly basis and to make appropriate changes. Honduras charges a customs administration tax of 0.5 percent on finished goods only, whereas Costa Rica has levied a tax of 1 percent of custom value since 1984.

The Guatemala Protocol gives Nicaragua a special status within the CACM, allowing this country "transitory preferential and asymmetrical treatment" in the areas of trade, finance, investment, and external debt to help it reconstruct and strengthen its productive and financial capacity.[12] Nicaragua established a temporary protection tariff (Arancel Temporal de Protección, or ATP, in Spanish) in July 1994, and added a general fiscal

10. SIECA (2000a, p. 2).
11. Article XXX of the Guatemala Protocol.
12. Article V, chapter VI.

stamp duty of 5 percent in July 1997. The ATP was phased out for most products by January 1999 and is currently applied to so-called "fiscal" goods, which include products such as mineral water, beer, ethyl alcohol, spirits, liqueurs, whisky, rum, gin, and tobacco.[13] ATP rates are scheduled to be phased out entirely by the end of 2001.[14]

A few disputes have disrupted trade among Central American countries during the past few years. For example, as a result of a diplomatic conflict, Nicaragua imposed a "patriotic" 35 percent tariff on all Honduran imports. On January 30, 2000, the Central American Court of Justice ruled against Nicaragua, calling for an end to the tariff. Moreover, a border conflict between Costa Rica and Nicaragua led Nicaragua in late 1999 to threaten to obstruct transit of Costa Rican exports to the rest of CACM members.

THE CUSTOMS UNION. After forty years of integration, the CACM is presently somewhere between an almost perfect free trade area and an imperfect customs union.[15] The General Treaty and later the Guatemala Protocol committed countries to enter into a customs union, and products were to be gradually included under the common external tariff.

The common external tariff system became very difficult to sustain in the late 1970s and during the economic crisis of the 1980s, but in 1990 the five countries decided to reestablish it, with a 20 percent ceiling. In May 1996 the Council of Ministers of Economic Integration approved the following parameters for the common external tariff: a 0 percent tariff on raw materials, intermediate goods, and capital goods not produced domestically; a 5 percent tariff on raw materials produced domestically; a 10 percent tariff for intermediate goods and capital goods produced domestically; and a 15 percent tariff for finished goods produced domestically.

In 1993 El Salvador, Guatemala, Honduras, and Nicaragua created the Central American Group of Four and announced the establishment of a customs union by April 1994. The initial union was not successful, however. On November 8, 1996, Guatemala and El Salvador initiated the process of creating a customs union between themselves, and on August 24, 1999, the presidents of the two countries declared that the customs union would be functioning on December 31, 2002. To meet this goal the two countries have harmonized 90 percent of their tariffs, created a customs

---

13. For more on this issue, see WTO (2000b).
14. WTO (1999b, p. 41).
15. SIECA (1999, p. 1).

union unit, approved an agreement covering investment and services, and coordinated their trade policy.[16] On August 29, 2000, Nicaragua and Honduras announced that they would join the customs union formed by Guatemala and El Salvador.[17] In another effort at deeper integration, El Salvador, Guatemala, and Nicaragua in May 2000 signed the Tri-National Declaration: Integration for the 21st Century, which reaffirmed their commitment to the creation of a customs union and outlined measures to be taken in the areas of international relations, macroeconomic policy, trade policy, infrastructure, energy, communication, immigration, and security.

THE COMMON MARKET. The ultimate goal of the General Treaty is to create a common market among the five member countries. To meet this objective, Central American countries have eliminated most tariffs on goods and are in the process of creating a customs union. Regulations have been adopted setting up regional legal frameworks for origin of goods, unfair business practices, safeguards, standardization measures, metrology, and authorization procedures, sanitary and phytosanitary measures and procedures, and dispute resolution.

External Trade Relations

In January 1991 Central American countries signed the Tuxtla Gutiérrez Declaration with Mexico with a view to negotiating a free trade agreement (FTA). After eight years of negotiations, El Salvador, Guatemala, and Honduras signed a free trade agreement with Mexico on June 29, 2000. Industrial tariffs are to be eliminated in eleven years, and tariffs on agricultural products in twelve years. Mexico is expected to begin to remove tariffs earlier. Costa Rica and Nicaragua, separately, negotiated free trade agreements with Mexico, while negotiations between Mexico and Panama are under way.

In April 1998 the Central American countries signed a free trade agreement with the Dominican Republic, which covers trade in goods and services, investment, and intellectual property rights, among other issues. The Dominican Republic will participate in the Central American Bank for Economic Integration, in the Alliance for Sustainable Development, and

16. For more on the customs union between Guatemala and El Salvador, see SIECA (2000b).

17. On this occasion, two resolutions were passed by the Council of Ministers for Economic Integration. See Resolution 56-2000 and Resolution 57-2000 (www.sieca/org.gt/publico/marco_legal/ Resoluciones/COMIECO/menu_de_resoluciones_del_comieco.htm).

in agreements on other areas of mutual interest, including tourism, health, and investment. The Dominican Republic is expected to ratify the agreement in the near future. The CACM countries and Chile also signed a free trade agreement, which is currently awaiting legislative approval in all the countries, except Costa Rica, which adopted the legislation in September 2000.

On March 21, 2000, Central America and Panama renewed negotiations on the mechanisms and rules of a modern trade agreement covering goods, services, investment, intellectual property rights, and government procurement.

Costa Rica initiated negotiations for a free trade agreement with Canada in July 2000. More recently, during the September 2000 Central America-Canada Summit, the heads of state announced that they would begin exploratory talks for a free trade agreement between the region and Canada. In 1999 Central American exports to the Canadian market amounted to $93 million, while Canadian imports to the region reached $254.2 million.

The CACM countries have held talks with MERCOSUR and the Andean Community. In April 2000 the heads of state of Brazil, the Dominican Republic, and the Central American countries agreed to support implementation of the Framework Agreement on Trade and Investment signed in April 1998 by MERCOSUR and the members of the Central American Integration System. El Salvador, Guatemala, Honduras, and the Andean Community reiterated their interest in a partial scope agreement to widen the list of products covered. The countries also expressed interest in an agreement on trade and investment with simple rules that would serve as the basis for future commitments under a free trade agreement that the two common markets agreed, on April 25, 1999, to negotiate.

The Andean Community

The Andean Community of Nations traces its origin to 1969, when Bolivia, Chile, Colombia, Ecuador, and Peru signed the Cartagena Agreement creating the Andean Pact (later called the Andean Group). Venezuela became a member in 1973, whereas Chile withdrew in 1976.[18]

18. As set out in the Cartagena Agreement, the main objectives of the group are to promote the balanced and harmonious development of the member countries under equitable conditions, to boost their growth through integration and economic and social cooperation, to enhance participation in the regional process with a view to the progressive formation of a Latin American common market, and to strive for a steady improvement in the standard of living of their inhabitants.

At its inception, the Andean Community represented an effort by a group of medium-size countries eager to expand the limited benefits they had been deriving from their participation in the Latin American Free Trade Association and to seek a counterbalance to the bigger economies in Latin America. Members aimed to establish a customs union and to progress in the coordination of policies in areas such as communications, transport, finance, investment, and industrial development. These efforts responded to an integration model based on the import-substitution principles that then dominated the development strategies of the Andean countries. The integration agreement, however, experienced a number of setbacks in its first several years. In the 1970s the common external tariff did not get approved, and the industrialization and liberalization programs failed to cover more than a few sectors. Nevertheless, Andean trade grew substantially, encouraged by the oil booms and the revenues from coffee production. In the 1980s, as a result of the debt crisis that spread over Latin America and a sharp reduction in commodity prices, members gradually abandoned the liberalization and industrialization programs and introduced new restrictions on trade. By the end of the decade, however, as widespread market-oriented reforms swept around the world, members began to make profound changes in their economic policies, and at the December 1989 presidential meeting held in the Galapagos Islands, members of the Andean community were ready to set aside the import-substitution model and to move toward establishment of a customs union.

The 1990s marked the beginning of a renewal for the Andean integration agreement. In 1993 Bolivia, Colombia, Ecuador, and Venezuela established a free trade zone and on February 1, 1995, the four countries implemented a common external tariff. (Peru joined the free trade area in 1997; see below.) Bolivia was allowed to keep its lower tariffs. Andean countries also updated their common legislation on foreign investment and intellectual property rights, adopted a common framework on services, negotiated preferential access for their exports to the United States and the European Union, and signed a framework agreement with MERCOSUR for the creation of a free trade zone.

The fact that Andean countries speak with a single voice in the Free Trade Area of the Americas (FTAA) negotiations constitutes further proof of their commitment to deepening integration among themselves. Necessary institutional and policy reforms, which modified the Cartagena Agreement, were introduced through the Trujillo Protocol, approved in March

1996, and the Sucre Protocol, approved in June 1997.[19] The Andean Group became the Andean Community of Nations. Thus, by the end of the decade, as the process celebrated its thirtieth anniversary, progress had been made in strengthening the institutional framework, establishing a customs union (with a presidential commitment to move on to a common market by 2005), and revitalizing the Andean Community's external relations. At the beginning of the twenty-first century, the community appeared determined to continue the march forward. On August 31–September 1, 2000, at the Brasilia Summit of Heads of State of the South American Countries, the Andean Community and MERCOSUR pledged "to start negotiations leading to the signing of a free trade agreement between the two groups as soon as possible and, in any case, by January 2002."

The Agreement Today: Legal and Institutional Framework

The Andean Community has developed a set of institutions patterned along the lines of those of the European Union, making it one of the most complex among the regional arrangements of the Western Hemisphere from an institutional standpoint. The Trujillo Protocol integrated the bodies and institutions within the organization into the Andean Integration System. The main bodies of this system are:

—Andean Presidential Council. The council, formally established by the Trujillo Protocol, is composed of the heads of state of the member countries and is the highest-level body of the Andean Integration System. It meets regularly once a year and in special sessions when required. The chairman of the council is appointed from among its members for a period of one year, on a rotating basis. The council is responsible for defining Andean subregional integration policy; orienting and promoting actions on matters of interest to the subregion as a whole; considering proposals submitted by the bodies and institutions of the Andean Integration System; and evaluating and studying the development and results of the process of Andean integration, as well as its relations with countries outside the community.

—Andean Council of Foreign Ministers. Composed of the ministers of foreign affairs of the member countries, this council is responsible for

19. The Cartagena Agreement went through another important change in December 1987 when members signed the Quito Protocol. The Andean Pact changed its name and was thereafter known as the Andean Group.

formulating and implementing the Andean Community's foreign policy and for ensuring the fulfillment of the objectives of Andean integration. It meets in regular session twice a year and in special session when advisable. The council expresses itself through declarations or through legally binding decisions, both of which must be adopted by consensus.

—Commission of the Andean Community. The plenipotentiary representatives from the governments of each member country (usually the minister in charge of trade and integration) constitute the commission, which functions as the main policymaking body of the Andean Integration System. Together with the Council of Foreign Ministers, the commission plays an important legislative role since its formal decisions are directly enforceable in member countries without requiring congressional ratification.

—General Secretariat of the Andean Community. Headquartered in Lima, Peru, the general secretariat is the executive body of the Andean Community under the direction of a secretary general. Established by the Trujillo Protocol, the secretariat replaced the former board of the Cartagena Agreement. It has the authority to present policy proposals for the consideration of the Andean commission. It also acts as the first instance or administrative phase in all cases of alleged noncompliance by member countries with Andean legislation.

—Court of Justice of the Andean Community. This is the judicial body of the Andean Community, headquartered in Quito, Ecuador, and composed of five judges, one from each member country. The court settles disputes, ensures the uniform application of the provisions of the legal system of the Andean Community through pretrial interpretations, and ensures the legality of community provisions by reviewing nullity actions that can be brought by any affected party against commission decisions or general secretariat resolutions that allegedly violate the community's legal system. As of 1996 the Andean Court was given authority to act as arbitrator and to rule on cases of omission or failure to act.

—Andean Parliament. The deliberative body of the Andean Community, the parliament is currently formed by representatives of the national congresses of member countries, but all of its members will be elected by direct and universal vote by the year 2002.

Several other institutions complete the Andean Integration System. The Andean Development Corporation, the financial arm of the process, has been very active in recent years in providing financing for projects that support and promote the integration process. The Andean Business

Advisory Council and the Andean Labor Advisory Council have been revitalized as means of increasing the role of these sectors of civil society in the integration process. Finally, there are the Latin American Reserve Fund, the Simón Bolívar Andean University, and the Social Conventions (Hipólito Unánue on health and Andrés Bello on educational, technological, and cultural integration).

The Agreement Today: Coverage

Since its formation, one of the main objectives of the Andean Community has been the establishment of a customs union among its members. Although that goal was not achieved within the ten-year period projected, progress has been made toward the establishment of a free trade area and, to a lesser extent, a customs union. Moreover, on May 27, 1999, the Eleventh Andean Presidential Council, meeting on the occasion of the thirtieth anniversary of the Cartagena Agreement, agreed to establish the Andean Common Market "by the year 2005 at the latest, creating the conditions for adding to the free circulation of goods, the free mobility of services, capital and persons in the subregion."[20]

To create the conditions for advancing regional economic integration, Andean countries have taken significant steps in the areas of services, investment, and intellectual property. The Andean Commission adopted Decision 439 on June 11, 1998, establishing a general framework of principles and rules for the progressive liberalization of trade in services within the subregion with the goal of attaining a common market in the sector by the year 2005. To this end, annual negotiations are envisaged for the gradual phase-out of discriminatory trade-restrictive measures maintained by each member country as identified in a national inventory.[21] The harmonization of national regulatory regimes in certain service sectors is also envisaged. Pursuant to Decision 439, new regimes have been adopted on telecommunications (Decision 462) and tourism (Decision 463), and discussions are under way on the adoption of decisions on financial and professional services. Decision 462 calls for the elimination of restrictions on

---

20. XI Andean Presidential Council, Act of Cartagena, May 23–27, 1999.
21. These inventories were to be prepared by the general secretariat and approved through a decision of the Andean Community Commission no later than July 2000.

all telecommunication services except radio and television broadcasting as of January 1, 2002.[22] This decision adds to the important body of provisions pertaining to transportation services that eliminate reserved cargo in sea transport, apply an "open skies policy" in air passenger transport, and incorporate the principles of freedom of operation, nondiscrimination, and free competition in land transport.[23]

In 1991 the Andean Community adopted a common regime on the treatment of foreign investment, which departed significantly from an earlier agreement on foreign investment that was geared to the import substitution model for economic growth.[24] Under Decision 291 restrictive elements of the old agreement—such as a requirement that a foreign investor obtain authorization from the host country before its establishment there, and limits on the transfer of funds related to investments—have been eliminated. The new regime accords foreign investors the same rights and obligations as it gives national investors, except as provided for in the national legislation of each member country. It also grants foreign investors the right to transfer abroad, in freely convertible currency, the proven net profits from their direct foreign investment as well as the proceeds of its total or partial liquidation. In general, however, treatment of foreign investment under the current regime, including the settlement of disputes, has been left to the national legislation of each member country. A new approach is currently under consideration. A working group established by the Andean Commission is in the process of elaborating a draft decision that would set up a common regime to promote investment in the region and harmonize the rules related to foreign investment in member countries.

The current intellectual property regime for all five countries of the Andean Community is found in four decisions issued by the Andean Commission. Decision 486, the Common Regime on Industrial Property,

22. The liberalization process has been organized in two stages, the first of which—free trade in all telecommunications services save basic local telephony, national and international long-distance calls, and ground mobile telephony—was implemented on January 1, 2000.

23. The provisions refer only to land transportation services provided for in the roads and border crossing points that form part of the Andean Road System. Moreover, the supply of those services must be authorized by both the country of origin and of destination. Progress in this area has been limited by conflicts among service providers that have prompted an ongoing process of revision of the regime by the Andean Community Commission.

24. Decision 291: Regime for the Common Treatment of Foreign Capital and Trademarks, Patents, Licensing Agreements and Royalties.

contains rules for the protection of patents, utility models, industrial designs, trademarks, geographical indications and appellations of origin, layout designs of integrated circuits, undisclosed information, and unfair competition. It also includes rules on enforcement of these rights. Decision 351 sets out a common regime on copyrights and related rights, Decision 391 does the same for access to genetic resources, and Decision 345 provides protection for plant breeders' rights.[25]

THE FREE TRADE AREA. Bolivia, Colombia, Ecuador, and Venezuela have participated in the Andean Free Trade Area since February 1993, when the list of exceptions to the tariff schedule was fully phased out for each country. Peru, which had suspended its commitments regarding the Liberalization Program in 1992, joined the Free Trade Area in July 1997, agreeing to a tariff reduction schedule that would lead to liberalization of 85 percent of items by the year 2000 and complete free trade in goods by 2005.[26] Pursuant to Article 3 of Decision 414, which allows for more rapid tariff phase-outs, Peru and Ecuador signed an agreement that eliminated tariffs in their reciprocal trade, as of August 1999, on around 42 percent of items still subject to phase-out in the Peruvian liberalization program with the rest of the Andean Community members. A phase-out schedule was also established for the remainder of the items traded between Peru and Ecuador, albeit with some exceptions, to be fully implemented by December 31, 2001.

The Andean Community rules of origin, designed to ensure that only products originating in the member countries benefit from the Andean Free Trade Area, are set out in Decision 416 of July 1997. These rules belong to the traditional or first-generation type, which determines origin using criteria such as fully manufactured goods, change in tariff subheadings, value added, and in some cases, specific requirements of origin. The system also includes procedures for appropriate certification, control, and enforcement.

25. Decision 486: Common Regime on Industrial Property, Sept. 14, 2000, entered into force on December 1, 2000. Decision 486 replaced Decision 344: Common Provisions on Industrial Property (Jan. 1, 1994). Decision 351: Common Provisions on Copyright and Neighboring Rights. Decision 345: Common Provisions on the Protection of the Rights of Breeders of New Plant Varieties. Decision 391: Common Regime on Access to Genetic Resources.
26. Commission of the Cartagena Agreement, Decision 414, July 30, 1997.

THE CUSTOMS UNION. Although the Andean Free Trade Area has been established—with totally liberalized trade among Bolivia, Colombia, Ecuador, and Venezuela and the gradual incorporation of Peru—obstacles preventing the full implementation of a common external tariff have made a customs union more difficult to attain. The common external tariff formally took effect on February 1, 1995, for all member countries except Peru.[27] The tariff has an average level of 13.6 percent and a four-level structure: a 5 percent tariff rate for raw materials and industrial inputs; 10 percent for intermediate inputs; 15 percent for capital goods; and 20 percent for final goods. However, Bolivia was authorized to continue applying its national schedule with tariffs of 5 and 10 percent. A special regime was established for Ecuador, allowing it to vary the common external tariff level by five percentage points for a specific list of products (initially, 930 items). Additionally, a list of exceptions (400 items for Ecuador and 230 items for Venezuela and Colombia) was to be reduced by 50 items a year, although total phase-out was delayed until June 2000. Currently, the phase-out is progressing but at a slower pace. Temporary suspensions are allowed in case of supply shortages and national emergencies. For 2,000 products included on the "List of Not Produced Goods," countries are authorized to lower the external tariff to 5 percent.[28]

The challenges encountered in the establishment of an Andean common external tariff are linked in many ways to the implementation of more open trade regimes during the 1990s that, in the case of some member countries, have included the adoption of flatter tariff schedules with much lower protection levels that allow little room for a complex common external tariff structure. Currently, ways to include a greater degree of flexibility in the design of the mechanism are being considered so as to allow for the establishment of the Andean Common Market within the 2005 deadline set by the heads of state.

A new Automotive Complementarity Agreement was signed on September 16, 1999, between Colombia, Ecuador, and Venezuela, superseding the previous arrangements in that sector. The agreement entered into force on January 1, 2000, for an extendable period of ten years. It maintains the common 35 percent external tariff on category 1 vehicles (light units with a maximum capacity of sixteen people and a maximum cargo capacity of 4.5 tons); and places a lower tariff on category 2 units (heavy

27. Commission of the Cartagena Agreement, Decision 370, November 26, 1994.
28. Andean Community General Secretariat, Resolution 262.

units surpassing the category 1 limits) of 15 percent for Colombia and
Venezuela and 10 percent for Ecuador. Vehicles that comply with specific
requirements of origin as set up by the general secretariat have free access to
the subregional market. The agreement was made compatible with WTO
obligations by removing the requirement for subregional local content.

THE COMMON MARKET AND BEYOND. According to the commitment adopted
at the Eleventh Andean Presidential Council, the Andean Common Market is to be operational by December 31, 2005, at the latest. This ambitious goal, reaffirmed by the heads of state at the Twelfth Andean Presidential
Council held in Lima on June 9–10, 2000, would result in the free circulation of goods, services, capital, and people among the member countries as
well as in the harmonization of their macroeconomic policies. As already
mentioned, progress has been achieved in establishing free trade for goods,
and steps have been taken in the areas of services, investment, and intellectual property.

With respect to the free circulation of people, the Twelfth Andean Presidential Council agreed to the use of a national identification document as
the only requirement for people from one member country to circulate
freely to another, as well as other complementary measures. Work is under
way to implement these commitments.

Finally, the subject of macroeconomic policy harmonization—one that
is usually associated with levels of integration that go beyond a common
market—has recently been given increased attention in the context of the
efforts toward establishing the Andean Common Market. Although the
subject had been discussed in the past, the Ninth Andean Presidential Council took a concrete step forward when it created the Advisory Council of
Treasury Ministers, Central Banks, and Economic Planning Bodies and
asked it to "draw up an Agenda for harmonizing monetary, exchange, financial, and fiscal policy." The advisory council has been holding annual
meetings with the purpose of complying with this ambitious objective. At
its fourth meeting, held in Lima, Peru, on June 8, 2000, the council reiterated its "firm intention to boost the harmonization of macroeconomic
policies and goals" starting with monetary and fiscal policies.

External Trade Relations

As part of its ambitious integration effort, the Andean Community
has developed a common foreign policy whose guidelines were laid down

in May 1999 by the Andean Council of Foreign Ministers.[29] On the economic front, the Andean Community has been actively engaged in trade
negotiations with third parties, has been participating with a single voice
in the FTAA negotiations, and has gained preferential access to the markets
of the United States and European Union through the Andean Trade Preference Act and the Special System of Andean Preferences, respectively.

Of particular importance are the ongoing negotiations with
MERCOSUR for the creation of a free trade area between the two blocs
pursuant to a framework agreement signed on April 16, 1998. As part of
this process, four of the members of the Andean Community (Colombia,
Ecuador, Peru, and Venezuela) signed economic complementarity agreements (ACEs) with Brazil in August 1999 (ACE 39) and with Argentina in
June 2000 (ACE 48). The latter provides preferential access to products
covering about 40 percent of the tariff schedule.[30] These agreements add
on to the agreement Bolivia had already signed with MERCOSUR in December 1996 (ACE 36) to establish a free trade area. The process got an
important boost with the recent agreement by the heads of state of the
member countries of MERCOSUR and the Andean Community to "start
negotiations leading to the signing of the free trade area as soon as possible
and, in any case, by January 2002."[31]

Additionally, negotiations between the Andean Community and the
Northern Triangle (El Salvador, Guatemala, and Honduras) started in March
2000 with the purpose of signing a tariff preferences agreement that would
eventually lead to the establishment of a free trade area between these countries. Preliminary talks were held in early 1997 with Panama for the signing
of a free trade agreement.

On October 30, 1998, the Andean Community countries signed an
agreement with the United States, their most important trading partner,
establishing a Council on Trade and Investment to serve as a forum for
dialogue. It held its first meeting in May 1999 in Cartagena de Indias,
Colombia. Exports from Bolivia, Colombia, Ecuador, and Peru to the U.S.
market benefit from tariff reductions granted under the Andean Trade Preference Act approved in 1991 by the U.S. Congress to support these countries' antinarcotic efforts. The Andean countries are seeking an extension

29. Andean Council of Foreign Ministers, Decision 458, May 25, 1999.
30. In the case of Paraguay and Uruguay, the bilateral partial scope agreements signed with these
countries by Colombia, Ecuador, Peru, and Venezuela have been extended until December 31, 2000.
31. The Brasilia Comuniqué. Meeting of the Presidents of South America. Brasilia, September 1,
2000.

of the program beyond its 2001 deadline, a reduction in the list of excluded products, and the incorporation of Venezuela as a beneficiary.[32]

The Caribbean Community and Common Market

The Caribbean Community and Common Market (CARICOM) was established by the Treaty of Chaguaramas, signed on July 4, 1973, by Barbados, Guyana, Jamaica, and Trinidad and Tobago. The treaty entered into force on August 1, 1973. The following year Antigua and Barbuda, Belize, Dominica, Grenada, Montserrat, St. Kitts-Nevis-Anguilla, St. Lucia, and St. Vincent and the Grenadines acceded to the treaty, thereby becoming CARICOM members.[33] The Bahamas joined the Caribbean Community, though not the Common Market, in 1983. Suriname became a member in 1995, and Haiti, which has formally been admitted to CARICOM, will become a member once it deposits its instruments of accession with the group's secretary general. The British Virgin Islands and the Turks and Caicos Islands count as associate members of CARICOM. (In addition, six Eastern Caribbean members of CARICOM are also organized into a subregional integration group, with a common monetary policy and currency; see box 3-1).

With a population of 6 million and a gross domestic product amounting to around $17 billion, CARICOM is the smallest of the regional integration arrangements in the Western Hemisphere. At the same time, it has the largest membership of any integration arrangement in the Americas.

Attempts at integration in the Caribbean region date back to 1958, when, under the auspices of the United Kingdom, ten dependent territories, all current members of CARICOM, formed the West Indies Federation. In the aftermath of the Second World War, the United Kingdom saw the federation primarily as an effective means of rationalizing the administration of its Caribbean territories. Soon after its formation, however, the federation began to disintegrate, as its two largest members—Jamaica and Trinidad and Tobago—gained independence from the United Kingdom and withdrew from the group.[34]

32. Venezuela currently benefits from the Generalized System of Preferences.
33. In 1980 Anguilla, which had been incorporated into a single British dependency along with St. Kitts and Nevis in the early nineteenth century, became a British dependency separate from St. Kitts and Nevis, which in turn gained its independence in 1983. Anguilla's associate membership status in CARICOM is currently under negotiation.
34. Duhamel (2000).

Box 3-1. *The Eastern Caribbean Subregion*

Subregional integration in the Eastern Caribbean region took place in parallel to broader integration initiatives among the larger group of Caribbean countries. In 1967 the government of the United Kingdom granted six Eastern Caribbean territories—Antigua and Barbuda, Dominica, Grenada, St. Kitts-Nevis-Anguilla, St. Lucia, and St. Vincent and the Grenadines—extended autonomy as West Indies Associated States. This Association was transformed into the Organization of Eastern Caribbean States (OECS) in 1981. OECS members have achieved a significant level of integration, as reflected by their common monetary policy and currency, as well as their common foreign and security policy.

Calls for strengthening and deepening ties among Caribbean islands did not end with the demise of the West Indies Federation. In fact, shortly after leaving the federation, the government of Trinidad and Tobago convened the first conference of heads of government and proposed the creation of a Caribbean Economic Community based on the integration model put into place by six Western European countries a few years earlier. As a step toward realizing that ambitious goal, representatives from Barbados, British Guiana, and Antigua announced plans in July 1965 to establish a free trade area. A few months later the three entities signed an agreement establishing the Caribbean Free Trade Area (CARIFTA). The implementation of CARIFTA was deliberately postponed while the new free trade area sought to expand its membership. CARIFTA became operational in 1968, the same year that several other Caribbean countries, including Jamaica, Trinidad and Tobago, and other former members of the West Indies Federation became members.

During the next few years trade among the Caribbean countries grew significantly. Trinidad and Tobago, for example, increased its exports to the Caribbean from around 50 percent of its total exports to more than 60 percent between 1967 and 1974.[35] The trade expansion within the region usually took place behind high protective tariff walls that insulated nascent Caribbean industries—particularly those in the larger economies

35. Bernal (1994).

of Barbados, Jamaica, and Trinidad and Tobago—from international competition.

In October 1972 the members of CARIFTA agreed to take further steps to transform the free trade area into a common market. Soon afterward, countries began to formulate a draft legal instrument, which was signed in Georgetown, Guyana, by all CARIFTA members except Antigua and Montserrat. Known as the Georgetown Accord, this instrument paved the way for the subsequent signing and entry into force of the Treaty of Chaguaramas establishing the Caribbean Community and Common Market.

The slower growth and increased economic volatility that coincided with the birth of CARICOM derailed many of its members' efforts to implement the measures necessary to comply with the common market principles set out in the Treaty of Chaguaramas. In fact, although an estimated 90 percent of intraregional imports to Barbados, Guyana, Jamaica, and Trinidad and Tobago faced no tariff or quantitative restrictions by the time CARICOM was founded in 1973, during the next ten years or so, many countries in the region reverted to protectionist policies and imposed quantitative restrictions and licensing requirements on imports originating in CARICOM countries.[36] As a result, intra-CARICOM trade suffered a sharp decline during most of the 1980s. Severe balance of payments crises and low rates of growth throughout the decade hindered repeated efforts at reviving the waning economic integration process in the Caribbean.

It was not until 1989, at the tenth meeting of CARICOM heads of government, that members were able to inject new impetus to the process of economic integration by recasting the objectives of the group regarding economic integration in terms of a single market and economy. This new initiative revolves around five main axes: the free movement of goods, services, and factors of production; the harmonization of laws and regulations affecting economic activities; the reform of CARICOM's institutions; the coordination of macroeconomic policies and foreign trade relations; and the implementation of a common external tariff. Although a single market and economy has yet to materialize, in recent years CARICOM countries and dependent territories have made significant progress in their efforts to achieve closer levels of economic integration.

36. Hall (1988).

The Agreement Today: Legal and Institutional Framework

The Treaty of Chaguaramas established two distinct entities: the Caribbean Community, and the Caribbean Common Market. In creating the Caribbean Community, the signatories of the Treaty of Chaguaramas sought to deepen economic integration among themselves, to coordinate their foreign policies, and to establish cooperative mechanisms in areas of common interest, including communications and information, culture, education, meteorology, disaster preparedness, energy development, science and technology, regional health development, and environmental protection.[37] The Caribbean Common Market, created as a means to attain the goal of deeper economic integration among the treaty's signatories, has three specific purposes: to strengthen coordination and regulation of the economic and trade relations among members; to achieve sustained expansion and continuing integration of the economies of members; and to attain a greater measure of independence and effectiveness in dealing with nonmembers.[38]

With a view to attaining the objectives of the Community and Common Market, CARICOM member states have recently taken significant steps toward rationalizing, restructuring, and strengthening the institutions first created by the Treaty of Chaguaramas. Protocol I, signed by CARICOM members in 1997, is devoted primarily to redefining the role, functions, and powers of the institutions of the Caribbean Community. The protocol identifies the Conference of Heads of Government and the Community Council of Ministers as the two principal organs of CARICOM.

The conference is the supreme organ of the Caribbean Community and has primary responsibility for providing policy guidance to the process of integration among the member countries. To this end, it has the power to issue policy directives to other bodies of the community, as well as to establish new organs. In addition, the conference has the authority to enter into agreements with third parties on behalf of the community. Composed of the heads of government of CARICOM members, the conference makes decisions by unanimous consent.

The second highest organ in CARICOM's hierarchy is the Community Council of Ministers. This body, which consists of ministers responsible for community affairs (and any other minister designated by member

---

37. Treaty Establishing the Caribbean Community and Common Market, Article 4.
38. Treaty Establishing the Caribbean Community and Common Market, Annex Article 3.

states), is responsible for "strategic planning and coordination," based on the policy decisions established by the conference, in the three areas covered by the Treaty of Chaguaramas: economic integration, functional cooperation, and external relations. To fulfill these broad functions, the council approves community programs and requests councils of ministers to develop specific proposals. In addition, the council approves the community budget and allocates resources for the implementation of community programs. It also promotes and monitors the implementation of community decisions in member countries. To carry out this responsibility, the council, following instructions of the conference, can issue directives to subsidiary organs and to the secretariat with a view to ensuring the timely implementation of community decisions. Several councils of ministers, with responsibilities in specific areas, assist the two principal bodies of the community in the performance of their functions: the Council for Trade and Economic Development, the Council for Foreign and Community Relations, the Council for Human and Social Development, and the Council for Finance and Planning.

The Treaty of Chaguaramas also created a secretariat, based in Georgetown. The secretariat services meetings of the community's governing organs, collects and disseminates to CARICOM members information on issues connected to the objectives of the community, provides technical assistance to countries, and coordinates the activities of donor agencies, among other functions. At the same time, the secretariat, which Protocol I refers to as the "chief executive officer" of the community, can carry out studies and make proposals to competent bodies on issues associated with furthering the objectives of the treaty. Finally, in 1997 CARICOM members set up the Caribbean Regional Negotiating Machinery for International Economic Negotiations (RNM), which services negotiations taking place between CARICOM and third countries in the context of the World Trade Organization, the Free Trade Area of the Americas, and the post-Lomé agreements with the European Union.[39] Like the Andean Community and MERCOSUR, CARICOM speaks with a single voice in the FTAA negotiations.

---

39. On June 23, 2000, the European Union and seventy-seven African, Caribbean, and Pacific (ACP) countries, including all members of CARICOM, signed the Cotonou Agreement, which replaced the Lomé Convention, since 1975 the basic framework for cooperation between the European Union and ACP countries. The Cotonou Agreement calls for the conclusion of new trading arrangements—or post-Lomé agreements—between the European Union and the ACP by the end of the year 2008.

The Agreement Today: Coverage

In the domain of trade policy, the Treaty of Chaguaramas contains provisions on tariffs and nontariff barriers, rules of origin, safeguards, anti-dumping and countervailing measures, subsidies, and standards. Like many other regional integration schemes in the hemisphere, CARICOM's rules of origin require that a good be "wholly produced" within CARICOM or, if the good is produced from materials originating in third countries, that "substantial transformation" occur within CARICOM.[40] With respect to safeguards, Articles 28 and 29 of the annex to the treaty allow CARICOM members to impose temporary trade restrictions in case of balance of payments difficulties or difficulties in particular industries. Article 19 of the annex authorizes CARICOM states and territories to take action against dumped or subsidized imports in conformance with members' domestic legislation and international obligations. Provisions in the areas of industrial standards and sanitary and phytosanitary measures are also contained in the annex. CARICOM members created the Caribbean Common Market Standards Council, an advisory body to the Council on Trade and Economic Development, with the specific objective of promoting the progressive development and harmonization of standards in the region.

Since the decision in 1989 to plan for a single market and economy, rule-making activity has intensified in many spheres that were previously not covered, or not covered in sufficient detail, by the Treaty of Chaguaramas. New or enhanced rules have been or are being formulated with respect to the free movement of goods, services, capital, and labor, as well as the harmonization of laws regarding customs, intellectual property, competition, corporate taxation, and dumping and subsidization.

Specifically, in the domain of services and investment, countries have negotiated Protocol II, which amends several articles of the Treaty of Chaguaramas to provide any CARICOM national with the right of establishment, the right to provide services, and the right to move capital across the member countries.[41] These provisions are complemented by various other instruments, including a 1993 arrangement allowing companies based in CARICOM to list on any of the region's stock exchanges and a 1995

---

40. The "substantial transformation" criterion is fulfilled when a good is classified under a different tariff heading from the materials used to produce it or when the good has a minimum percentage of "local content." In the case of CARICOM, a good is considered "local" when it has at least 65 percent local or regional value added.

41. See chapters 8 and 9 in this volume.

policy decision addressing the free movement of skilled persons. Several other protocols contribute to the basic legal framework for the establishment of the CARICOM single market and economy.[42] These protocols span a wide array of spheres underlying the functioning of a market economy, namely, trade policy (Protocol IV); competition policy, consumer protection, dumping, and subsidies (Protocol VIII); and dispute settlement (Protocol IX). In addition, there are three "sectoral" protocols: industrial policy (Protocol III); agricultural policy (Protocol V); and transportation policy (Protocol VI). Protocol VII (disadvantaged countries, regions, and sectors) establishes a framework for special and differential treatment targeted not only at the less-developed countries of CARICOM, but also at regions and sectors experiencing economic dislocation and requiring temporary support measures.

THE FREE TRADE AREA. CARICOM countries have largely succeeded in eliminating tariffs and nontariff barriers to imports of goods originating within the region, as provided for in Articles 15 (import duties) and 21 (quantitative import restrictions) of the Annex to the Treaty of Chaguaramas. The remaining exceptions to free trade can be grouped under two broad headings—health and security, and the development of CARICOM's less-developed countries.[43] On health and security issues, Article 23 (general exceptions) and Article 24 (security exceptions) allow CARICOM members to adopt measures necessary to protect, among other things, their essential security interests; public morals; human, animal, or plant life; industrial property or copyrights; and national treasures of artistic, historic, or archaeological value. CARICOM members can also impose import duties or quantitative restrictions on certain products (listed in Schedule I of the annex) in connection with "contractual obligations."[44] Only nine products remain listed on Schedule I.

To promote the development of less-developed members, the Treaty of Chaguaramas contains several provisions allowing them to apply import duties or quantitative restrictions on goods originating in the more devel-

42. There are a total of nine protocols amending the Treaty of Chaguaramas. All nine have been signed by CARICOM member states. Four are in effect and are being applied provisionally (Protocols I, II, IV, and VII).

43. The Treaty of Chaguaramas divides CARICOM members into less-developed countries and more-developed countries. The latter group includes Barbados, Guyana, Jamaica, and Trinidad and Tobago. The remaining CARICOM members are included in the less-developed category.

44. See Article 13 and Schedule I of the Annex to the Treaty of Chaguaramas.

oped countries of CARICOM (Barbados, Guyana, Jamaica, and Trinidad and Tobago). Currently, three less-developed countries—Belize, Dominica, and Grenada—include rum, cigarettes, and motor vehicles on this Schedule III list of exceptions. Apart from these exceptions, which are to expire in 2001, Article 56 of the treaty allows less-developed countries to promote the development of a particular industry by suspending CARICOM preferential treatment on imports from more-developed members. Before enacting measures under Article 56, however, a less-developed country must apply for permission from the Community Council of Ministers, which must approve the measures by majority decision. Nine products are currently covered by Article 56: curry powder, pasta products, candles, industrial gases, wheat flour, certain beverages, solar water heaters, and furniture of wood and upholstered fabric; their protection will expire in 2004. In a further effort to aid less-developed countries, CARICOM, in Schedule IX of the annex, allows them to subject imports of oils and fats products to a licensing requirement.

THE CUSTOMS UNION. Recent efforts by CARICOM members to deepen their level of economic integration have allowed the group to move beyond a free trade area and closer to a customs union. The 1973 Treaty of Chaguaramas provided for the establishment of a common external tariff—the central component of a customs union—but its implementation had fallen behind schedule by 1983. It was not until a special summit meeting in October 1992 that CARICOM formally adopted a new program to harmonize its members' tariff regimes, based on the proposals of a blue-ribbon panel of experts, appointed some time earlier to examine and make recommendations on the region's integration process, including the common external tariff.[45]

The decision to adopt this program was accompanied by a commitment on the part of CARICOM members to reduce the level of the external tariff. This development represented a significant policy shift away from the high import barriers that had characterized CARICOM's common protective policy in place since the group's founding. In the context of profound changes in the international economic environment in the latter half of the 1980s, CARICOM countries agreed on a four-phase schedule that would be implemented between 1993 and 1998 and would ultimately result in a common external tariff composed of six rates between 0 and 40

45. Gill (1997).

percent. The 40 percent ceiling would apply only to primary agricultural products, while textiles and apparel, general manufactures, and agro-industrial products would be subject to the next highest tariff levels. The lowest tariffs would apply to primary, intermediate, and capital inputs that were not available or produced locally. The remaining group of products would be subject to mid-range tariff levels. The implementation of the common external tariff has proceeded unevenly across countries: seven countries—Barbados, Grenada, Guyana, Jamaica, St. Lucia, St. Vincent and the Grenadines, and Trinidad and Tobago—have implemented the final phase of the reduction program. Belize and Montserrat were granted temporary delays.[46] The remaining countries have not yet implemented the entirety of the reduction program.

In parallel to their efforts to introduce and implement a common external tariff, CARICOM countries have gradually eliminated quantitative restrictions applied to imports from countries outside the community. As a result, quantitative restrictions no longer form part of the common external regime of CARICOM, except in the case of oils and fats products, which, as noted earlier, are subject to a special regime aimed at supporting the development of these sectors in less-developed countries.

THE COMMON MARKET AND BEYOND. As mentioned earlier, CARICOM in 1989 defined its future direction in terms of a single market and economy. This initiative contains elements of both a common market and an economic union, as it stipulates not only the free movement of goods, services, and factors of production, but also a more "comprehensive harmonization of laws affecting commerce and regulation of economic activities," and "more intensive coordination of macro-economic policy and planning, external trade and economic relations."[47] While significant steps have been taken in the area of trade in goods and services, efforts toward bolstering the movement of factors of production are still in their embryonic phase. The free movement of labor has perhaps advanced the most, as eleven member states of CARICOM have enacted legislation on the free movement of university graduates within the region. With respect to policy harmonization, countries recently began addressing the subject of fiscal harmonization, in particular the harmonization of both corporate tax structures and

46. Specifically, Belize was authorized to delay the implementation of each phase of the program by two years; Montserrat, on the other hand, was authorized to delay implementation of the common external tariff until 1998.
47. WTO (2000a).

incentive regimes for foreign direct investment. Ultimately, the extent to which the members of CARICOM fulfill the ambitious goals associated with their aspirations for closer economic integration will depend not only on their continued capacity to give specific content to the general principles of the single market and economy initiative, but also on their ability to implement existing disciplines, in particular those agreed upon during the 1990s.

External Trade Relations

During the 1990s CARICOM countries signed trade agreements with three countries of the Americas: Venezuela in 1992, Colombia in 1994, and the Dominican Republic in 1998. The agreements with Colombia and Venezuela contain nonreciprocal elements, that is, they grant preferential treatment to selected exports from CARICOM to Venezuela and Colombia without requiring that some or all CARICOM countries grant preferential treatment in return, at least during a specified period.[48] The agreement between CARICOM and the Dominican Republic, in contrast, eliminates tariffs for all goods (except those identified in annexes) traded between the Dominican Republic and the more-developed countries of CARICOM. Less-developed countries of CARICOM are not required to extend duty-free treatment to products originating in the Dominican Republic until the year 2005. In addition to merchandise trade, the agreement also specifies disciplines in the areas of services, investment, and government procurement.

Recently, the United States adopted the Caribbean Basin Trade Partnership Act, which accords preferential treatment to exports from most CARICOM members to the United States. The new U.S. law builds on previous programs commonly referred to as the Caribbean Basin Initiative.[49]

Outside the hemisphere CARICOM countries number among the seventy-seven African, Caribbean, and Pacific (ACP) countries that signed the Cotonou Agreement with the European Union on June 23, 2000. The agreement sets out a new framework for trade and cooperation between the European Union and ACP countries. In the area of trade the Cotonou Agreement grants, for a "preparatory" period of eight years from the entry into force of the agreement's trade provisions (March 1, 2000), nonreciprocal

---

48. See chapter 5 in this volume for a description of the CARICOM-Colombia and the CARICOM-Venezuela agreements.

49. For a discussion of the Caribbean Basin Initiative, see chapter 5 in this volume.

preferential treatment for products originating in the ACP countries that is substantially equivalent to the preferential regime established by the fourth Lomé Convention, the agreement governing relations between the European Union and ACP countries prior to the Cotonou Agreement. During the preparatory phase the two parties have agreed to conclude additional agreements with a view to the progressive elimination of all barriers to trade between them. For the Caribbean countries the principal products benefiting from the preferential regime include bananas, rum, and rice.

MERCOSUR

The presidents of Argentina, Brazil, Paraguay, and Uruguay signed the Treaty of Asunción on March 26, 1991, with the objective of establishing the Common Market of the South (MERCOSUR). The treaty called for the free circulation of goods, services, and factors of production among member countries by January 1, 1995, through the elimination of tariffs and nontariff barriers, the adoption of a common external tariff and a common trade policy, the coordination of macroeconomic and sectoral policies, and the harmonization of the members' legislation in relevant areas.

In 1999 MERCOSUR encompassed a population of 213 million and a gross domestic product of almost $1.1 trillion. Brazil is MERCOSUR's largest member, accounting for 70 percent of its gross domestic product (GDP) and for almost one-third of Argentina's exports, about 35 percent of Uruguay's, and 40 percent of Paraguay's. Chile and Bolivia became associate members of MERCOSUR in 1996 and 1997, respectively.

Two key events led to the establishment of MERCOSUR. First, the return to democracy in Argentina and Brazil in the 1980s contributed to the building of a new alliance between these two countries. Although they, along with Paraguay, had signed an agreement in 1979 ending a long dispute over the use of the Paraná River waters, it was the election of presidents Raúl Alfonsín in Argentina in 1983 and José Sarney in Brazil in 1985 that furthered the integration process in the Southern Cone. The first tangible step toward integration was taken in 1986 when Argentina and Brazil concluded a bilateral economic cooperation agreement. The Program for Integration and Economic Cooperation was negotiated in the framework of the Latin American Integration Association (and was based on the industrial and trade strategy that had given rise in the 1950s to the import-substitution model in Latin America). The agreement between Argentina and Brazil took a sectoral approach to expanding bilateral trade between the two countries. It included numerous protocols in areas such as capital goods, technological cooperation, and the nuclear and auto industries.

The debt crisis of the 1980s and the structural reforms that followed produced fundamental changes in the integration strategy espoused by Argentina and Brazil. By the late 1980s and early 1990s, both countries had embraced trade liberalization. In 1988 they signed the Treaty of Integration, Cooperation, and Development, which entered into force a year later. The treaty laid out the legal framework for economic integration between Argentina and Brazil and built on principles already laid out in the earlier bilateral agreement. The treaty aimed at eliminating all tariffs and nontariff barriers and creating a common market between the two partners within a period of ten years. It also promoted the harmonization and coordination of their policies in the economic sphere. In June 1990, as economic liberalization and privatization were intensifying in both countries, Argentina and Brazil signed the Act of Buenos Aires to speed up the integration process and to establish a common market by the end of 1994. A meeting of high-level representatives of Argentina, Brazil, Chile, Paraguay, and Uruguay held in Brasilia in August of the same year to discuss the creation of a common market in the Southern Cone, led to the signing of the Treaty of Asunción in March 1991.[50] Chile, which had an external tariff of 11 percent, lower than the common external tariff level set by MERCOSUR, elected not to join MERCOSUR in 1991 but became an associate member in 1996 after signing a trade agreement with the group in the framework of the Latin American Integration Association. Bolivia followed Chile a few months later and became an associate member in 1997.

Following the transition period and the signing of the Protocol of Ouro Preto on December 17, 1994, the members of MERCOSUR concentrated their efforts and resources on implementing the results of their negotiations to that date and on deepening integration in the direction of a common market. The Protocol of Ouro Preto also introduced special agreements in the automotive and sugar sectors, which foresaw the establishment of a common automotive policy and the phasing out of tariffs in intrazone trade in sugar by 2000.

By January 1995 MERCOSUR had achieved one of its main goals, with 88 percent of the goods on which tariffs were levied already under the common external tariff.[51] Intra-MERCOSUR trade grew at a fast pace until

50. ECLAC (1992, p. 17).
51. Valls Pereira (1999).

1997. Between 1991 and 1996, intraregional trade as a share of the total exports of MERCOSUR countries increased from 8 percent to 21 percent. As MERCOSUR member countries gradually phased out tariffs on the imports of member countries and as the common external tariff was implemented, the value of total exports from MERCOSUR countries rose from $47 billion in 1990 to $84 billion in 1997, while imports grew from $32 billion to $106 billion during the same period.

The region experienced a temporary slowdown in the wake of the 1997 Asian financial crisis and the recession that followed in Brazil and Argentina in 1998–99. MERCOSUR's trade volume shrank by 20 percent in 1999. In late April 2000 the finance and foreign ministers of Argentina and Brazil met in Buenos Aires "to relaunch" MERCOSUR. They agreed "to remove the cause of some of the recent friction by bringing their economies into closer harmony. To that end, they have set a timetable for a 'mini-Maastricht'—a set of economic-convergence targets similar to those in the Maastricht treaty that led to the euro."[52]

Almost ten years after the signing of the Treaty of Asunción, there is no doubt that MERCOSUR has been a success, even though it has yet to reach all the objectives set forth in that treaty. The relaunching of the MERCOSUR endorsed in late June 2000 by all the members, the commitment to sign a free trade agreement with the Andean Community by January 2002, and MERCOSUR's participation as a single bloc in the FTAA negotiations are a clear indication that members are committed to move forward collectively.

The Agreement Today: Legal and Institutional Framework

The Treaty of Asunción provided several important instruments for establishing the common market, a provisional institutional structure for the transition period, and the mechanisms for deciding on the definitive structure of the common market.[53] The treaty spells out the four elements necessary to form a common market:

—the free movement of goods, services, and factors of production between countries through, among other things, the elimination of customs duties and nontariff restrictions on the movement of goods, and any other equivalent measures;

52. *The Economist*, "Mercosur's Trial by Adversity," May 27, 2000.
53. Haines Ferrari (2000).

—the establishment of a common external tariff and the adoption of a common trade policy in relation to nonmembers or groups of nonmember countries, and the coordination of positions in regional and international economic and commercial forums;

—the coordination of macroeconomic and sectoral policies between the member states in the areas of foreign trade, agriculture, industry, fiscal and monetary matters, foreign exchange and capital, services, customs, transport and communications, and any other areas that may be agreed upon, in order to ensure proper competition between the member states; and

—the commitment by members to harmonize their legislation in the relevant areas in order to strengthen the integration process.[54]

The treaty also contains four annexes: the first included a program for tariff reduction with different timetables for the smaller members (Paraguay and Uruguay), and the other three annexes address rules of origin, dispute settlement, and the formation of working groups. At the institutional level the treaty established a Common Market Council, made up of the ministers of foreign affairs and economy of the four member countries; and the Common Market Group, made up of representatives of public entities of the national governments. The Common Market Council is in charge of the political direction of the integration process, while the Common Market Group oversees the implementation of the agreement under the coordination of the foreign ministries of the member countries. The headquarters of the administrative secretariat was established in Montevideo, Uruguay.

The Protocol of Ouro Preto established the organizational structure of MERCOSUR. In addition to reaffirming the role of the Common Market Council and the Common Market Group, the protocol added the MERCOSUR Trade Commission, the Joint Parliamentary Commission, the Economic-Social Consultative Forum, and the MERCOSUR Administrative Secretariat. The Common Market Council, Common Market Group, and MERCOSUR Trade Commission are the three intergovernmental organs with decisionmaking powers.

The Common Market Council formulates policy for the bloc through formal decisions. Its main purpose is to ensure that members are in compliance with the MERCOSUR agreements and that the objective of creating a common market is met. The Common Market Group is the executive organ of MERCOSUR and issues binding resolutions in line with its

54. Article 1, Treaty of Asunción.

mandate, which is threefold: to ensure that the Treaty of Asunción and all the ancillary protocols and agreements signed under the authority of MERCOSUR are respected by its members; to establish work programs that advance the bloc's integration toward a common market; and to negotiate on behalf of MERCOSUR, with the participation of representatives from its member countries, agreements with third countries, groups of countries, and international entities.

The MERCOSUR Trade Commission ensures that the common commercial policy mechanisms agreed to by the member countries are applied consistently. The commission follows up on members' trade policies and reviews developments in the areas under its competence, such as intra-MERCOSUR commercial rules and disciplines, tariffs and goods classification, and sectors such as textiles and automotive.

The Economic-Social Consultative Forum is the only forum with direct participation and representation from the private sector. It provides a venue for promoting the economic and social development of MERCOSUR as a region, through analysis and evaluation of the impact of integration policies on the region. The forum works in cooperation and consultation with public and private national and international entities.

The principal organs of MERCOSUR are assisted in their work by working groups, ad hoc groups, meetings of high-level officials in specialized areas, and technical committees and commissions. The administrative secretariat of MERCOSUR provides support for meetings and maintains the information and documentation infrastructure for members.

The Agreement Today: Coverage

Additional protocols were negotiated to supplement the Treaty of Asunción and to provide rules and disciplines in specific areas. In the area of investment, MERCOSUR countries signed two agreements. The Protocol of Colonia for the Reciprocal Promotion and Protection of Investments in MERCOSUR, signed on January 17, 1994, requires that each MERCOSUR member grant investments of investors of other members treatment no less favorable than that it accords to investments of its own investors or those of third countries. The protocol also prohibits performance requirements, guarantees the free transfer of funds related to investment, provides for compensation in the event of expropriation, and includes an investor-state dispute resolution mechanism in addition to a state-to-state dispute resolution mechanism. The second agreement is the Protocol for the Promotion and Protection of Investment of Third States. Signed on August 5, 1994, the so-called Buenos Aires Protocol addresses the entry of foreign investment from sources outside MERCOSUR. It allows each member to promote and admit investment from third countries in accordance with its laws and regulations. Neither protocol has entered into force.

In December 1996 MERCOSUR countries signed a protocol that sets out guidelines for a common competition policy in the region. The Protocol for the Defense of Competition foresees that each member will establish an autonomous competition agency, that national competition laws will apply to all economic activities, and that the member countries will share a common view about the interplay between competition policy and other government actions.

In the area of services, MERCOSUR member states signed the Protocol of Montevideo in December 1997 with the aim of phasing out restrictions on trade in services over a ten-year period, beginning from the implementation of the protocol (which is not yet in effect). MERCOSUR members carried out a first round of negotiations for an initial exchange of commitments in 1998.

More recently the four member countries set out to reactivate MERCOSUR and take steps to improve the functioning of the subregional agreement. On June 29–30, 2000, MERCOSUR members held the Eighteenth Meeting of the Common Market Council in Buenos Aires. Member countries' presidents, along with those of Chile and Bolivia, also met during this time, approving a series of decisions to reactivate MERCOSUR. Among the issues that blocked progress toward greater trade liberalization in the MERCOSUR area and that the member countries decided to address as part of the reactivation plan were the common external tariff, including related measures such as special import regimes and rules of origin; market access restrictions; measures to facilitate customs procedures; public policies that have a negative effect on competition, as well as competition policy and government procurement issues more generally; trade in services; and the effective incorporation of MERCOSUR legislation into the national legal framework of each of the member countries (the so-called "internalization" of MERCOSUR legislation into national legislation).

THE FREE TRADE AREA. Most tariffs on goods were eliminated between June 1991 and December 1994. Adjustment lists negotiated in 1994 called for a progressive phase-out of the remaining tariffs between January 1, 1995, and December 31, 1998, for Argentina and Brazil and between January 1,

1996, and December 31, 1999, for Uruguay and Paraguay. The tariff reductions were to be gradual, across-the-board, and automatic. The auto and sugar sectors, however, are under a special regime (Box 3-2).

THE CUSTOMS UNION. Between 1991 and 1995 the members of MERCOSUR engaged in a series of negotiations to establish a common external tariff, which has been in force since January 1, 1995. MERCOSUR did not achieve its goal of having a complete customs union by 1995, however, and the deadline was extended to 2006 for full implementation by all members and in all sectors.[55] Capital goods will be covered as of January 1, 2001, whereas the implementation of the common external tariff for computer goods and telecommunications products has been delayed until 2006. As mentioned above, sugar and autos are covered under special arrangements in the Protocol of Ouro Preto. A common policy on these issues is to be adopted by the year 2000 for Argentina and Brazil and by 2001 for Paraguay and Uruguay.

THE COMMON MARKET AND BEYOND. The goal of closer macroeconomic policy coordination is a key element in the relaunching of MERCOSUR's integration process. Although two ad hoc working groups were created to examine trade and macroeconomic coordination in June 1999, progress was very limited on that front until the fall of 2000 when member countries announced the harmonization of their fiscal statistics.[56] The next step, to be implemented in 2001, is to set fiscal targets and convergence goals. These initiatives could eventually be followed by common exchange policies and a single currency.

External Trade Relations

MERCOSUR's external agenda has gained momentum throughout 1999 and 2000. The group announced in July 2000 that negotiations would be initiated to incorporate Chile as a full member into the agreement (Chile has been an associate member since 1996) and to expand trade integration

---

55. WTO (1999a, p. 30).

56. The working groups are the Macroeconomic Coordination Committee, which is to consider, among other things, an action program for greater macroeconomic convergence, and the Trade Coordination Committee. See Inter-American Development Bank (1999).

between MERCOSUR and the Andean Community, with a view toward creating a free trade zone in South America. Chile requested full membership in MERCOSUR in July 2000 during Chilean president Lagos' trip to Brazil. At the Nineteenth Meeting of the Common Market Council, held in Florianopolis, Brazil, on December 14–15, 2000, the president of Chile reiterated the political will of his administration to continue the gradual incorporation of Chile into MERCOSUR at all the institutional levels. On Chile's full incorporation into the customs union the president expressed the need to make progress in succeeding stages on agreeing, when the appropriate moment comes, on the form, reference, terms, and deadlines.

Chile and MERCOSUR will have to overcome a difficult issue involving tariff rates before Chile integrates fully into MERCOSUR. Chile's uniform import tariff rate is currently 9 percent and will decrease by one percentage point a year until it reaches 6 percent in 2003. Meanwhile, external tariff rates for MERCOSUR range from 10 percent to 30 percent for various products, with an average rate of 14 percent. Chile does not want to raise its duties. Chile has made it clear throughout the meetings it has held with its MERCOSUR counterparts that it would like to maintain its trade autonomy vis-à-vis third parties. On December 6, 2000, Chile and the United States launched the negotiation of a free trade agreement. Chile has signed a NAFTA-type agreement with Canada and Mexico.

In April 1998 the member countries of MERCOSUR and the Andean Community took the first step toward the negotiation of a common free trade area by signing a framework agreement for the creation of a free trade area that encompasses various areas of cooperation between the two blocs. Andean Community members negotiated a set of preferential agreements with Brazil in August 1999 and completed a similar set of negotiations in June 2000 with Argentina. Negotiations to reduce barriers to trade between the two subregional blocs were confirmed during the Summit of South American Presidents, held in Brasilia at the end of August 2000. An agreement is expected to be the cornerstone of a larger free trade area in South America, to be completed by 2002. Initial meetings between representatives of the two blocs following the Brasilia Summit indicated that some areas that could deliver early results were considered to be telecommunications, transport, sanitary measures and standards, and physical infrastructure development. Finally, in December 2000 MERCOSUR members signed a framework agreement with South Africa with a view to exploring the possibility of signing a free trade agreement with that country in the future.

Box 3-2. *Sugar and Autos in MERCOSUR*

Disagreements among members of MERCOSUR over trade in two sectors, sugar and autos, have prevented the organization from moving closer to a customs union.

The Sugar Sector

Sugar was originally exempted from the tariff structure negotiated by MERCOSUR members. Under the Protocol of Ouro Preto, the sector is to be fully integrated into the MERCOSUR scheme and liberalized accordingly by 2001. Since 1992 Argentina has applied a tariff of 23 percent to sugar imported from Brazil in response to Brazil's practice of subsidizing its sugar production (in particular, the production of sugar cane). Negotiations between MERCOSUR members to eliminate Brazil's subsidy schemes and Argentina's tariff on the product have been ongoing since 1995, and various studies have been undertaken as part of the process of seeking a negotiated solution. These efforts have led to a better understanding of the sector in the region but have yielded few practical results. Brazil maintains that it has eliminated most distortionary practices (such as regulations on prices and quantities) and that the remaining programs affect a very small proportion of sugar cane production.

Sugar figured prominently on the agenda for relaunching MERCOSUR in April 2000. At the end of August the Argentine Congress approved a law that extended duties on sugar indefinitely. The government later intervened, extending the tariffs on sugar imports only until the end of 2005. The positions of all four countries still diverge on the treatment of tariffs on this product. At a special meeting on September 26, 2000, member countries presented new proposals. Brazil requested that tariffs on sugar be reduced gradually and eliminated by January 2001, while Argentina insisted on extending the date for the total elimination of tariffs, and Paraguay proposed the longest period for phasing out tariffs, with the maintenance of the status quo until 2008, and the gradual elimination of sugar tariffs over the next twelve years.

The Automotive Sector

MERCOSUR was expected to have a functioning internal market for autos by the beginning of the year 2000, free of competition-distorting domestic incentives and with a common external tariff as established in Decision CMC 29/94. Trade in this sector represents approximately one-third of all the import and export transactions within MERCOSUR. Brazil and Argentina account for 95 percent of the auto sector trade within the region.

At meetings before April 1998 several important advances were made toward reaching agreement. Discussions stalled in April over numerous issues, such as asymmetries caused by subnational investment incentives in the sector and the treatment of the smaller members of the bloc (Paraguay and Uruguay). By March 2000 Brazil and Argentina were able to agree on several important elements of an eventual agreement. One of these was a common external tariff for the categories of vehicles and auto parts to be covered by the agreement, to be achieved through a gradual increase in the tariff rate until the parties achieve full convergence to the common external tariff on all trade in the sector.

Argentina and Brazil signed an auto agreement on June 30, 2000, with the proviso that negotiations would follow shortly for the incorporation of Paraguay and Uruguay. The agreement is designed to be in force until January 2006, at which time MERCOSUR would have complete free trade in the auto sector.

The agreement established that to be considered a product of MERCOSUR and benefit from duty-free status, a vehicle must have 60 percent MERCOSUR content; Argentina further required that 30 percent of the domestic content had to be Argentine-made. Argentina issued Executive Decree 660 on August 1, giving full domestic force to the auto agreement. The decree specified that in determining the 30 percent local content, imported parts were to be excluded from the rules-of-origin calculations. Brazil contended that the decree effectively increased the Argentine content to 48 percent or more. A disagreement arose on this issue between the two partners. On November 21, 2000, Argentina and Brazil agreed that local content for Argentina would be 30 percent (25 percent for commercial vehicles) of the parts and 44 percent of the vehicle (37 percent for commercial vehicles and trucks). At the Nineteenth Meeting of the MERCOSUR member states, held in Florianopolis on December 14–15, 2000, Uruguay and Paraguay joined the agreement.

References

Bernal, Richard L. 1994. "CARICOM: Externally Vulnerable Regional Economic Integration." In *Economic Integration in the Western Hemisphere*, edited by Roberto Bouzas and Jaime Ros. University of Notre Dame Press.

BID-CEPAL. 1998. "La integración centroamericana y la institucionalidad regional." Inter-American Development Bank/United Nations Economic Commission for Latin America and the Caribbean, Washington, D.C.

Duhamel, Anne. "Le marché commun de la Communauté du bassin des Caraïbes." *Les Notes d'information du GRIC* (www.unites.uqam.ca/gric/CARICOM.htm [November 12, 2000]).

ECLAC (United Nations Economic Commission for Latin America and the Caribbean). 1992. *Panorama reciente de los procesos de integración en América Latina y el Caribe.* LC/R. 1189. Santiago, Chile. September.

Gill, Henry S. 1997. "CARICOM and Hemispheric Trade Liberalization." In *Integrating the Hemisphere: Perspectives from Latin America and the Caribbean*, edited by Ana Julia Jatar and Sidney Weintraub. Washington, D.C.: Inter-American Dialogue.

Granados, Jaime. 1999. *La Integración Comercial Centroamericana: Un marco interpretativo y cursos de acción plausible.* Washington, D.C.: Inter-American Development Bank.

Inter-American Development Bank. 1999. "Integration and Trade in the Americas." *Periodic Note.* Washington, D.C. (October).

Haines Ferrari, Marta, ed. 2000. *The MERCOSUR Codes.* London: British Institute of International and Comparative Law.

Hall, Kenneth O. 1988. "The Caribbean Community." In *International Economic Integration,* edited by Ali M. El-Agraa. Basingstoke, U.K.: Macmillan Press.

Lizano, Eduardo, and José Manuel Salazar-Xirinachs. 1999. "The Central American Common Market and Hemispheric Free Trade." In *Integrating the Hemisphere, Perspectives from Latin America and the Caribbean*, edited by Ana Julia Jatar and Sidney Weintraub. Washington, D.C.: Inter-American Dialogue.

SIECA (Central American Economic Integration Secretariat). 1999. "La Unión Aduanera Centroamericana." Guatemala City.

———. 2000a. "Avances de la integración económica centroamericana 1995–2000." Guatemala City.

———. 2000b. "Informe de las actividades y avances del proceso de la unión aduanera Guatemala y El Salvador." Guatemala City.

Valls Pereira, Lia. 1999. "Toward the Common Market of the South: Mercosur's Origins, Evolution, and Challenges." In *MERCOSUR: Regional Integration, World Markets,* edited by Riordan Roett. Boulder: Lynne Rienner.

WTO (World Trade Organization). 1999a. "Trade Policy Review Mechanism-Argentina." Geneva. April.

———. 1999b. "Trade Policy Review Mechanism-Nicaragua." Geneva.

———. 2000a. *Caribbean Community and Common Market: Biennial Report on the Operation of the Agreement.* WT/REG92/R/B/1. Geneva. April 12.

———. 2000b. *General Treaty on Central American Economic Integration.* WT/REG93/R/B/1/G/L/358. Geneva. March 27.

MARYSE ROBERT

4 | *Free Trade Agreements*

E conomic reforms recently implemented by Latin American and Caribbean countries have engendered a substantial increase in the number of free trade agreements negotiated at the bilateral and regional levels. When these countries abandoned the import-substitution model in the mid-1980s and early 1990s, they embraced reforms aimed at dismantling protectionist measures in their own markets and at promoting a more open and dynamic pattern of integration into the world economy. Their trade policy is now based on a three-pronged approach where unilateral, regional, and multilateral liberalization mechanisms reinforce one another.

Free trade agreements newly negotiated by developing countries go beyond the reduction of tariffs in a few sectors. Issues ranging from tariffs and nontariff barriers to services, intellectual property, investment, and dispute settlement are now covered by these agreements, which often serve to lock in unilateral liberalization achieved at the domestic level. In the Americas, the North American Free Trade Agreement (NAFTA) between Canada, Mexico, and the United States, which was signed on December 17, 1992, and entered into force on January 1, 1994, has led to the negotiation of several free trade agreements. To gain credibility and confidence and to benefit from the signaling effects that a free trade agreement generates, numerous countries in the Western Hemisphere have entered into commitments similar to those of the NAFTA. These agreements lay the foundation for a stronger and more competitive economy; improve market access for goods, services, and investment; and provide a rules-based framework upon which trade and investment among partner countries can grow.

Mexico has been particularly active in promoting the NAFTA model, having negotiated agreements with Bolivia, Chile, Costa Rica, the Group of Three (Colombia, Mexico, and Venezuela), Nicaragua, and the Northern Triangle (El Salvador, Guatemala, and Honduras). Canada concluded an agreement of the same type with Chile in 1996 with the objective of facilitating Chile's accession to NAFTA, whereas Central American countries negotiated agreements with the Dominican Republic and Chile that have many of the same features as NAFTA. Finally, seeking to broaden markets in order to achieve economies of scale, the Caribbean Community and Common Market (CARICOM) countries and the Dominican Republic signed a bilateral free trade agreement in August 1998 (see table 1-1 in chapter 1).

At the end of the year 2000, several countries in the Americas were negotiating modern free trade agreements, including Costa Rica and Canada, Central America and Panama, Mexico and Panama, Mexico and Trinidad and Tobago, Mexico and Peru, Mexico and Ecuador, Chile and the United States, and the Andean Community and MERCOSUR. Others, such as Canada and the CA-4 Group (El Salvador, Guatemala, Honduras, and Nicaragua), were exploring the possibility of negotiating a free trade agreement.

After discussing the origin of NAFTA, its provisions, and its institutions, this chapter reviews the main elements of all the free trade agreements signed between countries of the region.

The North American Free Trade Agreement (NAFTA)

Continental integration has been achieved in several phases in North America. Until 1989 corporate strategies, government policies, and sectoral agreements had been the main instruments enabling producers to rationalize their operations and become more efficient. The 1980s marked a turning point in the relationship among the three countries. First, Canada announced in 1985 that it would seek freer trade with the United States. The Canada-U.S. Free Trade Agreement was signed on January 2, 1988, and entered into force on January 1, 1989. The agreement removed trade barriers in goods between the two countries and reduced several impediments to trade in services and to investment.[1]

Mexico undertook a series of ambitious economic reforms in the mid-1980s. On the trade front, Mexico joined the General Agreement on Tariffs and Trade (GATT) in 1986, lowering its maximum tariffs to 20 percent and eliminating import licenses on all but 20 percent of imports. In 1989 Mexico signed a framework agreement with the United States mandating a series of sectoral trade negotiations. A year later Mexico approached the United States about negotiating a free trade agreement. Canada also announced that it would join the talks. The NAFTA negotiations began in Toronto on June 12, 1991, and ended at the Watergate Hotel in Washington, D.C., on August 12, 1992.[2] Two side agreements, one on labor cooperation and one on environmental cooperation, were negotiated in 1993 and implemented in parallel to NAFTA. They were designed to facilitate greater cooperation between the NAFTA countries and to promote the effective enforcement of each country's laws and regulations. NAFTA and the two side agreements entered into force on January 1, 1994.

The NAFTA Provisions

NAFTA provides for the progressive elimination of all tariffs and other barriers to trade on goods qualifying as North American. Tariffs (from baseline rates in effect on July 1, 1991) between the United States and Mexico, and between Canada and Mexico either were eliminated in 1994 or are being phased out in five, ten, and, in a few cases, fifteen years. Tariff elimination between Canada and the United States followed the schedule set forth under the Canada-U.S. Free Trade Agreement, which means that all tariffs covered by that agreement were phased out by January 1, 1998. The three NAFTA countries implemented a first round of accelerated tariff elimination by July 1, 1997. A second round of accelerated tariff elimination took effect on August 1, 1998, covering approximately $1 billion in trade. Effective January 1, 2001, NAFTA parties further accelerated the elimination of tariffs on a number of products. The estimated value of

1. The agreement represented an event of historical proportion for Canada. Since the 1867 Confederation, the country had considered the idea of free trade with the United States on several occasions. For more on the Canada-U.S. Free Trade Agreement, see Hart, Dymond, and Robertson (1994).

2. For more on NAFTA, see Cameron and Tomlin (2000), Johnson (1994), Robert (2000), Rubio (1992), and von Bertrab (1996).

90 MARYSE ROBERT

two-way trade in the goods on the Canadian and Mexican lists is approximately $140 million. NAFTA allows parties to apply safeguards during the tariff elimination period, which is the ten-year period that began on January 1, 1994.[3] Mexico and Canada, and the United States and Mexico can impose, for a period not exceeding three years in most cases, temporary import barriers to protect domestic producers from serious injury due to increased imports from the other NAFTA country. These bilateral actions apply to originating goods.[4] There is also a NAFTA provision for emergency actions taken under GATT Article XIX. Special safeguard provisions apply to agricultural products and to textiles and apparel products.

NAFTA allows for national treatment in trade in goods, but most-favored-nation (MFN) treatment is specifically mentioned only for trade in automotive products. All three members are bound by the MFN principle set out in GATT Article I, however. NAFTA contains an MFN clause covering cross-border trade in services, investment, and financial services.

The agreement also provides for the removal of duty drawback after a seven-year transition period. It extended for two more years (from January 1994 to January 1996) the full duty drawback available under the Canada-U.S. Free Trade Agreement. Under duty drawback programs, tariffs paid on imported components used in exported goods are waived or rebated. On January 1, 2001, Mexican *maquiladoras* and U.S. foreign trade zone firms started paying duties on all non–North American components and raw materials used to manufacture goods for NAFTA duty-free treatment. To prevent double taxation, limited drawback programs on goods are available as long as these goods are subject to duties in the free trade area.

NAFTA provides for import prohibitions and restrictions to be abolished between the parties, except to the extent permitted by GATT Article XI on the elimination of quantitative restrictions. It prohibits customs user fees on originating goods and provides for customs cooperation and enforcement.

There are five general NAFTA rules of origin for products made or assembled in North America with inputs originating from within or from outside the region. In a free trade area, rules of origin have two functions. First, they specify criteria determining which goods not entirely produced within the area are entitled to duty-free treatment. They also aim at

---

3. The transition period expires on January 1, 2008, for a few items in the NAFTA schedule of the United States and Mexico.

4. The bilateral safeguard in the Canada-U.S. Free Trade Agreement was incorporated into NAFTA.

preventing *trade deflection*. Unlike customs unions, members of a free trade area do not have a common external tariff. Thus, without rules of origin, imported goods would enter the free trade area through the country with the lowest tariff. It is worth noting that NAFTA establishes a customs union for certain categories of computer products. The three countries are moving toward a common MFN rate for these products. Annex 308.1 requires each party to reduce its MFN rate in five stages, starting on January 1, 1999. The chapter on rules of origin will not apply to these products at the end of the five-year transition period.

Goods wholly produced in North America qualify for NAFTA's preferential tariff treatment. Under the rule governing changes in tariff classifications, "depending on the good involved, NAFTA requires non-NAFTA components to be in a different HS [Harmonized System, also known as the Harmonized Commodity Description and Coding System] chapter, heading, subheading, or tariff item than the final product if the latter is to receive the agreement's preferential duty treatment."[5] Other goods qualify for preferential treatment if they undergo a change in tariff classification and also contain at least 50 or 60 percent regional value content based on either the transaction value method (sale price of a good minus costs associated with duties and freight) or the net-cost method. A different regional value content requirement applies to automotive products, which must use the net-cost method. Finally, certain goods qualify for preferential treatment if they meet the regional value content requirement even without undergoing any tariff shift. A special de minimis provision allows goods that do not comply with the NAFTA rules of origin but contain no more than 7 percent of nonoriginating material to be eligible for NAFTA preferential duty.

Two separate bilateral agreements were negotiated in agriculture. Tariffs between Mexico and the United States were removed immediately or are being eliminated over five, ten, or fifteen years. Tariffs between Canada and Mexico are also subject to a transition period of up to fifteen years. The Canada-U.S. Free Trade Agreement, which governs agricultural trade between Canada and the United States, does not include tariff reductions. Although NAFTA allows Canada to keep its supply-management system— that is, to maintain trade barriers in the dairy, poultry, and egg sectors— this system was later modified as a result of the Uruguay Round, and the quotas converted to tariff quotas. A few agricultural measures in NAFTA

5. U.S. General Accounting Office (1993, p. 29).

relating, for example, to domestic support and export subsidies apply to the three parties. The NAFTA chapter on agriculture also includes provisions on sanitary and phytosanitary measures.

NAFTA incorporates other goods-related sections on textiles and apparel and automobiles, as well as a chapter on energy. The agreement includes a chapter on standards-related measures, which covers both goods and services. The government procurement chapter also encompasses provisions on goods and services and mirrors the World Trade Organization (WTO) Agreement on Government Procurement. The chapter on competition policy calls for cooperation among national authorities.

Services in NAFTA are dealt with in several chapters. In addition to those already mentioned, services are included in chapter 11 on investment, chapter 12 on cross-border services, chapter 13 on telecommunications, chapter 14 on financial services, and chapter 16 on temporary entry for business persons. NAFTA innovates in that it requires parties to liberalize all their discriminatory measures in the area of cross-border services, financial services, and investment (which covers both goods and services), except those that are specifically listed in the annexes to the agreement.

Although very similar in its form, structure, and content to the WTO Agreement on Trade-Related Aspects of Intellectual Property Rights (TRIPS), the NAFTA chapter on intellectual property represents higher standards of protection and enforcement. Dispute settlement provisions include the general dispute settlement procedures, which do not apply to the chapter on competition policy, the review and dispute settlement in antidumping and countervailing duty matters, the investor-state dispute settlement mechanism, and the provision of the chapter on financial services requiring each party to maintain a separate roster to serve as financial services panelists. Finally, NAFTA includes a chapter on exceptions, which includes provisions on general exceptions, national security, taxation, balance of payments, disclosure of information, and cultural industries.

The NAFTA Side Agreements

The side accord on labor ensures that each country retains the full right to establish its own domestic labor standards and to adopt or modify accordingly its labor laws and regulations. Each country must allow for the review of its labor law and may request that an independent evaluation committee of experts (ECE) be established to examine another party's patterns of practice in enforcing labor laws protecting various aspects of worker

rights and safety.[6] If after consideration of a final evaluation report, a country believes that there is still a persistent pattern of failure by another country, it may request further consultation and the establishment of an arbitral
panel. Under the side agreement, "After considering the matter, the Arbitral Panel may issue a ruling on which the Parties may agree on an 'action
plan.' If the action plan is not implemented, the Panel may impose a monetary enforcement assessment."[7] If a party fails to pay the assessment, the
other party may suspend the application to that party of NAFTA benefits
in an amount no greater than the assessment imposed by the panel.

The side accord on environmental cooperation requires each party to
ensure that its laws provide for high levels of environmental protection.
Each party agrees to enforce its environmental laws effectively, using in-
spectors to monitor compliance and pursuing the necessary legal means to
seek appropriate remedies for violations. The agreement also includes a
dispute settlement mechanism allowing a panel to impose a monetary enforcement assessment. If this amount is not paid, the other party may suspend NAFTA benefits in an amount no greater than that sufficient to collect
the monetary enforcement assessment.

The NAFTA Institutions

The Free Trade Commission is the central institution of the North
American Free Trade Agreement. Composed of the trade ministers from
each of the three countries, the commission supervises the implementation
of the agreement and oversees the work of NAFTA's committees, working
groups, and other subsidiary groups. It also helps to resolve disputes that
may arise between member countries regarding the implementation of the
agreement. In April 1999 ministers completed an operational review,
launched in 1998, to examine the structure, mandates, and future priorities of the NAFTA work program.

More than twenty-five working groups, committees, and other subsidiary bodies (task forces and technical working groups) have been established to implement the agreement, to make suggestions on how to further
liberalize trade among the three parties, and to "provide an apolitical arena

6. Prohibition of forced labor, labor protections for children and young people, minimum employment standards, elimination of employment discrimination, equal pay for women and men, prevention of occupational injuries and illnesses, compensation in cases of occupational injuries and illnesses,
and protection of migrant workers.
7. Signatory Countries' Obligations under the NAALC (www.naalc.org [December 17, 2000]).

for the discussion of issues and, through early dialogue on contentious points, the possible avoidance of disputes."[8] Each committee and working group is cochaired by a representative of each country. Key issues addressed by these groups include trade in goods, rules of origin, customs, agricultural trade and subsidies, standards, investment and services, cross-border movement of business people, government procurement, and alternative dispute resolution.

The NAFTA Secretariat is located in each member country. It administers the dispute settlement provisions of the agreement under chapter 14 (financial services), chapter 19 (review and dispute settlement in antidumping and countervailing duty matters), and chapter 20 (institutional arrangements and dispute settlement procedures) and has certain responsibilities related to chapter 11 (investment). Each national section of the secretariat maintains a "court-like registry" relating to panel, committee, and tribunal proceedings. As the commission may direct, the secretariat supports the work of other committees and groups established under NAFTA.

Other NAFTA institutions include the Commission for Labor Cooperation, which comprises a ministerial council, composed of labor ministers, and a secretariat. The council oversees the implementation of the side agreement on labor, supervises the activities of the secretariat, and promotes trinational activities on a broad range of labor-related issues. National administrative offices, located in the ministries responsible for labor in each of the three countries, help implement the agreement. The secretariat, now based in Washington, D.C., serves as the general administrative arm of the Commission for Labor Cooperation, undertakes research and analysis on labor issues, and provides support to the council of labor ministers, as well as to evaluation committees of experts and arbitral panels established by the council.

The Commission for Environmental Cooperation consists of a council of ministers, a secretariat, and a joint public advisory committee. The council is composed of environment ministers from each of the parties. The secretariat, located in Montreal, provides technical, administrative, and operational support to the council and to any committees and groups established by the council. It is also responsible for management of submissions on enforcement matters. Any person or nongovernmental organization may make submissions to the secretariat asserting a party's failure to

8. See Canada, Department of Foreign Affairs and International Trade. "Institutions of the NAFTA" (www.dfait-maeci.gc.ca/nafta-alena/inst-e.asp [December 17, 2000]).

enforce its environmental laws effectively. Consideration of such submissions may result in a decision by the council to direct the secretariat to develop a factual record. The joint public advisory committee provides advice to the council. It is composed of fifteen citizens, five from each country, representing a broad range of interests.[9]

NAFTA-Type Agreements

As mentioned earlier in this chapter, several free trade agreements signed between countries of the hemisphere have been modeled on the North American Free Trade Agreement in terms of their structure, scope, and coverage (table 4-1). Like NAFTA, most of these agreements aim, through their principles and rules—including national treatment, most-favored-nation treatment, and transparency—at eliminating barriers to trade in, and facilitate the cross-border movement of, goods and services between the territories; promoting conditions of fair competition in the free trade area; increasing substantially investment opportunities in the territories of the parties; providing adequate and effective protection and enforcement of intellectual property rights; creating effective procedures for the implementation and application of the agreement, for its joint administration, and for the resolution of disputes; and establishing a framework for further bilateral, trilateral, regional, and multilateral cooperation to expand and enhance the benefits of the agreement.

Central America-Mexico

On January 11, 1991, the presidents of Mexico and the five Central American countries signed the Declaration of Tuxtla Gutiérrez, Chiapas, calling for the creation of a free trade area in goods by December 31, 1996. On November 20, 1992, the six countries signed the Multilateral Framework Agreement for the Trade Liberalization Program between the governments

9. Two other institutions were created under the auspices of NAFTA. The North American Development Bank (NADB) and its sister organization, the Border Environment Cooperation Commission (BECC), operate under the November 1993 agreement between the United States and Mexico. Their mandate is to work in a joint effort to preserve and promote the health and welfare of border residents and their environment. Specifically, the two institutions were established to address problems related to water supply, wastewater treatment, and municipal solid waste management in the border region (the area within 100 kilometers, or 62 miles, north and south of the international boundary between the two countries). For more on these institutions, see (www.nadbank.org) and (www.cocef.org).

Table 4-1. *Main Chapters in NAFTA-Type Agreements*

Chapter	NAFTA	Costa Rica-Mexico	Mexico-Nicaragua	Mexico-Northern Triangle	Group of Three	Bolivia-Mexico	Canada-Chile	Chile-Mexico	Central America-Dominican Republic	Central America-Chile
Objectives, general definitions[a]	x	x	x	x	x	x	x	x	x	x
National treatment, market access for goods	x	x	x	x	x[b]	x	x	x	x	x
Rules of origin	x	x	x	x	x	x	x	x	x	x
Customs procedures	x	x	x	x	x	x	x	x	x	x
Energy[c]	x	...	...	...	...	...	...	...	...	...
Agriculture, sanitary, and phytosanitary measures	x	x	x[d]	x[d]	x	x	...	x[e]	x[e]	x[e]
Standards	x	x	x	x	x	x	...	x	x	x
Government procurement[f]	x	x	x	...	x	x	...	...	x	x
Investment	x	x	x	x	x	x	x	x	x	x[g]
Cross-border trade in services	x	x	x	x	x	x	x	x	x	x
Temporary entry for business persons	x	x	x	x	x	x	x	x	x	x
Financial services[h]	x	...	x	...	x	x	...	...	...	...
Air transportation	...	...	...	...	...	...	x	x	...	x
Telecom	x	...	x	x	x	x	x	x	x	x
Safeguards	x	x	x	x	x	x	x	x	x	x
Competition policy	x	...	...	...	x	...	x	...	x	x
Unfair trade practices/antidumping and countervailing duty matters[i]	...	x	x	x	x	x	x[j]	...	x	x

Review and dispute settlement in anti-dumping and countervailing duty matters	x	...	...	...	...	...	x	x
Intellectual property	x	x	x	x	x	x	x	x
Publications, notification and administration of laws	...	x	x	x	x	x	x	x
Administration of the agreement[k]	x	x	x	x	x	x	...	x
Dispute settlement	x	x	x	x	x	x	x	x
Exceptions	x	x	x	x	x	x	x	x
Final provisions	x	x	x	x	x	x	x	x

a. Most agreements also include a preamble.

b. There is a chapter on automobiles in this agreement.

c. Energy is covered under market access in most free trade agreements.

d. Agriculture and sanitary and phytosanitary measures are in two separate chapters.

e. The chapter covers sanitary and phytosanitary measures. Agriculture is covered under market access.

f. Eighteen months after the entry into force of the Mexico-Northern Triangle free trade agreement, parties must start negotiating an agreement on government procurement. In the case of Chile-Mexico, parties must do so one year after the entry into force.

g. The investment rules are those of the bilateral investment treaties signed by each Central American country with Chile. Article 10.02 states that Parties may at any time decide—but must within two years of the entry into force of the agreement analyze the possibility—to broaden the coverage of these rules.

h. Chile and Mexico agree to start negotiations on financial services no later than June 30, 1999.

i. Chile and Mexico agree to start negotiations on the elimination of antidumping one year after the entry into force of their free trade agreement.

j. Parties exempt each other from the application of antidumping duties when a tariff on a good reaches zero or on January 1, 2003, whichever comes first.

k. The issue of the administration of the agreement is addressed in the section on dispute settlement in NAFTA and in the Canada-Chile Free Trade Agreement.

of Costa Rica, El Salvador, Guatemala, Honduras, Mexico, and Nicaragua (*Acuerdo Marco Multilateral para el Programa de Liberalización Comercial entre los Gobiernos de Costa Rica, El Salvador, Guatemala, Honduras, México y Nicaragua*). The agreement reiterated the decision taken in Tuxtla Gutiérrez to create a free trade area and established a few parameters for the bilateral negotiations between Mexico and each Central American country.

COSTA RICA-MEXICO. The Costa Rica-Mexico Free Trade Agreement was signed on April 5, 1994, in Mexico City and entered into force on January 1, 1995. It was the first in a long series of NAFTA-type free trade agreements signed by Mexico. The agreement had been preceded by a partial scope agreement signed by the two countries on July 22, 1982, under Article 25 of the Montevideo Treaty of the Latin American Integration Association (ALADI), which allows association members to negotiate trade agreements with nonmember countries from Latin America. Under the partial scope agreement and its successive protocols, Mexico accorded preferential access to some Costa Rican products.

As in NAFTA, tariffs are being phased out in four main stages: upon the agreement's entry into force, and after five, ten, and fifteen years. Duties on approximately 70 percent of Mexican products entering the Costa Rican market and close to 80 percent of Costa Rican products entering the Mexican market were eliminated when the agreement entered into force. Tariffs on approximately 12 percent of Mexican products and 7 percent of Costa Rican products were removed in annual stages over the next five years. On January 1, 2004, tariffs will have been eliminated on 95 percent of Costa Rican products entering the Mexican market and on 97 percent of Mexican products entering the Costa Rican market. By January 1, 2009, virtually all tariffs will have been eliminated. About 2 percent of Mexican products and 1 percent of Costa Rican products are excluded.[10]

In addition to the chapters on objectives and general definitions, and on national treatment and market access for goods, the agreement contains chapters on agriculture and sanitary and phytosanitary measures, rules of origin, customs procedures, safeguards, standards, cross-border trade in services, investment, temporary entry for business persons, government procurement, intellectual property, information and transparency, administration of the agreement, dispute settlement, exceptions, and final provisions (covering accession, withdrawal, and entry into force). It does not

10. Costa Rica, Foreign Trade Ministry (1998).

include chapters on energy and basic petrochemicals, telecommunications, financial services, and competition policy. The intellectual property chapter does not cover patents, industrial designs, and layout designs of integrated circuits. Unlike NAFTA, which refers to review and dispute settlement only in antidumping and countervailing duty matters, the Costa Rica-Mexico Free Trade Agreement incorporates provisions on unfair trade practices.

Two-way trade between Mexico and Costa Rica increased from $157.5 million in 1995 to $536 million in 1999. Mexican exports to Costa Rica reached $345 million in 1999, representing more than 6 percent of all Mexican exports to Latin America. Mexican imports of Costa Rican goods totaled $191 million.

MEXICO-NICARAGUA. Nicaragua was the second Central American country to negotiate a NAFTA-type agreement with Mexico. The free trade agreement was signed on December 18, 1997, and took effect on July 1, 1998. Seventy-six percent of tariffs on Nicaraguan exports to Mexico and 45 percent of tariffs on Mexican exports to Nicaragua were removed when the agreement entered into force. The remaining tariffs are being phased out in five, ten, and fifteen years.

The agreement is very similar to NAFTA. It includes chapters on objectives and general definitions, national treatment and market access for goods, agriculture, sanitary and phytosanitary measures, rules of origin, customs procedures, safeguards, unfair trade practices, standards, cross-border trade in services, investment, temporary entry for business persons, telecommunications, financial services, government procurement, intellectual property, transparency, administration of the agreement, dispute settlement, exceptions, and final provisions. The agreement does not include a chapter on competition policy or energy. The chapter on intellectual property does not cover patents, industrial designs, and layout designs of integrated circuits.

In the aftermath of the devastation in Nicaragua caused by Hurricane Mitch in the fall of 1998, two-way trade fell by 13 percent in 1999 to a total of $72 million. Mexican exports to Nicaragua amounted to $57.4 million, and Mexican imports of Nicaraguan goods reached $14.8 million.

MEXICO-NORTHERN TRIANGLE. Mexico and countries of the Northern Triangle—El Salvador, Guatemala, and Honduras—signed a free trade agreement on June 29, 2000. Four years after they had been launched, negotiations resumed at the second Tuxtla Summit in 1996, and ended on May 10, 2000. With this free trade agreement, Mexico has concluded a NAFTA-type agreement with all Central American countries.[11] Before completing this agreement, Mexico had signed a partial scope agreement with Guatemala on September 4, 1984, with El Salvador on February 6, 1986, and with Honduras on October 13, 1990, under Article 25 of the Montevideo Treaty, granting some products of these countries preferential access to the Mexican market. These agreements were renewed several times.

Approximately 57 percent of Mexico's exports to the Northern Triangle will benefit from duty-free treatment upon the entry into force of the agreement. Tariffs on an additional 15 percent of goods are to be removed within three to five years. Mexico is to eliminate duties on 65 percent of the Northern Triangle's exports when the agreement takes effect, and 24 percent are to be liberalized within three to five years. Also, 30 percent of Mexico's agricultural exports will be duty free upon the entry into force of the agreement, another 12 percent will be liberalized over the next five years, and 41 percent between five and eleven years.

The Mexico-Northern Triangle free trade agreement includes chapters on objectives and general definitions, national treatment and market access for goods, agriculture, sanitary and phytosanitary measures, rules of origin, customs procedures, safeguards, unfair trade practices, standards, cross-border trade in services, investment, temporary entry for business persons, telecommunications, financial services, intellectual property, transparency, administration of the agreement, dispute settlement, exceptions, and final provisions. It does not include chapters on government procurement, competition policy, or energy. Eighteen months after the entry into force of the agreement, however, the parties must start negotiating a chapter on government procurement, which will have a broad coverage and accord national treatment.[12] Utility models not covered in NAFTA are included in the chapter on intellectual property. Layout designs of integrated circuits are excluded.

11. It is worth noting that at the third Tuxtla Summit held in San Salvador on July 17, 1998, the five Central American countries and Mexico reiterated their commitment to initiate, once the free trade agreements between Mexico and all these countries have been finalized, the processes to move toward a single agreement. See *III Cumbre Tuxtla Centroamérica-México, Declaración Conjunta de la III Reunión de Jefes de Estado y de Gobierno de los Países Integrantes del Mecanismo de Diálogo y de Concertación de Tuxtla*, San Salvador, El Salvador, July 17, 1998, paragraph 37.

12. See Article 21-02 of the Mexico-Northern Triangle Free Trade Agreement.

The Northern Triangle is Mexico's single largest trading partner in Latin America. The three countries account for 25 percent of all Mexican exports to the region, which is the equivalent of Mexico's total exports to Argentina, Brazil, and Chile.

Group of Three

The leaders of Colombia, Mexico, and Venezuela, known as the Group of Three, signed a free trade agreement on June 13, 1994, on the eve of the fourth Ibero-American Summit held in Cartagena, Colombia. The agreement entered into force on January 1, 1995. The Group of Three traces its origin to the Contadora Group (Colombia, Panama, Mexico, and Venezuela), set up in 1983 to help resolve the political conflicts and promote the peace process in Central America during the 1980s. Countries of the Contadora Group were later supported in their efforts by those of the Lima Group (Argentina, Brazil, Peru, and Uruguay). In 1986 these countries formed the Rio Group.[13] In November 1989, at a meeting of the Rio Group, the Group of Three, which had been established in April, agreed to move toward economic integration. A year later, in September 1990, the leaders of the three countries decided to initiate talks on the possibility of signing a free trade agreement. Their trade ministers met for the first time in Puerto Vallarta, Mexico, in November 1990.

Tariffs between Colombia and Mexico and between Mexico and Venezuela are being phased out at an annual rate of 10 percent, leading to a free trade area by 2005. As noted in chapter 3, tariffs were eliminated between Colombia and Venezuela as part of the Andean Free Trade Area, which has been in place since February 1993.

In addition to objectives and general definitions, the free trade agreement includes chapters on national treatment and market access for goods, automobiles, agriculture and sanitary and phytosanitary measures, rules of origin, customs procedures, safeguards, unfair trade practices, standards, cross-border trade in services, investment, temporary entry for business persons, telecommunications, financial services, government procurement, state enterprises, intellectual property, transparency, administration of the agreement, dispute settlement, exceptions, and final provisions. The

---

13. The Rio Group now counts nineteen members: Argentina, Bolivia, Brazil, Colombia, Costa Rica, Chile, the Dominican Republic, Ecuador, El Salvador, Guatemala, Honduras, Mexico, Nicaragua, Panama, Paraguay, Peru, Uruguay, Venezuela, and Guyana, representing the Caribbean Community.

agreement does not include a chapter on energy, and the chapter on intellectual property does not cover patents, industrial designs, and layout designs of integrated circuits.

Provisions on national treatment and market access for goods, automobiles, agriculture, rules of origin, safeguards, unfair trade practices, state enterprises, and intellectual property do not apply between Colombia and Venezuela, both members of the Andean Community.

Mexico's exports to Venezuela account for approximately 12 percent of all Mexican exports to Latin America, whereas its exports to Colombia represent 10 percent of total Mexican exports to Latin America. Bilateral trade between Colombia and Mexico increased by 35 percent between 1994 and 1999, reaching $625 million in 1999, whereas bilateral trade between Mexico and Venezuela rose by almost 60 percent between 1994 and 1999, reaching $754 million in 1999.

Bolivia-Mexico

After two years of negotiations, Bolivia and Mexico signed a free trade agreement on September 10, 1994, which entered into force on January 1, 1995. The signing took place at the end of the Rio Group meeting, held in Rio de Janeiro on September 9–10, 1994. Bolivia became the third Andean country to enter into a NAFTA-type free trade agreement with Mexico. The trade relationship between the two countries had been governed until then by the Regional Tariff Preference of the Latin American Integration Association under Articles 5 and 18 of the Montevideo Treaty.

The deal immediately slashed tariffs on 97 percent of Mexican exports to Bolivia and on 99 percent of Mexican imports from Bolivia. Approximately 98 percent of all products are to be free of trade duties within ten years of the entry into force of the agreement. The remaining 2 percent of goods are to be completely liberalized by 2010.

The agreement incorporates chapters on objectives and general definitions, national treatment and market access for goods, agriculture and sanitary and phytosanitary measures, rules of origin, customs procedures, safeguards, unfair trade practices, standards, cross-border services, investment, temporary entry for business persons, telecommunications, financial services, government procurement, intellectual property, transparency, administration of the agreement, dispute settlement, exceptions, and final provisions. The agreement does not include a chapter on competition policy or energy. Unlike NAFTA, the chapter on intellectual property includes a section on utility models but does not cover layout designs of integrated circuits.

Total trade between the two countries increased from $35.8 million in 1994 to $42.4 million in 1999. Mexican exports to Bolivia account for the bulk of this trade, reaching $34.6 million in 1999.

Canada-Chile

The Canada-Chile Free Trade Agreement was signed on December 5, 1996, and entered into force on July 5, 1997. The agreement was intended to be an "interim" agreement before Chile joins NAFTA. In the preamble the parties resolved to facilitate Chile's accession to NAFTA.

Duties on most originating goods were removed when the agreement took effect. Close to 90 percent of goods are now duty free. On November 4, 1999, on the occasion of the second meeting of the Canada-Chile Free Trade Agreement Commission, the two countries signed an agreement to speed up the elimination of tariffs covering approximately CDN$25 million in goods. Tariffs on some industrial goods and resource-based products are to be eliminated within a maximum of five years of the entry into force of the agreement. Duties on textiles and apparel are being removed in up to six years for Canada.

The agreement includes chapters on objectives; general definitions; market access for goods; rules of origin; customs procedures; investment; cross-border trade in services; telecommunications; competition policy; temporary entry for business persons; publication, notification and administration of laws; antidumping and countervailing duty matters; institutional arrangements and dispute settlement procedures; exceptions; and final provisions. There is no chapter on government procurement, financial services, intellectual property rights, energy, sanitary and phytosanitary measures, or standards. The agreement, however, includes some provisions related to intellectual property rights (see chapter 10). The agreement also innovates in that the parties exempt each other from the application of antidumping duties when a tariff on a good reaches zero or on January 1, 2003, whichever comes first.[14] As in NAFTA, there are two parallel agreements on labor and environmental cooperation.[15]

---

14. See Article M-03 of the Canada-Chile Free Trade Agreement. For more on this issue, see chapter 11 of this volume.

15. These agreements are different from the NAFTA side agreements.

Annual trade between the two partners reached approximately $525 million in 1999, which represented a slight increase of 8 percent from 1995. The relationship is particularly strong in investment because Canada is Chile's second largest foreign investor (and the first in mining).

Chile-Mexico

On September 22, 1991, Chile and Mexico signed a free trade agreement covering only trade in goods. The agreement entered into force on January 1, 1992. As trade between the two partner countries steadily grew, they decided to deepen the coverage of their 1991 agreement, and on April 17, 1998, during the second Summit of the Americas, signed a more comprehensive free trade agreement modeled on NAFTA.

Most tariffs that had not been eliminated under the first agreement were removed immediately at the entry into force of the second agreement on August 1, 1999. Like the other NAFTA-type agreements, the free trade agreement between Chile and Mexico contains specific chapters on objectives and general definitions, national treatment and market access for goods (including a section on automobiles), rules of origin, customs procedures, safeguards, sanitary and phytosanitary measures, standards, investment, cross-border trade in services, air transport services, telecommunications, temporary entry of business persons, competition policy, intellectual property, transparency, administration of the agreement, dispute settlement, exceptions, and final provisions. The agreement does not have a chapter on energy, government procurement, unfair trade practices, or financial services. The parties agreed, however, to start negotiations on government procurement and the elimination of antidumping one year after the agreement entered in force. The agreement further stipulated that the parties were to start negotiations on financial services no later than June 30, 1999.[16] The chapter on intellectual property does not cover patents, industrial designs, trade secrets, and layout designs of integrated circuits.

Annual two-way trade increased substantially in the 1990s, from $188 million in 1991 to $1.26 billion in 1999. Mexico's exports to Chile represented 9.7 percent of its total exports to Latin America in 1999, compared with 6.8 percent to Argentina and 10.6 percent to Brazil.

---

16. See Article 20-08 of the Chile-Mexico Free Trade Agreement.

Central America-Dominican Republic

The Central America-Dominican Republic Free Trade Agreement between Costa Rica, El Salvador, Guatemala, Honduras, Nicaragua, and the Dominican Republic was signed in Santo Domingo on April 16, 1998. The protocol to the agreement, which includes the goods that are excluded from the agreement, was signed on November 29, 1998, by Costa Rica, El Salvador, Guatemala, and the Dominican Republic. Honduras signed the protocol on February 4, 2000, and Nicaragua on March 13, 2000.

The agreement, which applies bilaterally between each Central American country and the Dominican Republic, is modeled after NAFTA. It includes chapters on objectives, general definitions, national treatment and market access for goods, rules of origin, customs procedures, sanitary and phytosanitary measures, standards, unfair trade practices, safeguards, investment, cross-border trade in services, temporary entry of business persons, government procurement, intellectual property, competition policy, dispute settlement, exceptions, administration of the agreement, transparency, and final provisions. There is no chapter on telecommunications, financial services, or energy. The chapter on intellectual property essentially refers to the WTO TRIPS Agreement. The investment chapter does not provide a right of establishment for investments and investors of the other party, as NAFTA does. The government procurement chapter does not contain any threshold for the procurement of goods or services, which implies that, all else equal, the agreement is more liberalizing than NAFTA on this issue.

Two-way trade between the Central American countries and the Dominican Republic increased from $38.6 million in 1994 to $95.2 million in 1998. Costa Rica and Guatemala, with $33 million and $29 million, respectively, in exports and $6.3 million and $1.4 million in imports in 1998 are the Dominican Republic's largest Central American trading partners.

Central America-Chile

The free trade agreement between Central America and Chile was signed on October 18, 1999. It applies bilaterally between each of the five Central American countries and Chile. Tariffs between Costa Rica and Chile will be eliminated in four periods—immediately upon the entry into force of the agreement, and within five, twelve, and sixteen years. In the case of Nicaragua, Chile will eliminate its tariffs in five main periods—immediately upon the agreement taking effect or within four, five, seven, or fifteen years. Nicaragua will remove its tariffs on Chilean goods immediately or in two, four, nine, or fifteen years. El Salvador will eliminate its tariffs immediately or in five, eight, ten, or sixteen years, whereas Chile will remove its duties on Salvadoran goods immediately or in three, five, eight, or ten years. Upon the entry into force of the agreement, 95 percent of Costa Rican exports will enter the Chilean market duty free. That percentage for Nicaragua and El Salvador, respectively, is 77 percent and 83 percent for products. Market access negotiations with Guatemala and Honduras have not been completed.

The agreement contains chapters on objectives, general definitions, national treatment and market access for goods, rules of origin, customs procedures, sanitary and phytosanitary measures, unfair trade practices, safeguards, standards, investment, cross-border trade in services, air transport, telecommunications, temporary entry of business persons, government procurement, competition policy, dispute settlement, exceptions, administration of the agreement, transparency, and final provisions. There is no chapter on intellectual property or financial services. The investment rules are those of the bilateral investment treaties signed by each Central American country with Chile, but the investment chapter stipulates that parties may at any time decide to broaden the coverage of these investment rules and must analyze the possibility of doing so within two years of the agreement entering into force. The chapter on government procurement, like that in the Central America-Dominican Republic agreement, does not include any threshold.

Two-way trade between Central America and Chile grew from $59.2 million in 1994 to $103.2 million in 1998. Costa Rica, Guatemala, Nicaragua, and El Salvador exported goods to Chile worth respectively $19.6 million, $11.8 million, $4.9 million, and $1.4 million, respectively, in 1998, whereas Honduras exported only $29 thousand in goods.

CARICOM-Dominican Republic Free Trade Agreement

The free trade agreement between CARICOM and the Dominican Republic was signed on August 22, 1998. A protocol to implement the agreement was signed on April 28, 2000. Tariffs will be phased out on about twenty product headings by January 1, 2004. Goods in this category include such items as anthuriums, ginger lilies, and orchids; coffee; sausage; bacon; pasta; biscuits; jams and jelly; passion fruit juice; rum; essential oils, perfumes and toilet waters; boxes and containers; tableware and plastic items; certain footwear items; and mattresses. Approximately fifty products have been excluded, including soft drinks, chocolates, cosmetics, juices, some agricultural goods, and oils and fats. The tariff on all other items will be eliminated upon the entry into force of the agreement.

The agreement covers trade in goods, trade in services, investment, and dispute settlement. Parties agreed to work toward the adoption of an agreement on government procurement to encourage and facilitate greater participation by their economic entities in business opportunities arising from government procurement activities. The parties also agreed to develop and adopt an agreement on intellectual property rights, taking into account the rights and obligations provided for in the WTO TRIPS Agreement and other relevant agreements to which all the member states of CARICOM and the Dominican Republic are signatories.

References

Cameron, Maxwell A., and Brian W. Tomlin. 2000. *The Making of the NAFTA: How the Deal Was Done*. Cornell University Press.

Costa Rica, Foreign Trade Ministry. 1998. *Tratado de Libre Comercio entre la República de Costa Rica y los Estados Unidos Mexicanos*. San José: COMEX.

Hart, Michael, with Bill Dymond and Colin Robertson. 1994. *Decision at Midnight: Inside the Canada-US Free-Trade Negotiations*. UBC (University of British Colombia) Press.

Johnson, Jon R. 1994. *The North American Free Trade Agreement: A Comprehensive Guide*. Aurora, Ontario: Canada Law Book.

Robert, Maryse. 2000. *Negotiating NAFTA: Explaining the Outcome in Culture, Textiles, Autos, and Pharmaceuticals*. University of Toronto Press.

Rubio, Luis. 1992. *¿Cómo va a afectar a México el tratado de libre comercio?* Mexico City: Fondo de Cultura Económica.

U.S. General Accounting Office. 1993. *North American Free Trade Agreement: Assessment of Major Issues*. Vol. 2. Washington, D.C.

Von Bertrab, Hermann. 1996. *El redescubrimiento de América: Historia del TLC*. Mexico City: Nacional Financiera/Fondo de Cultura Económica.

KARSTEN STEINFATT

5 | *Preferential and Partial Scope Trade Agreements*

Nonreciprocal preferential trade arrangements are one-way concessions involving the elimination or reduction of tariffs and other barriers to imports on a selected group of products originating in beneficiary countries. With the addition of Part IV on "Trade and Development" to the General Agreement on Tariffs and Trade (GATT) in 1965, the principle of nonreciprocity became firmly ingrained in multilateral trade rules. Since then many industrialized countries have unilaterally extended preferential tariff rates to certain export items of developing countries under the Generalized System of Preferences (GSP).[1] Apart from general preferential schemes applied by the United States and Canada, there are five nonreciprocal preferential programs between countries of the hemisphere: the Caribbean Basin Initiative, the Andean Trade Preference Act, CARIBCAN, and the agreements between the Caribbean Community and Common Market (CARICOM) and Venezuela and CARICOM and Colombia.

The author wishes to acknowledge the help of Jorge Mario Martínez in preparing the section on the Caribbean Basin Initiative. Elizabeth Cadena, Larisa Caicedo, and the CARICOM Secretariat provided useful background information for the section on the CARICOM Agreements. Finally, the section on the Latin American Integration Association is based on a draft by Donald R. Mackay.
1. The Canadian equivalent of the United States GSP is known as General Preferential Tariff (GPT).

This chapter provides an overview of the principal features characterizing each of these five nonreciprocal preferential agreements. It also explains the Latin American Integration Association (ALADI), an intergovernmental organization that covers a vast array of trade agreements (preferential and nonpreferential) between countries in the Americas.

Caribbean Basin Initiative

The Caribbean Basin Initiative (CBI) is the name commonly used to refer to two broad nonreciprocal preferential programs—the 1983 Caribbean Basin Economic Recovery Act (CBERA) and the 1990 Caribbean Basin Economic Recovery Expansion Act (CBEREA)—providing preferential access to the United States market for exports originating in Central America and the Caribbean. The recent enactment of Title II of the Trade and Development Act of 2000 further expands the benefits available under the CBI by adding several products of key export interest to Central American and Caribbean countries to the list of products allowed to enter the United States free of duty.

U.S. president Ronald Reagan announced the Caribbean Basin Initiative in February 1982 as armed conflict threatened to engulf the countries of Central America. By promoting the growth of Caribbean Basin exports and reducing the region's dependence on exports of agricultural products and raw materials, proponents of the CBI saw the program as a potent tool to advance political stability in the region. The Caribbean Basin Economic Recovery Act, which specifies the unilateral tariff preferences that constitute the core of the CBI, was passed by the U.S. Congress in July 1983 and signed into law by President Reagan a month later.

The benefits of the CBI program became available to twenty beneficiary countries or dependent territories as of January 1, 1984: Antigua and Barbuda, Barbados, Belize, the British Virgin Islands, Costa Rica, Dominica, the Dominican Republic, El Salvador, Grenada, Guatemala, Haiti, Honduras, Jamaica, Montserrat, the Netherlands Antilles, Panama, St. Kitts and Nevis, St. Lucia, St. Vincent and the Grenadines, and Trinidad and Tobago.[2] Aruba, the Bahamas, and Guyana were designated as CBI beneficiaries in subsequent years, while Nicaragua acquired that status after President

2. 19 U.S.C. 2702(b) lists the countries potentially eligible for benefits under the economic recovery act. It is only when the U.S. president signs a proclamation designating these countries as beneficiaries that they can receive the benefits specified under the program.

Reagan's successor, George Bush, announced the lifting of economic sanctions against the country in March 1990. Panama's status as a beneficiary country was suspended in March 1988 and restored in December 1989, when a democratically elected government replaced the regime headed by General Manuel Noriega. Honduras lost part of its benefits for a two-month period in 1998, when the U.S. Trade Representative found that the country had failed "to provide adequate and effective protection of intellectual property rights."[3] Today, only Anguilla, Cayman Islands, Suriname, and Turks and Caicos Islands are potentially eligible for the benefits but have not requested to be designated as beneficiary countries. In 1999, however, both Anguilla and Suriname expressed interest in taking full advantage of the benefits offered by the program.[4]

Originally, the CBERA was to expire after ten years. In 1990, however, the U.S. Congress passed the Caribbean Basin Economic Recovery Expansion Act, which made the program permanent and also expanded its product coverage. The privileged access to the U.S. market enjoyed by beneficiary countries under the new act was partially eroded in January 1994, when the North American Free Trade Agreement came into force. NAFTA eliminated all barriers to trade between Canada, Mexico, and the United States, leading CBI countries to call for "NAFTA-parity" for products of export interest to them.[5]

The CBI was given new impetus on May 18, 2000, when U.S. president Bill Clinton signed the Trade and Development Act of 2000, which includes the Caribbean Basin Trade Partnership Act. The new legislation became effective on October 2, 2000, with the decision by President Clinton to extend its benefits to all twenty-four CBI countries. The new law is to remain in effect until the earlier of two dates: September 30, 2008, or the date the Free Trade Area of the Americas enters into force.

As a result of this legislation, the list of Caribbean products that do not receive preferential treatment is now limited to a small group of agricultural products, principally rice, sugar, and tobacco. Imports of these com-

3. U.S. International Trade Commission (1999, p. 2).
4. U.S. International Trade Commission (1999, p. 1).
5. Ever since the announcement in 1990 that Mexico and the United States had agreed to form a free trade area, CBI countries voiced concerns about the possible trade- and investment-diverting consequences of such an agreement, especially in light of the similarity in comparative advantage and resource endowments between Mexico and some CBI countries. There exists a vast literature seeking to document the effects of NAFTA on Central American and Caribbean economies. See, for example, Federación de Entidades Privadas de Centroamérica y Panamá (1992), Leamer and others (1995), ECLAC (1996), and Gitli and Arce (2000).

modities into the United States, irrespective of source, are subject to restrictions in the form of tariff rate quotas.[6] Products that now receive preferential treatment but that were previously excluded from the CBI include textiles, apparel, certain footwear, canned tuna, petroleum and petroleum derivatives, and certain watches and watch parts.[7] Of these, the preferential treatment afforded to certain textiles and apparel is of particular significance to CBI countries and will likely have the greatest impact on these countries' export performance in the coming years.[8] Under the new legislation, apparel made in Caribbean Basin countries from U.S. fabrics formed from U.S. yarns is granted tariff- and quota-free treatment. Duty- and quota-free treatment will also be available for apparel made in the Caribbean Basin from fabrics determined to be in "short supply" in the United States, as well as for designated "hand-loomed, handmade, or folklore" articles. Other apparel articles, including certain knit apparel made in CBI countries from fabrics formed in the Caribbean Basin region from U.S. yarns pay no import duties but are subject to quotas. These quotas will increase by 16 percent annually for three years after the enactment of the legislation. Since the U.S. legislation only specifies overall quotas, the responsibility for allocating the quotas among the beneficiary countries lies with those countries.

The Caribbean Basin Trade Partnership Act introduces new and more specific criteria that the U.S. president is required to take into account when designating a beneficiary country.[9] These new criteria, which are intended to add to, rather than to replace, the criteria established by previous CBI legislation, make explicit reference to international agreements and domestic legislation. For example, the president must take into account

6. Tariff rate quotas provide for the application of a specific tariff to imports of a particular good up to a specified quantity, and a different (usually higher) tariff to imports of the same good that exceed that quantity.

7. U.S. House of Representatives, *Trade and Development Act of 2000 (H.R. 434),* Section 211.

8. It should be noted, however, that before enactment of the partnership act, certain imports of textiles and apparel from Caribbean Basin countries, though excluded from the CBI, entered the United States at preferential rates of duty under essentially two schemes. The first was the so-called 807 provision, which required Caribbean countries to pay import duties (below the most-favored-nation [MFN] rate) only on the Caribbean "value added" portion of apparel assembled from U.S. fabric, cut to shape in the United States, and sewn in the Caribbean region. Under the second scheme, named the special access program, qualifying textile and apparel products were exempted from U.S. quotas (but not from MFN rates of duty) on condition that the beneficiary country enter into a bilateral textile agreement limiting imports into the United States of certain other textile and apparel products that do not have sufficient U.S. content.

9. U.S. House of Representatives, *Trade and Development Act of 2000 (H.R. 434),* Section 211.

the extent to which countries provide intellectual property protection consistent with or greater than that afforded under the World Trade Organization (WTO) Agreement on Trade-Related Aspects of Intellectual Property Rights or whether countries have taken steps to eliminate the worst forms of child labor, as defined in section 507(6) of the U.S. Trade Act of 1974. The president must also consider the extent to which countries apply procedures in government procurement equivalent to those included in the WTO Agreement on Government Procurement, as well as the extent to which they have sought to become parties to or to implement the Inter-American Convention Against Corruption.

Similar to other nonreciprocal preferential agreements, the new partnership act establishes rules of origin to ensure that the benefits afforded by the program accrue only to beneficiary countries. Here, beneficiary countries are treated as if they were parties to NAFTA. Accordingly, goods are eligible for preferential treatment if they meet the rules of origin requirements set out in chapter 4 of NAFTA.[10]

Finally, the new Caribbean Basin legislation requires the United States International Trade Commission (USITC) to submit a biennial report to Congress and the president analyzing "the economic impact of [the legislation] on United States industries and consumers and on the economy of the beneficiary countries."[11] In the past, USITC reports have found the overall effect on the U.S. economy to be minimal. Meanwhile, U.S. consumers have seen their welfare increase as a result of U.S. imports of the twenty main categories of products entering the country under preference laws. The USITC has also found that the preferential treatment has played an instrumental role in supporting beneficiary countries' efforts to expand, strengthen, and diversify their export sectors. The case studies conducted by the USITC have also shown, however, that the benefits from the program have varied considerably across countries.

Andean Trade Preference Act

On December 4, 1991, U.S. president George Bush signed into law the Andean Trade Preference Act (ATPA), a package of trade measures granting preferential treatment to a wide range of products imported into the United States from Bolivia, Colombia, Ecuador, and Peru. The objective

10. U.S. House of Representatives, *Trade and Development Act of 2000 (H.R. 434)*, Section 211.
11. U.S. House of Representatives, *Trade and Development Act of 2000 (H.R. 434)*, Section 211.

of ATPA is twofold: first, to promote broad-based economic development in the Andean region; and second, to provide economic incentives in support of Andean countries' efforts to shift resources away from coca cultivation and cocaine production.

The origin of ATPA can be traced back to the Andean Summit held in Cartagena, Colombia, in February 1990, where President Bush and his Andean counterparts discussed joint efforts that might be taken to combat illegal drug trafficking.[12] In this context the leaders underscored the positive role that broader access to the U.S. market could play in expanding the economic alternatives to drug-crop cultivation and production in the Andean region. The conclusions reached at the Cartagena Summit materialized a few months later, when President Bush announced his intention to implement a package of unilateral trade benefits specifically aimed at the four Andean countries. Included in this package was ATPA, which became operative on July 2, 1992, with the designation of Bolivia and Colombia as ATPA beneficiaries by President Bush. Ecuador and Peru acquired beneficiary status the following year. The program is scheduled to remain in effect through December 3, 2001.

Although modeled after the Caribbean Basin Initiative, ATPA is a narrower program that does not grant eligible countries many of the nontariff benefits extended through CBI legislation. Like that legislation, however, ATPA specifies certain criteria that countries must fulfill in order to be designated as program beneficiaries.[13] Such criteria relate primarily to the protection of intellectual property rights, worker rights, and the rights of U.S. investors in beneficiary countries. To date, no country has lost its benefits under ATPA on the basis of the criteria specified in the legislation.[14]

Tariff preferences established by ATPA apply to a wide range of products.[15] In 1999 almost one-fifth of the $9.8 billion worth of goods exported from the four Andean countries to the United States entered under ATPA.[16] A small group of products, including leather handbags, luggage, flat goods, work gloves, and leather apparel, do not enter the United States duty free, but they do benefit from reduced tariffs. Textile and apparel

12. For a detailed account of the origin of the ATPA, see Smith (1992).
13. 19 U.S.C. 3202.
14. U.S. International Trade Commission (2000, p. 2).
15. 19 U.S.C. 3203.
16. 19 U.S.C. 3203.

articles, certain footwear, canned tuna, petroleum and petroleum derivatives, certain watches and watch parts, certain sugar products, and rum are excluded from the program. Lastly, ATPA does not eliminate tariff rate quotas established by the United States for sugar, beef, and some other agricultural commodities, nor does it waive generally applicable sanitary and phytosanitary requirements for imports of food.

ATPA also contains rules of origin to which Andean products must conform to qualify for preferential tariff treatment. These rules ensure that only goods wholly grown, produced, manufactured, or, if made from non-ATPA inputs, substantially transformed in the four Andean countries receive preferential treatment. Essentially, the cost of the materials originating in the four countries, and the processing costs incurred in one or more of them, must equal at least 35 percent of a product's customs value for that product to enter the United States at reduced or zero tariff rates under ATPA.[17] The 35 percent threshold can be met through the use of inputs from any of the four Andean countries. Inputs from Puerto Rico, the U.S. Virgin Islands, and countries designated under the Caribbean Basin Economic Recovery Act also count as "local" products.

Finally, under ATPA the USITC is required to issue biennial reports analyzing the economic impact of ATPA "on United States industries and consumers and in conjunction with other agencies, the effectiveness of [the Act] in promoting drug-related crop eradication and crop substitution efforts of beneficiary countries."[18] The USITC has consistently found the overall effect of ATPA on the economy of the United States to be minimal and concentrated on a small group of U.S. producers. At the same time, imports of the leading product categories receiving tariff preferences under ATPA have translated into net welfare gains for U.S. consumers. Most USITC reports have concluded that the program has had a small, albeit positive, effect on the economies of beneficiary countries, usually as a result of additional investment in sectors that receive tariff preferences. Also, the report for the year 2000 attributes a small part of the downward trend in illicit coca production in the Andean region to ATPA.[19]

17. 19 U.S.C. 3203.
18. 19 U.S.C. 3204(b). The reporting requirement in ATPA was amended by the Trade and Development Act of 2000. Instead of preparing annual reports, the U.S. International Trade Commission is now required to submit reports every other year.
19. U.S. International Trade Commission (2000).

CARIBCAN

At the urging of Caribbean leaders, Canada's Prime Minister Brian Mulroney in late 1985 proposed an economic and trade development assistance program named CARIBCAN. The program, which was enacted on June 15, 1986, seeks to provide an avenue for Caribbean countries to enhance their export earnings and attract investment, while at the same time promoting economic cooperation and integration between Canada and countries in the Caribbean. To this end, CARIBCAN unilaterally eliminates Canadian tariffs on an extensive list of products originating in eighteen eligible countries or dependent territories in the Caribbean.[20] Over the years this list of preferences has expanded to include all Caribbean imports except textiles, clothing and footwear, and goods subject to MFN rates of duty above 35 percent.[21] In 1999, only CDN$65.3 million of the CDN$550 million worth of goods imported by Canada from CARIBCAN countries entered under CARIBCAN preferential tariffs. The bulk of Canadian imports from the region (over CDN$400 million) received duty-free treatment on a most-favored-nation (MFN) basis.[22] The principal Caribbean products benefiting from CARIBCAN's preferential treatment are iron ores and bars, cane sugar, fish, spirits, and certain agricultural products.

Like other one-way preferential schemes, CARIBCAN establishes rules of origin to ensure that the benefits it provides accrue only to producers in beneficiary countries. Specifically, for a product to qualify for duty-free treatment under CARIBCAN, at least 60 percent of its price must originate in one or more beneficiary countries or Canada.[23] Finally, CARIBCAN differs from the U.S. preferential schemes in that it does not make its preferences contingent on the fulfillment of certain requirements by beneficiary countries.

---

20. The countries eligible to receive the duty-free treatment under CARIBCAN are Anguilla, Antigua and Barbuda, the Bahamas, Barbados, Belize, Bermuda, the British Virgin Islands, the Cayman Islands, Dominica, Grenada, Guyana, Jamaica, Montserrat, St. Kitts and Nevis, St. Lucia, St. Vincent and the Grenadines, Trinidad and Tobago, and the Turks and Caicos Islands.

21. Products that were originally excluded from the program but that are currently covered include leather luggage and garments, certain vegetable fiber products, lubricating oils, and methanol. See WTO (1996, 1999, p. 25).

22. WTO (2000, p. 2).

23. WTO (2000, p. 2).

CARICOM-Venezuela and CARICOM-Colombia

The Agreement on Trade, Economic and Technical Cooperation Between the Caribbean Community and Common Market (CARICOM) and the Government of the Republic of Venezuela was first proposed by Venezuelan president Carlos Andres Perez during a meeting of CARICOM heads of government in St. Kitts in 1991. Signed in October 1992, the agreement entered into force on January 1, 1993. Almost two years later, CARICOM countries and dependent territories signed a similar agreement with Colombia, which became effective on January 1, 1995. Both agreements were concluded under the provision for nonreciprocal partial scope agreements of ALADI (the Latin American Integration Association), of which Colombia and Venezuela are members. Consequently, the two preferential schemes are open to accession by other members of the association.

The core objective of the two agreements is to strengthen economic ties between their respective members through the promotion of trade—particularly exports from the Caribbean Community to Colombia and Venezuela—and investment flows. To this end, the agreements establish three-tier liberalization programs whereby tariffs on a first group of CARICOM exports to Colombia and Venezuela (Annex I) are eliminated upon the entry into force of the agreements, tariffs on a second group of goods (Annex II) are reduced in annual stages until reaching zero, and tariffs on the remaining products (Annex III) receive MFN treatment.[24] In the case of CARICOM-Venezuela, goods listed under Annex II are subject to four annual 25 percentage point reductions; in the case of CARICOM-Colombia, duties on goods included in Annex II are slashed by 33.3 percentage points each year for three years. To a certain extent, the products covered by both agreements fall under the same broad categories, which include live trees and plants; cut flowers; coffee, tea, and spices; iron and steel; electrical machinery; and mechanical appliances. In some instances, however, products that appear in one annex in one agreement appear in a different annex in the other agreement, thus subjecting the same products to different liberalization regimes. Such is the case for fish, fruit and vegetables, and certain articles of apparel and clothing, which are included in

24. According to Article 5 of the CARICOM-Colombia Agreement, Annex III contains products that, in addition to receiving MFN treatment on the part of Colombia, "may receive preferential treatment in Colombia beginning in the fourth year after the entry into force of the Agreement, following negotiations between the Parties."

Annex I of CARICOM-Colombia and in Annex II of CARICOM-Venezuela.

The two preferential schemes require CARICOM to grant MFN treatment and to refrain from applying nontariff barriers—other than those in force or authorized by the Treaty Establishing the Caribbean Community—to all imports from Colombia and Venezuela. In calling explicitly for "postponed reciprocity," however, CARICOM-Colombia takes the obligations of four CARICOM member states—Barbados, Guyana, Jamaica, and Trinidad and Tobago, also known as the "more-developed countries" of CARICOM—a step further. Specifically, Article 6 stipulates that these countries provide preferential treatment to an agreed list of products of export interest to Colombia four years after the entry into force of the agreement. Within this framework, in May 1998 Colombia and CARICOM countries signed a protocol agreeing to eliminate tariffs on an identified set of products from both Colombia and the CARICOM more-developed countries effective as of June 1, 1998. The protocol also calls for the implementation of a mechanism whereby duties on a second set of identified products are reduced by 25 percentage points each year beginning in January 1999. Altogether then, the protocol added 207 goods, including lubricating oils, fish, and chemicals, to the list of products from CARICOM countries receiving some form of preferential treatment from Colombia. At the same time, more than 1,000 products originating in Colombia now enjoy some form of preferential treatment when exported to CARICOM's more-developed countries.[25] These goods include tobacco, agricultural machinery, chemicals, and textiles.

To ensure that the benefits associated with preferential treatment accrue exclusively to signatories, both agreements contain rules of origin specifying the products that are entitled to receive tariff preferences.[26] Moreover, members can apply safeguard provisions in the event of injury (or the threat thereof in the case of the CARICOM-Colombia agreement) to domestic production or when facing balance of payments difficulties. The agreements' clauses on unfair trade practices also envisage the application of

25. Venezuela has reportedly submitted a formal request for the extension to Venezuelan products of the preferential tariffs granted to Colombia by CARICOM's most-developed countries. CARICOM and Venezuela are expected to begin negotiating on this topic beginning in the first quarter of 2001.

26. With a view to establishing definitive rules of origin, Article 9 of the CARICOM-Colombia agreement calls for a review of the rules of origin set forth in Annex IV after three years of the entry into force of the agreement. The protocol signed between CARICOM countries and Colombia in May 1998 modified the rules of origin contained in the original agreement.

antidumping and countervailing measures by the signatories in conformance with domestic legislation.

Finally, both agreements establish a "joint council" responsible not only for administering the preferential programs, but also for settling any disputes that may arise in connection with their application. The joint councils must meet at least once a year and can propose measures that help the Parties better achieve the objectives of the Agreements.

The Latin American Integration Association

On August 12, 1980, eleven Latin American countries (Argentina, Bolivia, Brazil, Chile, Colombia, Ecuador, Mexico, Paraguay, Peru, Uruguay, and Venezuela) signed the Treaty of Montevideo and instituted the Latin American Integration Association (ALADI, in Spanish) with a view to furthering the treaty's long-term objective of gradually creating a Latin American common market. ALADI traces its ancestry to 1960, when Mexico and six South American countries established the Latin American Free Trade Association. Relying largely on the instrument of negotiated annual tariff reductions, this free trade association sought to eliminate barriers to trade among its members by 1972. Although efforts to expand the association's geographical scope were successful—by 1967, the group counted eleven countries among its members—efforts to liberalize trade relations became reduced to bilateral tariff-cutting exercises usually involving largely unimportant sectors. Disenchanted with this slow pace of liberalization, five members of the group (Bolivia, Chile, Colombia, Ecuador, and Peru) established the more ambitious Andean Pact in the late 1960s.[27]

The transformation of the Latin American Free Trade Association into the Latin American Integration Association gave new impetus to the process of economic integration in Latin America. At the outset, the new initiative adopted a "flexible" approach to integration, relying mainly on sector-based bilateral or plurilateral negotiations. Beginning in the 1990s, however, the agreements concluded under the "flexible" approach lost some of their significance when ALADI members entered into more comprehensive and far-reaching agreements such as MERCOSUR (the Common Market of the South, composed of Argentina, Brazil, Paraguay, and Uruguay) and the Group of Three (Colombia, Mexico, and Venezuela).

---

27. Venezuela joined this group in 1973, and Chile withdrew from it in 1976.

Institutional Structure

Articles 28 and 29 of the Treaty of Montevideo identify three governing bodies for ALADI: the Council of Foreign Affairs Ministers, the Conference on Evaluation and Convergence, and the Committee of Representatives. The council is ALADI's highest organ, responsible for providing political guidance to the process of integration among the association's members. Council members are the ministers of foreign affairs of the member countries. The Conference on Evaluation and Convergence, made up of plenipotentiaries, examines the functioning of the integration process and seeks to foster convergence between existing agreements. The Committee of Representatives is a permanent political body and negotiating forum responsible for analyzing and agreeing on the initiatives necessary to achieve the objectives espoused by the Treaty of Montevideo. Its resolutions must be adopted by a two-thirds majority, with each member casting one vote. ALADI also has a secretariat, based in Montevideo, which is designed to support the negotiations between ALADI members.

Structure of the ALADI System

To reach its objective of a Latin American common market in a "gradual and progressive" manner, the Treaty of Montevideo provides a variety of instruments to facilitate the integration of its members:[28]

—regional tariff preferences whereby ALADI members grant each other tariff preferences on a reciprocal basis;

—regional scope agreements, which require the participation of all ALADI members and include schemes that grant nonreciprocal tariff preferences to ALADI's "less-developed countries" (Bolivia, Ecuador, and Paraguay); and

—partial scope agreements, which do not require the participation of all ALADI members and include commercial and economic implementation agreements.

As countries in Latin America began embracing broad trade liberalization schemes in the late 1980s and early 1990s, both regional tariff preferences and regional scope agreements, as well as "selective" partial scope agreements (those negotiated on a product-by-product basis or those that cover all products but do not eliminate barriers to trade completely), lost

28. Treaty of Montevideo, Chapter II.

some of their economic significance. Indeed, with the heightened pace of trade liberalization in the hemisphere, these agreements gave way to "new generation" partial scope agreements, which provide for automatic, preferential programs for the elimination of tariff and nontariff barriers to trade in all goods, with some exceptions (table 5-1). A large majority of the twenty-six "selective" partial scope agreements and all of the new generation partial scope agreements are registered with ALADI as economic complementarity agreements, or ACEs (for their Spanish acronym).

Most of the exceptions specified in partial scope agreements concluded under the ALADI framework tend to be shared exceptions, that is, they appear in more than one agreement. Most of these affect the automotive sector, oil and oil-based products, agricultural products, plastics, textiles, clothing, and footwear.

Reaching beyond ALADI

The introspective attitude that largely characterized most countries in Latin America in the years preceding and immediately following the creation of ALADI has long dissipated. As they turned their backs on economic theories of the 1970s and early 1980s that called for the creation of partial trade liberalization agreements among a handful of countries in the hemisphere, ALADI members increasingly sought to engage partners outside of the group's boundaries. Soon, under provisions of the Treaty of Montevideo, particularly Article 25, that foresee the formation of agreements with third parties, new agreements were being forged between ALADI and non-ALADI countries.[29]

The more engaged strategy of ALADI members vis-à-vis third countries has recently led to changes in the group's membership. On August 26, 1999, Cuba became the twelfth member of ALADI. At the time of its entry, Cuba had already signed agreements with nine of the eleven ALADI members under the framework of Article 25. Of these agreements, those

29. For agreements concluded between ALADI and non-ALADI members outside the framework of ALADI, Article 44 of the Treaty of Montevideo requires that the ALADI member extend any benefits granted to a third party to all members of the association. In this context, the ALADI Council of Ministers approved the Interpretative Protocol of Article 44 of the Montevideo Treaty in June 1994. The protocol allows members that have granted preferences to third countries the right not to have to apply the MFN clause embodied in Article 44, provided negotiations are launched to compensate ALADI members. Mexico ratified this protocol, and invoked it in September 1994, in the context of its membership in NAFTA.

Table 5-1. *New Generation Agreements in ALADI*

Agreement	Signatories	Date of signing
ACE 18	Argentina, Brazil, Paraguay, Uruguay	Nov. 29, 1991
ACE 23	Chile, Venezuela	April 2, 1993
ACE 24	Chile, Colombia	Dec. 6, 1993
ACE 31	Bolivia, Mexico	Sept. 10, 1994
ACE 32	Chile, Ecuador	Dec. 20, 1994
ACE 33	Colombia, Mexico, Venezuela	June 13, 1994
ACE 35	Chile, MERCOSUR	Sept. 30, 1996
ACE 36	Bolivia, MERCOSUR	Dec. 17, 1996
ACE 38	Chile, Peru	June 22, 1998
ACE 41	Chile, Mexico	Sept. 22, 1991

Source: ALADI Secretariat, El Sistema de Preferencias de la ALADI, ALADI/SEC/Estudio 128 (27 June 2000).
Note: ACE is the Spanish acronym for economic complementarity agreement.

signed with Bolivia, Colombia, Ecuador, and Peru were negotiated in parallel to the Uruguay Round and include provisions on services, intellectual property, and technical barriers to trade. ALADI members are in the process of updating previous agreements with Cuba or, in the case of Chile, which had no preexisting agreement with the Caribbean island, negotiating new arrangements to take into account Cuban membership in the regional organization.

References

ECLAC (United Nations Economic Commission for Latin America and the Caribbean). 1996. *Las exportaciones de países pequeños en el Mercado de EE.UU: efectos del TLCAN y la devaluación mexicana*. Mexico City.

Federación de Entidades Privadas de Centroamérica y Panamá (FEDERICAP). 1992. *U.S.-Latin American Relations in the 1990s: A New Partnership for Development and Competitiveness: A Caribbean Basin Proposal*. San José.

Gitli, Eduardo, and Randall Arce. 2000. "Los desbalances de los países de la Cuenca del Caribe frente al TLCAN: La industria de la confección." *Integración y Comercio* 11 (May-August): 109–34.

Learner, E., and others. 1995. "How Does the North American Free Trade Agreement Affect Central America?" Policy Research Working Paper 1464. World Bank, Washington, D.C.

Smith, Guy C. 1992. "The Andean Trade Preference Act." *Denver Journal of International Law and Policy* 21 (Fall): 149–58.

U.S. International Trade Commission. 1999. *Caribbean Basin Economic Recovery Act, 14th Report 1998.* Washington, D.C. (September).

———. 2000. *Andean Trade Preference Act: Impact on U.S. Industries and Consumers and on Drug Crop Eradication and Crop Substitution, Seventh Report.* Washington, D.C. (September).

WTO (World Trade Organization). 1996. *Canadian Tariff Treatment for Commonwealth Caribbean Countries: 1996 Report of the Government of Canada on the Trade-Related Provisions of CARIBCAN.* WT/L/175. Geneva (September 16).

———. 2000. *Canada—Tariff Treatment for Commonwealth Caribbean Countries: Report of the Government of Canada on the Trade-Related Provisions of CARIBCAN Under the Decision of 14 October 1996.* WT/L/365. Geneva (October 26).

———. 1999. *Trade Policy Review: Canada 1998.* Geneva (March).

PART III

*Trade Rules
in the Americas*

DONALD R. MACKAY
MARYSE ROBERT
ROSINE M. PLANK-BRUMBACK

6 Trade in Goods and Agriculture

The negotiation of rules governing the commercial exchange of goods has traditionally been the heart of any individual trade negotiation and is the foundation upon which trade policy rests. Assuring open and reciprocal access to markets for agricultural products has proved more difficult, although limited progress has been achieved in the Uruguay Round of Multilateral Trade Negotiations and at the regional and bilateral levels in the Americas.

The decade of the 1990s developed into a wonderful laboratory for tracking the unprecedented level of trade negotiations and trade and tariff liberalization among countries in the Americas. At the start of the decade, few of the countries in the Western Hemisphere had liberalized their tariffs. By the mid-1990s, however, a definitive trend toward bilateral and plurilateral trade and tariff liberalization had become so entrenched that by the end of the decade, it was almost difficult to keep track of which country was negotiating trade and investment agreements with which other country or group of countries.[1]

All customs unions and modern free trade agreements covered in this volume provide for the liberalization of tariffs and most nontariff barriers.

1. For more on trade liberalization in the hemisphere, see Devlin and Estevadeordal (2000), Estevadeordal (1999), and Devlin, Estevadeordal, and Garay (1999).

A few trade agreements negotiated under the framework of the Latin American Integration Association (ALADI in Spanish) also provide for the gradual removal of duties or preferential duty treatment on most goods. These agreements are those signed by Chile with Colombia, Ecuador, MERCOSUR (Common Market of the South), Peru, and Venezuela, and the Bolivia-MERCOSUR and Mexico-Uruguay agreements. Other trade agreements, partial in scope and also negotiated under the ALADI framework, cover fewer tariff lines.[2]

Tariff liberalization for goods and agricultural products is not the only issue confronting trade negotiators, however. They must also address new challenges presented by the growth of global commercial interchanges. Rules of origin, in particular, have become much more complex as globalized production processes make it difficult to establish a country of origin. Early regimes based on established percentages of "value added," found largely in ALADI and the Canada-U.S. Free Trade Agreement, have gradually given way to "tariff shift" models for determining eligibility for preferential tariff treatment. Another important dimension of market access has to do with safeguard measures, that is, temporary import barriers designed to protect domestic producers from serious or material injury due to increased imports from the other party.

Liberalization of Trade in Goods and Agriculture: Convergences and Divergences

From the perspective of trade in goods and agricultural products, liberalization approaches under customs unions, free trade agreements, and nonreciprocal preferential arrangements are vastly different from each other, although each category of agreements has tended to follow a broadly consistent approach in its treatment of the issues. The most pronounced difference between the categories lies in their basic structures. Customs unions, by their nature, seek to establish conditions of internal free trade along with the presentation of a common face, in market access terms, externally. Negotiating customs unions—not to mention the task of implementing the results—has thus tended to be quite difficult because agreement is

2. See table 5-1 in chapter 5 for the dates that these agreements were signed. On December 29, 1999, Mexico and Uruguay signed an agreement that deepened the Economic Complementarity Agreement they had signed in 1986 under the ALADI framework. The new agreement covers 90 percent of the tariff lines and also includes provisions on rules of origin, safeguards, unfair trade practices, sanitary and phytosanitary measures, standards, and dispute settlement.

required not only on the various schedules for internal tariff reduction, but also on the establishment of common external tariff regimes. Free trade agreements, in contrast, are designed to eliminate internal barriers to trade while preserving each participant's external commercial independence. Nonreciprocal preferential arrangements provide for unilateral concession and therefore are divergent in that respect.

Customs unions have often encountered difficulties in establishing common external tariffs in all products and therefore have required provisions allowing for limited and specified exceptions. Similarly, parties to free trade agreements have found it necessary to provide for a limited number of exceptions, especially in the areas of agricultural goods, textiles, and auto-related products.

In addition to trade liberalization and tariff elimination, this chapter also notes similarities and differences in the rules of origin and safeguards contained in the many trade agreements among countries in the hemisphere. Rules of origin are tools that allow governments to determine the country of origin of a good or service. In a free trade area, they are essentially discriminatory instruments that help determine which good or service is entitled to preferential treatment. Safeguard measures enable a party to a trade agreement to take an emergency action in response to a surge in imports in cases where such an increase constitutes a substantial cause of serious, or in some cases, material injury, or threat thereof.

The chapter concludes with the issues confronting negotiators in the FTAA negotiations and assesses the progress already achieved in the Americas in the area of trade in goods.

Trade Liberalization: Universal Coverage and Exceptions

By and large, free trade agreements and customs unions, particularly those of more recent vintage, have tended to adopt a framework of universal, or near universal, coverage in their liberalization programs. Nearly all of these agreements, however, fail to cover certain areas and sectors. In no area is this more true than for the agricultural sector, or various parts of it, where few liberalization efforts have been successful. Parties to the North American Free Trade Agreement, for instance, were unable to agree on a single set of agricultural rules. NAFTA incorporates three bilateral agreements, including the rules governing agricultural trade between the United States and Canada under their earlier free trade agreement. Exceptions for agriculture and agricultural products reflect the particular sensitivities of each participating country.[3] Other examples of sectors where liberalization has proved very challenging, at least until recently, are the automotive and sugar sectors in MERCOSUR (see chapter 3).

For the most part, tariff reductions have taken place as scheduled; in some cases they have even been accelerated above and beyond what was initially called for in the agreements. In 1997 and 1998 the three NAFTA countries, for example, implemented two rounds of accelerated tariff elimination, the last one of which covered approximately $1 billion in trade. On January 1, 2001, NAFTA partners agreed to accelerate the elimination of tariffs on a number of products rather than wait until January 2003, as originally provided for in the agreement. NAFTA-type agreements also include tariff acceleration provisions. Although commercial pressures have not arisen and the original timetables have remained essentially unchanged in most cases, accelerated tariff elimination took place under the Canada-Chile free trade agreement and under the agreement between Costa Rica and Mexico.[4] Free trade agreements negotiated in the latter half of the 1990s, for example those negotiated by Chile, Mexico, and Canada, have tended to follow the NAFTA model. Although individual liberalization schedules were drafted to reflect bilateral or in some cases plurilateral interests, their basic structure and even organization are generally convergent with NAFTA. MERCOSUR has been largely successful in removing products from the initial lists of exclusions allowed in the agreement's initial phase. Other agreements that have been recently "revitalized," such as the Andean Community and the Caribbean Community and Common Market (CARICOM), have either met their initial market access obligations or are in the process of doing so. The Central American Common Market (CACM) has succeeded from the very beginning in eliminating most tariffs on goods and has shortened the list of products not entitled to duty-free treatment. Currently, tariffs apply only for roasted coffee, alcoholic beverages, and petroleum products.

Rules of Origin

Parties to a trade agreement grant each other preferential access. To ensure that goods containing materials from a third country have under-

---

3. For example, supply-managed products (poultry and dairy products) for Canada, sugar and sugar-containing products for the United States.

4. Canada Department of Foreign Affairs and International Trade (1999); *La Nación* (1999).

gone sufficient processing within the preferential trading area, trade agreements include provisions on rules of origin. A good that satisfies the rules of origin is classified as "originating" and therefore is entitled to preferential tariff treatment.

Two main rules of origin are contained in trade agreements in the Americas. The value added approach generally defines a maximum percentage of third country processing or components that can be included for a good to qualify for preferential tariff treatment. This approach suffers from severe limitations because it is highly dependent on fluctuations in a wide range of factors that determine the price and cost of a good. It is also administratively very burdensome for customs administrations that must audit the cost of these materials because accounting methods vary widely throughout the world. Moreover, low-wage countries are at a disadvantage when using this method because they must use a higher percentage of originating components to qualify for the preferences.

The "tariff shift" model requires a determination that a party has modified a good or product enough to change its classification in the Harmonized Commodity Description and Coding System (often referred to as Harmonized System, or HS), thus making it eligible for preferential tariff treatment.[5] This method is not without problems. It does not always ensure that there will be a substantial transformation in the production of a good. In fact, the Harmonized System was not designed for determining product origin, but for statistical and classification purposes.

Broadly speaking, examples of both the value added approach and the tariff shift model are found in integration arrangements in the Americas, and often the same country may apply different regimes, or significant variations of a particular regime, to different trading partners. The change in tariff classification, for example, is most closely associated with NAFTA and the NAFTA-type agreements. But NAFTA does not have a pure tariff shift approach because regional content requirements—subject to different accounting methodology—are also included. In addition, rules of origin in NAFTA are product specific in some sectors such as the automotive sector and textiles and apparel.[6]

---

5. Rules of origin based on a change in tariff classification are generally applied at the two-digit chapter level, the four-digit heading level, the six-digit subheading level, or the eight-digit tariff item level (as for some goods in NAFTA) of the Harmonized System. For an excellent overview of the rules of origin in trade agreements in the Americas, see Garay and Cornejo (1999).

6. For more on the NAFTA rules of origin, see chapter 4 of this volume.

The value added approach has been most closely associated with ALADI and is often called the ALADI model. Resolution 78 of ALADI defines a good as originating if it has undergone a change in tariff classification in its HS heading (four digits) or has a regional value content of 50 percent or higher of the free-on-board (FOB) cost of the good. This approach is found, in one form or another, in MERCOSUR and the Andean Community. MERCOSUR requires a change in tariff heading and 60 percent value added content for some goods. MERCOSUR also has specific rules of origin for sectors such as data processing, chemicals, and iron and steel. The Andean Community regime was adopted in 1997 and includes four categories of goods.[7] The first category covers goods entirely produced in the region. The second category encompasses goods that include non-Andean materials. To qualify as originating, these goods must undergo processing in the region, that is, there must be a change in tariff classification, and the cost, insurance, and freight (CIF) price of nonoriginating materials should not exceed 50 percent of the FOB value of the final merchandise in the case of Colombia, Peru, and Venezuela, and 60 percent in the case of Bolivia and Ecuador. The third category includes merchandise resulting from an assembly operation, for which the requirement is the previously mentioned value added for each of the five members. The last category covers goods subject to special requirements of origin. The system also includes procedures under which the Andean Community's secretariat may impose sanctions on national officials who issue "irregular" certificates of origin.

Different rules are sometimes applied to countries that may be at different levels of development. There are no differences in treatment in terms of rules of origin within MERCOSUR itself, for example, but the trade agreement that MERCOSUR concluded with Bolivia does contain special treatment for Paraguay and Bolivia. MERCOSUR's agreement with Chile also includes less restrictive rules for Paraguayan goods. Similarly, the Andean Community permits special treatment in the case of Ecuador and Bolivia.

The main rule of origin in the Central American Common Market is a change in tariff classification. This general rule may be accompanied by additional requirements such as regional content. Like NAFTA and the NAFTA-type agreements, the CACM also includes provisions allowing for accumulation and a de minimis rule. The provision on accumulation permits a producer to aggregate his production with that of another producer

7. See Andean Community Decisions 416 and 417.

from the CACM for the purpose of determining if a good qualifies for preferential treatment. The de minimis rule ensures that a good that does not meet the rule of origin but contains only 7 percent (10 percent until year 2000) of nonoriginating materials does qualify as originating.

CARICOM also borrows from both models. Protocol IV stipulates that goods produced in CARICOM countries wholly or partly from materials imported from outside CARICOM must undergo a tariff shift to be eligible for preferential treatment. Protocol IV also provides that goods that have been consigned in another member state for repair, renovation, or improvement may be reimported under preferential treatment so long as the value of materials imported from outside CARICOM does not exceed a certain percentage (65 percent when the repair or improvement is done in a more-developed country and 80 percent when it is done in a less-developed country).

Safeguards

NAFTA and most NAFTA-type agreements allow for bilateral safeguard mechanisms, but these mechanisms have time limits ("sunset provisions") and are permitted only during the tariff elimination period. Special safeguard provisions also apply to agricultural products and to textiles and apparel products. NAFTA and NAFTA-type agreements allow for global safeguards against imports from third parties, which apply on a most-favored-nation (MFN) basis, permitting each party to retain its rights and obligations under Article XIX of the 1994 General Agreement on Tariffs and Trade (GATT) and the World Trade Organization (WTO) Agreement on Safeguards. Although allowed under Article XIX of GATT 1947, safeguard measures were rarely used because governments often preferred to protect their domestic industries through "grey area" measures, outside the GATT framework, such as voluntary export restraints (VERs), where exporting countries would restrain exports "voluntarily." Automobiles, steel, and semiconductors were the principal targets of voluntary export restraints and orderly marketing arrangements. The WTO Agreement on Safeguards prohibits these measures and also sets time limits on safeguard actions (four years up to a maximum of eight years). A country can apply a safeguard measure if an import surge has caused or threatens to cause serious injury. Safeguard measures must be applied on a MFN basis. According to a WTO explanation, however, "the agreement does describe how quotas can be allocated among supplying countries, including in the exceptional circumstance where imports from certain countries have increased disproportionately quickly."[8] A developing country has to supply more than 3 percent of a product to be subject to a safeguard measure; and, collectively, developing countries with less than a 3 percent import share must account for more than 9 percent of total imports.

CARICOM Protocol IV on Trade Policy allows a member to apply safeguard measures if an increase in imports of a product from another member state results in a substantial decrease in demand for the like domestic product. Members may not, however, discriminate among the sources of supply or the nationality of the suppliers.[9] Under Protocol VII, no CARICOM country can impose safeguard measures on imported products originating in disadvantaged (less-developed) CARICOM countries where those imports make up less than 20 percent of the importing country's market for that product.[10]

The Andean Community's Cartagena Agreement provides that when a product originating in the subregion is being imported in such quantities or conditions as to cause a "disturbance" in the domestic production of specific products of a member country, that member country may apply corrective measures that are nondiscriminatory and temporary in nature, subject to pronouncement of the general secretariat.[11] The Andean Community countries have only rarely resorted to safeguard measures. Bolivia and Ecuador can be the targets of agricultural and industrial safeguards only in exceptional cases when the general secretariat has determined that imports from these countries are causing serious adverse effects.[12]

MERCOSUR allows global safeguard measures in the case of a surge in imports from a nonmember state.[13] The Central American Common Market permits the application of safeguard measures when a causal link

8. See the WTO website at (www.wto.org/english/thewto_e/whatis_e/tif_e/agrm7_e.htm).

9. Article 26 of CARICOM Protocol IV (Trade Policy) and Article 59 of CARICOM Protocol VII (Disadvantaged Countries, Regions, and Sectors).

10. CARICOM Protocol VII defines "disadvantaged countries" as (a) the less-developed countries; or (b) member states that may require special support measures of a transitional or temporary nature by reason of: (1) impairment of resources resulting from natural disasters; or (2) the adverse impact of the operation of the CARICOM Single Market and Economy on their economies; or (3) temporary low levels of economic development; or being a highly-indebted poor country designated as such by the competent intergovernmental organization.

11. Article 109 of the Cartagena Agreement.

12. Article 129 of the Cartagena Agreement.

13. MERCOSUR/CMD/DEC No. 04/97 Annex II.

has been demonstrated between a surge in imports from third countries and the existence of serious injury or threat thereof to a domestic industry.

Thus, in one form or another, countries tend to view emergency measures as either transitory in nature or legitimately subject to disciplined oversight. Although the elimination of trade barriers has also been accompanied by the adoption of import-relief mechanisms, for large economies in the hemisphere antidumping duties are the preferred instrument for relief, as noted in chapter 11. Safeguard measures represent a valid alternative for small open economies, because they are less administratively burdensome than antidumping measures. The only requirement to apply a safeguard action is to determine whether a surge in imports has caused serious injury to a domestic industry.

Trade in Goods and Agriculture in the FTAA

The thirty-four countries negotiating the Free Trade Area of the Americas (FTAA) have spent a considerable amount of time and resources discussing issues of trade in goods and agricultural products. Between the Miami and Santiago summits, that is, between December 1994 and April 1998, these discussions were conducted in a series of working groups. Leaders at the Santiago Summit authorized formal negotiating groups, which have been meeting regularly since then. Discussions on market access and agricultural issues started in 1995, although agricultural discussions were initially subsumed in the Working Group on Subsidies, Antidumping, and Countervailing Duties. When formal negotiations were launched, the twelve working groups were reconfigured into nine negotiating groups, including one devoted specifically to agriculture.

By the end of 2000 the Negotiating Group on Market Access (NGMA) had met eleven times, and the Negotiating Group on Agriculture (NGAG) ten times. Given perhaps the broadest mandate of any of the nine negotiating groups, the NGMA was charged with designing a hemispheric regime that would address tariff and nontariff barriers (as well as other equivalent measures), rules of origin, customs procedures, safeguards, and standards and technical barriers to trade.

Much of the preparatory phase (1995–97) was spent on generating, collecting, and collating information that would be critical to conducting actual negotiations on trade in goods and agriculture. For the market access group, this preparatory phase involved attempting to construct a hemispheric trade and tariff database that did not previously exist. The database would have to cover the range of tariffs (many countries would record bound, applied, and several different schedules of preferential tariffs in their national submission) and associated trade patterns so that the value of negotiated outcomes could somehow be measured.

The working group dealing with agricultural issues, particularly the issue of domestic and export subsidies, found itself similarly challenged to develop a common base of information. The group spent considerable time examining subsidy practices outside of the hemisphere, particularly those practices in the European Union, which remains a major agricultural exporter to the Americas and whose subsidies therefore have an impact on the competitive situation in individual markets.

Market Access Objectives in the FTAA

At their meeting in San José in March 1998, trade ministers established the following objectives for the FTAA negotiations in market access:

—Consistent with the provisions of the WTO, including GATT Article XXIV (1994) and its Understanding on the Interpretation of Article XXIV of the General Agreement on Tariffs and Trade 1994, to progressively eliminate tariffs, and nontariff barriers, as well as other measures with equivalent effects, that restrict trade between participating countries.

—All tariffs will be subject to negotiation.

—Different trade liberalization timetables may be negotiated.

—To facilitate the integration of smaller economies and their full participation in the FTAA negotiations.

Ministers also established the following objectives for the negotiations on rules of origin and customs procedures:

—Development of an efficient and transparent system of rules of origin, including nomenclature and certificates of origin, to facilitate the exchange of goods without creating unnecessary obstacles to trade.

—Simplification of customs procedures, in order to facilitate trade and reduce administrative costs.

—Creation and implementation of mechanisms to exchange information on customs issues among FTAA countries.

—Development of effective systems to detect and combat fraud and other illicit customs activities, without creating unnecessary obstacles to foreign trade.

—Promotion of customs mechanisms and measures that ensure operations are conducted with transparency, efficiency, integrity and responsibility.

As discussed in chapter 7, ministers also established objectives for standards and technical barriers to trade.

The San José Declaration further specifies that the objectives of the Negotiating Group on Market Access shall apply to trade in agricultural products. Ministers, recognizing the interaction between market access and agriculture, instructed the NGMA and the Negotiating Group on Agriculture to identify any areas that might merit further ministerial consideration and to report their results to the Trade Negotiations Committee (TNC) no later than December 2000. In San José the NGAG was given the challenging task of addressing sanitary and phytosanitary measures, agricultural export subsidies, and other trade-distorting practices that affect trade in agricultural goods.

Customs-Related Business Facilitation Measures

At their meeting in Toronto in November, 1999, ministers agreed to a number of specific business facilitation measures, concentrating on customs procedures and enhanced transparency in response to the priorities identified by business communities (these are covered in detail in chapter 14). Ministers agreed to implement, beginning on January 1, 2000, eight specific measures that would "contribute significantly to the conduct of business in the hemisphere by reducing transaction costs and creating a more consistent and predictable business environment." These measures cover temporary importation or admission of certain goods related to business travelers; express shipments; simplified procedures for low value shipments; compatible electronic data interchange (EDI) systems and common data elements; a harmonized commodity description and coding system; customs information and dissemination/Hemispheric Guide on Customs Procedures; codes of conduct for customs officials; and risk analysis and targeting methodology.[14] An ad hoc Group of Experts on (Customs-related) Business Facilitation Measures is reporting to the Trade Negotiations Committee on the progress each of the thirty-four FTAA countries achieve regarding the primary elements identified for each of these eight measures, including technical assistance activities.[15]

14. The Hemispheric Guide on Customs Procedures, containing information for all thirty-four countries, was updated as of November, 2000, and posted on the FTAA home page at (www.ftaa-alca.org).

15. See FTAA document TNC/cbf/w/01/Rev.6. An updated version can be downloaded from (www.ftaa-alca.org/Alca_e.asp).

Hemispheric Trade and Tariff Database

To further transparency, trade ministers affirmed in Toronto that information on tariffs and trade flows prepared for the Negotiating Group on Market Access should be disseminated through the FTAA Home Page and periodically updated.[16] The information on the database consists of official country submissions for the following information:

—National customs tariffs, based on the 1996 version of the Harmonized System (HS96) at the most detailed tariff line level with corresponding product description;

—For each tariff line, as applicable: MFN bound tariff rates; MFN applied tariff rates; and preferential tariff rates and the countries to which they apply, as well as other taxes, charges, and measures that affect the applied tariff.

—Import and export statistics by trading partner in value and volume at the most detailed level of the appropriate customs tariff.

This information is updated annually, with tariffs available in March, and trade flows in September. This database will be an essential tool for negotiators in the next phase of tariff negotiations.

In November 2000 the Negotiating Group on Market Access finalized its report to the Trade Negotiations Committee. The report contained proposed options for modalities and procedures for tariff negotiations, a report on the interaction between the negotiating groups on market access and agriculture, and draft normative texts on tariffs, nontariff measures, safeguards, rules of origin, customs procedures, and technical barriers to trade. As in other FTAA negotiating groups and bodies, the Negotiating Groups on Market Access and Agriculture have benefited from the expertise and analytical support of the Tripartite Committee (Organization of American States, Inter-American Development Bank, and United Nations Economic Commission for Latin America and the Caribbean), and, according to the division of labor between these institutions, most particularly the Inter-American Development Bank.

Challenges for the Future

The countries of the Western Hemisphere have taken significant steps toward liberalizing trade in goods. This was particularly true in the 1990s,

16. The "Hemispheric Trade and Tariff Data Base for Market Access" was posted at (alca-ftaa.iadb.org/eng/ngmadb_e.htm).

when subregional arrangements were deepened and several free trade agreements were concluded. The FTAA will build on all these agreements and multilateralize the liberalization trend present in all the subregions of the hemisphere.

Some of the specific issues that the drafters of the normative texts on market access issues must address under an eventual FTAA agreement are:

—The timetable for agreement on methods and modalities for tariff negotiations including base tariffs (WTO bound rate, applied rate), reference periods (base year or average), tariff nomenclatures (future updates of the harmonized system), schedules and pace of tariff elimination, types of tariff concessions (linear or preferential percentage margins), and methods for determining concessions (formula or request-offer);

—The timetable and modality for establishing FTAA rules of origin, including whether in the normative text on rules of origin, primary reliance for certification should be placed upon certifying authorities or upon the economic operators involved in the transactions, and the need to take advantage of new technologies;

—The consideration of how to accommodate differences in the levels of development and size of economies in the hemisphere, including those of the smaller economies;

—Establishment of a database on nontariff measures, including the exchange of notifications and counternotifications;

—The need, if any, for safeguard provisions under the FTAA beyond those existing under GATT Article XIX (1994) and the WTO Agreement on Safeguards;

—The linkage, if any, to the timetable for reduction and elimination of agricultural export subsidies.

Taking into account all the agreements negotiated or trade and tariff negotiations under way between FTAA participating countries, it is a useful exercise to attempt to map out the web of tariff relationships yet to be liberalized.

Canada would have to negotiate removal of duties with Central America, the Andean Community, MERCOSUR, the Dominican Republic, and Panama. The eventual outcome of the current Canada-Costa Rica negotiations and the possible negotiation and conclusion of a free trade agreement between Canada and the other Central American republics implies that Canada would face four negotiations of potential technical complexity or political difficulty in the FTAA. It is assumed that minimal tariff concessions would have to be negotiated with CARICOM given the existence of Canada's General Preferential Tariff and the CARIBCAN program.

The United States would face negotiations with Central America, CARICOM, the Dominican Republic, Panama, the Andean Community, and MERCOSUR. U.S. preferential arrangements (both its Generalized System of Preferences and those granted under the Caribbean Basin Initiative) might serve as a basis for the first four partners, leaving three sets of significant negotiations. As of December 2000 the United States was negotiating a bilateral free trade agreement with Chile.

Mexico, essentially, would have to negotiate with CARICOM, the Dominican Republic, and MERCOSUR to complete its tariff liberalization agenda in the hemisphere. As of December 2000 Mexico was negotiating with Panama, Peru, and Ecuador.

Central America would be required to negotiate with the United States, CARICOM, the Andean Community, and MERCOSUR, assuming that negotiations currently under way with Canada and Panama would have been completed. As noted above, the negotiations with the United States could probably use, as a basis, existing unilateral preferential arrangements.

CARICOM is in a somewhat unique position. Although the region enjoys preferential access to several external markets, it has taken on very few commitments for its own part. With the exceptions of its nonreciprocal agreements with Colombia and Venezuela, and the recent free trade agreement with the Dominican Republic, the region has few "models" to turn to.

The Dominican Republic has negotiated free trade agreements with Central America and CARICOM. Therefore, the country would face negotiations with Canada, the United States, Mexico, Panama, the Andean Community, Chile, and MERCOSUR.

Panama, like CARICOM, has entered into very few trade agreements with FTAA countries. As of December 2000, it was negotiating with Mexico and with Central America. Therefore, in the FTAA, Panama has to negotiate removal of duties with Canada, the United States, CARICOM, the Andean Community, Chile, and MERCOSUR.

The Andean Community countries, for the most part, have to negotiate with Canada, the United States, Central America, CARICOM, the Dominican Republic, and Panama. Negotiations with MERCOSUR are under way. The two groupings have a commitment to sign a free trade agreement by January 2002. Colombia and Venezuela, the two most important members of the Andean Community, have already made tariff and other market access concessions to CARICOM. These could conceivably be broadened to include the remaining members of the Andean Community. The main challenge for the community will lie in its negotiations with Canada and more particularly with the United States. Both will come to the table with commercially significant requests.

MERCOSUR will need to negotiate with Canada, the United States, Mexico, the Dominican Republic, Panama, Central America, and CARICOM. The negotiation with the United States, and potentially with Canada and Mexico in selected sectors, will be challenging. The key to a fully tariff liberalized hemisphere does truly lie in this one negotiating relationship with the United States, among many.

Like Mexico, Chile sits in the best position of all. It has basically completed its market access negotiating agenda, with only three partners left on its scorecard: CARICOM, the Dominican Republic, and Panama. Supported and encouraged by the most outward looking trade policy in the region, Chile has had remarkable success in diversifying its commercial relations. Domestic reforms in Chile, and particularly its unilateral reduction of barriers to trade—including significant unilateral tariff reductions—have served to prepare the country well. As of December 2000 Chile and the United States were negotiating a free trade agreement.

Several challenges in the area of trade in goods lie ahead, but the number of trade agreements concluded between countries of the Americas illustrates that further progress can be achieved. Lots of events or dates are characterized as being groundbreaking in stature or significance, or marking one sort of a turning point or another. It nonetheless remains true that the 1990s represented a unique time for trade liberalization in the Americas, with a remarkable freeing up of bilateral, plurilateral, and subregional trading relationships. A quantitative analysis, which is beyond the scope of the present endeavor, would surely show that more than 80 percent of all trade conducted in the hemisphere is now conducted under the framework of one liberalizing agreement or another. The decade has witnessed the birth and the implementation of the NAFTA, the MERCOSUR agreement, and a wide range of bilateral agreements between Mexico, Chile, Central America, and Canada. Subregions linked by older integration schemes have been subject to the demonstration effect and have sought actively to rejuvenate their arrangements; these include the Andean Community, the Central American Common Market, and CARICOM. At the same time, many countries have reached out to nontraditional partners (Chile and Central America and recent efforts between Canada and Costa Rica and CARICOM and the Dominican Republic, to name but a few) in their need to find open new markets in support of export-led growth and investment. These arrangements have almost all been of the "new generation," but at their heart they have remained grounded in the traditional exchange of concessions that has always characterized agreements on trade in goods.

References

Canada. Department of Foreign Affairs and International Trade. 1999. *International Trade Minister Signs Tariff Acceleration Agreement with Chile.* Ottawa (November 4).

Devlin, Robert, and Antoni Estevadeordal. 2000. *What's New in the New Regionalism in the Americas.* Washington, D.C.: Inter-American Development Bank.

Devlin, Robert, Antoni Estevadeordal, and Luis J. Garay. 1999. *The FTAA: Some Longer Term Issues.* Buenos Aires: INTAL.

Estevadeordal, Antoni. 1999. *Negotiating Preferential Market Access: The Case of NAFTA.* Buenos Aires: INTAL.

Garay, Luis J. S., and Rafael Cornejo. 1999. "Rules of Origin in Free Trade Agreements in the Americas." In *Trade Rules in the Making: Challenges in Regional and Multilateral Trade Negotiations*, edited by Miguel Rodríguez Mendoza, Patrick Low, and Barbara Kotschwar. Brookings/Organization of American States.

La Nación. 1999. "México dijo sí a carne y leche." San José: January 16.

BARBARA R. KOTSCHWAR

7 | Standards and Technical Barriers to Trade

The regulatory measures taken by governments to ensure the safety of their populace and environment are becoming more prominently placed on the trade agenda. It is a known and accepted fact that standards and technical regulations that aim to protect health and safety may restrict trade. As tariff barriers have fallen over the last two decades, however, the trade effects of nontariff technical regulations have become more obvious. As a result, standards and technical regulations are becoming an important component of international trade agreements.

There has been a commensurate increase in the incidence of issues related to technical regulations in the multilateral trade arena: during the first five years of operation of the World Trade Organization's Dispute Settlement Understanding (DSU), twenty-five cases (13 percent of the total) referenced standards-related provisions. In its first year of operation, one-fourth of the DSU's cases—eleven out of forty-four—made reference to the standards provisions of the WTO contained in the Agreement on Technical Barriers to Trade and the Agreement on the Application of Sanitary and Phytosanitary Measures.[1]

1. Hufbauer, Kotschwar, and Wilson (2000, table 4).

Although few quantitative data are available to measure the actual impact of technical barriers to trade, the numbers that do exist bear out the worries of negotiators who are trying to stem the trade impact of such regulations. In a much-cited 1996 study, economists with the Organization for Economic Cooperation and Development (OECD) found that differing standards and technical regulations, combined with the cost of testing and compliance certification, could constitute between 2 and 10 percent of overall production costs—not an insignificant amount, especially for smaller firms.[2] More recently a team of economists at the World Bank found that the harmonization of a European Union standard on aflatoxin, a toxin that has been identified in cereals, fruits, and nuts, would cause African exports of cereals to fall by 51 percent.[3]

The particular challenge presented to trade negotiators is that these technical barriers are aimed at achieving legitimate public goals and serve, at least theoretically, to correct a market distortion. Standards and technical regulations are set to protect health, safety, and the environment and to promote consumer and producer efficiency. When they are set to address such legitimate objectives, their removal or relaxation is thus undesirable. In this they differ from tariffs, which create a market distortion by driving a wedge between the market price and the true price of a good and with respect to which the ultimate goal of trade negotiators is elimination. However, these measures can also effectively be used to discriminate against imports and, when applied arbitrarily or in a discriminatory way, may introduce new distortions, keep out foreign goods, or sustain rent-seeking behavior. This may occur when standards of an importing country are enforced through testing and certification requirements that are difficult or expensive for foreign manufacturers or producers to access.

Conformity assessment procedures—the technical procedures, such as testing, verification, inspection, and certification, performed to ensure that a product meets the specifications set out in regulations and standards— are especially susceptible to becoming barriers to trade. Barriers arise when these procedures are unclear or not well publicized or when differences among standards in different countries are not justified by the objective that they aim to fulfill. Generally, exporters bear the cost of these procedures and can be dissuaded from entering a market if the cost of fulfilling that market's regulations is too high. Such costs are especially daunting to

---

2. Organization for Economic Cooperation and Development (1996).
3. Otsuki, Wilson, and Sewadeh (2000).

small and medium-size enterprises. Barriers result from the duplication of effort associated with separate conformity assessment procedures, which are needed in cases where mandatory product specifications differ from country to country, even where countries rely on international standards. The goal for the negotiator whose aim is to facilitate trade is to make these objectives compatible in a manner that restricts trade as little as possible while continuing to meet the needs for which the standards were developed.

In the context of international trade agreements, an important distinction is made between a "standard" and a "technical regulation." Both standards and technical regulations set out specific characteristics of a product such as its size, shape, design, functions, and performance; the way it is labeled or packaged; and the related process and production methods. The difference between standards and technical regulations is one of compliance. Technical regulations are those standards adopted by governments as representing legal specifications; conformity with these is mandatory and is enforced by official agencies. In contrast, conformity with standards, which are often promulgated by nongovernmental bodies and associations, is voluntary and enforced by the market. Thus, if a product does not meet the requirement of a technical regulation in an importing country—for example, if an automobile exceeds emissions levels as specified by the U.S. Environmental Protection Agency—that product will not be allowed on the U.S. market. If a product does not meet a voluntary standard, however, it is free to enter the country. It may, however, not find much of a market. Producers of Betamax videotapes are free to sell their wares in the United States. They may meet resistance, however, from a population of VHS VCR owners.

Although the economic effect of general and food safety standards is similar, this chapter focuses on the standards and technical regulations that are not considered to be sanitary or phytosanitary measures. The potential of standards and technical regulations to act as barriers to trade was first formally recognized at the multilateral level during the Tokyo Round, with the negotiation of the Agreement on Technical Barriers to Trade, also known as the Standards Code, which came into effect in 1980. Along with a number of other Tokyo Round codes, this was a voluntary, plurilateral agreement, with obligations applying only to members who chose to sign on. Initially there were thirty-two signatories; by 1993 forty-six countries (including six FTAA participants) had agreed to the obligations of the Standards Code. With the Uruguay Round Agreement on Technical Barriers to Trade (the TBT Agreement), standards issues were brought into the mainstream of international trade negotiations and under the single undertaking were made obligatory for all WTO members. The TBT Agreement expands and strengthens the scope and coverage of international disciplines on standards and technical regulations and provides a comprehensive set of guidelines for the regulation of technical barriers to international trade. Because the WTO requires all its members to adhere to the TBT Agreement, a much larger number of countries are bound by its obligations than were committed to the Standards Code.[4]

In the TBT Agreement, the definition of standards and technical regulation is expanded to cover processes and production methods as well as characteristics of manufactured products.[5] The TBT Agreement includes more language on rules guiding how a product is manufactured or grown.[6] Where the Standards Code set the rules for the central governments that signed it, the TBT Agreement expanded coverage to include local, nongovernmental, and private standards-setting bodies. This is a significant development: in many countries standards-related activities are undertaken by organizations at the subfederal level or are the initiative of nongovernmental actors such as industry consortiums or associations. Under the Uruguay Round obligations, governments are responsible for "taking positive measures" to ensure observance by their local and nongovernmental bodies.[7] The general principles for the development and implementation of standards for central governments, local government bodies, and nongovernmental and regional standardizing bodies are set out in Annex 3, the "Code of Good Practice." New disciplines were developed to increase the transparency of standards-related work done at the bilateral and regional level and information-sharing requirements were enhanced. Third parties were given the right to comment "in good time" on standards-related work done by other countries in regional or bilateral forums. Additionally, TBT-related disputes were to be settled under the procedures of the Dispute Settlement Understanding incorporated into the WTO structure.

---

4. As of December 2000, 140 countries are members of the WTO.

5. WTO Agreement on Technical Barriers to Trade, Annex 1.

6. Under the Tokyo Round Code, dispute settlement procedures could be used if process or production requirements were believed to be used as a means of avoiding obligations on product characteristics.

7. For a discussion of the history of the Uruguay Round negotiations on Standards and Technical Barriers to Trade, see Croome (1996).

The TBT Agreement aims to provide guidelines by which technical regulations and voluntary standards least restrict trade and sets out the basic principles for addressing their development and implementation and for procedures to ensure that these are met, including testing, certification, laboratory accreditation, recognition, and quality system registration programs. Its provisions apply to all levels of government and cover all industrial and agricultural products. The TBT Agreement does not cover services and does not apply to government procurement activities. Nor does it apply to sanitary and phytosanitary measures, which are addressed in a separate Agreement on the Application of Sanitary and Phytosanitary Measures.[8]

The TBT Agreement has four main policy objectives. The first objective, which underpins the others, is to uphold the key principles of *nondiscrimination* and the avoidance of *unnecessary obstacles to trade*. The second is to encourage members to recognize each other's standards and testing procedures as *equivalent*. This means that if two countries have different ways to fulfill the same objective, they should accept each other's ways of fulfilling these objectives. Such acceptance eliminates the cost to businesses in one country of having to adjust production to fit some particular specifications of another country when both countries' specifications meet the same objectives. The third broad objective is for national and regional standards to be based, to the greatest extent possible, on international standards. The fourth objective, and the one in which the greatest strides were made during the Uruguay Round negotiations, is to enhance the exchange of information among the member governments and to increase transparency in the standards-setting process.

Provisions on Standards-Related Measures in Subregional Arrangements in the Americas

Although the TBT Agreement provides a shared set of guidelines for regulations and standards-related activities for the countries of the Americas, many subregional integration agreements, especially recent ones, include comprehensive disciplines on standards, technical regulations, and conformity assessment. These provisions vary in length, depth, and breadth. Some agreements contain legal language elaborating comprehensive disciplines,

---

8. This agreement covers measures relating to pests or diseases in animals or plants and contaminants of food.

while others focus instead on carrying out cooperative activities and in developing common policies in this area. Many of the agreements make reference to the WTO and extend transparency requirements to the subregional level; in others, the provisions differ in scope, coverage, or substance from WTO provisions. The remainder of this chapter is devoted to examining the guidelines and activities in standards-related issues among the countries of the Americas with a view to identifying commonalities and divergences in the ways countries have chosen to address these issues in their subregional arrangements.

There is a fundamental difference in approach among the subregional arrangements in fulfilling the objective of avoiding unnecessary technical barriers to trade. Those agreements that strive for deeper integration, the customs unions and the arrangements whose objective is formation of a common market, aim toward *harmonization* of standards, technical regulations, and certification criteria. Free trade areas, including NAFTA, the Group of Three (G-3), and the bilateral free trade agreements signed by Mexico subsequent to negotiating NAFTA and by Chile and the Dominican Republic, favor *promoting compatibility*. This latter trend shows an increasing commonality of structure in bilateral and plurilateral agreements: as a result of the bilateral agreements negotiated by Canada and especially Mexico, NAFTA rules and disciplines have been "exported" to other Latin American countries. Although two main approaches exist in the hemisphere, these mechanisms are not mutually exclusive at the regional level, and the challenge now is for countries to select the bundle of elements that will bring them closest to fulfilling the FTAA objective.

Aiming for Harmonization: The Customs Unions

MERCOSUR (Common Market of the South) is the largest subregional integration arrangement that aims toward deep integration and places great importance on the harmonization of rules and practices among the members. Although neither the founding Treaty of Asunción nor the 1994 Protocol of Ouro Preto contains specific language regarding standards-related measures, MERCOSUR has been very active in coordinating national regulations on standards-related activities. Under the Treaty of Asunción ten working groups were created, of which one, SGT-3, is responsible for technical regulations. Related directives are issued though resolutions of the Common Market Group, including GMC Resolution 02/92, which established a MERCOSUR Standardizing Committee and provided for the creation of sectoral standardizing committees.[9] The main objectives of this standardizing policy are to harmonize the technical regulations identified by member countries as obstacles to this trade, to make national conformity assessment structures compatible, and to develop a common methodology for elaborating a common MERCOSUR standards regime.[10] To date, MERCOSUR has elaborated a significant number of common standards. In 1996 and 1997 MERCOSUR concluded "association" agreements with Bolivia and Chile, which free trade among the countries and pave the way for future entry into the customs union. These agreements also include provisions on technical regulations and associated issues.

The Andean Community began to address standards-related issues in the early 1980s, with Andean Decision 376 in 1983, which was reformed and supplemented in 1997 by Decision 419. The 1996 Trujillo Protocol establishing the Andean Community gave the governing commission responsibility for overseeing the Andean System of Standardization, Accreditation, Testing, Certification, Technical Regulations, and Metrology. A number of common standards have been elaborated, and many joint cooperative activities undertaken.

In the Central American Common Market (CACM), Article 26 of the Guatemala Protocol to the General Treaty of Economic Integration in Central America obligates members to harmonize and adopt common standards and technical regulations. This is further elaborated in the Central American Regime on Standards-Related Measures, Metrology, and Authorization Procedures. Attempts to promote a regional standardizing infrastructure have, to date, not been brought to fruition.

Detailed provisions on standards are not included in the treaty setting up the Caribbean Community and Common Market (CARICOM), but the policy objective is made clear in Article 42, which recognizes "the desirability to harmonize as soon as practicable such provisions imposed by law or administrative practices as affect the establishment of the Common Market in the following areas," including industrial standards and labeling of food and drugs. In 1992, as part of CARICOM's modification of its integration process, Protocol III on Industrial Policy was introduced, which

9. The sectoral committees include electrical power, steel, electronics and telecommunications, toys, cement and concrete, machines and equipment, automobiles, tires, rings and valves, plastics, information technology, dentistry, medicine and hospital care, paper and cellulose, quality control, welding, furniture, and the environment.

10. GMC Resolution 152/96 December 13, 1996, and GMC Resolution 61/97, December 13, 1997.

addresses standards and technical regulations in Article 47. Although the protocol has not yet been signed by all members, the discussion of CARICOM here refers to these provisions.

Free Trade Agreements: Promoting Compatibility

Unlike the customs unions, which seek for deeper integration of approaches to standardization, the free trade agreements all aim to make measures more compatible. All of the plurilateral, and the majority of bilateral, free trade agreements contain provision on standards-related issues. Chapter 9 of NAFTA addresses standards-related measures. The Group of Three agreement among Colombia, Mexico, and Venezuela elaborates provisions quite similar to those in NAFTA. The bilateral free trade agreements also explicitly address standards in their provisions. All of the bilateral free trade agreements signed by Mexico contain provisions on standards measures that are similar to those contained in NAFTA and the Group of Three agreement. The bilateral agreements signed by the Dominican Republic with CARICOM and with Central America also contain elaborate provisions on technical barriers to trade. The Canada-Chile agreement is notable in that it includes no provisions at all on standards or technical barriers to trade.

Convergence and Divergence

The WTO TBT Agreement refers to definitions set out by international standardizing bodies, such as the International Organization on Standardization and the International Electrotechnical Commission, and the United Nations system (with the caveat that their context should be taken into account), specifically ISO/IEC Guide 2. The main areas covered in the agreement—"technical regulation," "standard," and "conformity assessment procedures"—are defined along with explanatory notes.

NAFTA introduces an innovation in terminology, employing the term *standards-related measures* referring to and substituting for "a standard, technical regulation or conformity assessment procedure."[11] This usage was subsequently incorporated into the Group of Three agreement and the bilateral free trade agreements signed by Mexico, Chile, and the Dominican Republic, as well as by the CACM.

11. North American Free Trade Agreement, Article 915.

The WTO and the NAFTA-like agreements all define conformity assessment procedures as procedures "used, directly or indirectly, to determine that relevant requirements in technical regulations or standards are fulfilled."[12] NAFTA elaborates on this definition, including mention of sampling, testing, inspection, evaluation, verification, monitoring, auditing, assurance of conformity, accreditation, registration, or approval. Approval procedures are defined separately as "any registration, notification or other mandatory administrative procedure for granting permission for a good or service to be produced, marketed or used for a stated purpose or under stated conditions."[13] The free trade agreements signed by Mexico, Chile, and the Dominican Republic contain similar definitions (except the Central America-Dominican Republic agreement does not include approval procedures in its definitions).

A principal concept in both the WTO and NAFTA-type agreements is that of *legitimate objectives*. This term does not appear in the WTO section on definitions but rather is included as part of Article 2.2 of the TBT Agreement as "inter alia, national security requirements; the prevention of deceptive practices; protection of human health or safety; animal or plant life or health, or the environment."[14] The NAFTA definition, set out in Article 915, includes safety; protection of human, animal or plant life or health; the environment; and consumers; unlike the WTO, it includes sustainable development but omits national security. The CARICOM-Dominican Republic agreement follows this definition. The Mexico bilateral agreements and the Central America-Dominican Republic agreement employ a mixture of the WTO and NAFTA terms, mentioning all of the common factors and omitting both national security and sustainable development. The Central America-Chile definitions follow the WTO, including national security but not sustainable development. The Andean Community does not use the term *legitimate objectives*.

Policy Objectives

Table 7-1 summarizes the policy objectives within the various trade agreements in the Americas. MERCOSUR's goal in this area is to identify technical barriers to trade flows among the members and then to harmonize

---

12. WTO TBT Agreement, Annex 1.
13. NAFTA, Article 915.
14. WTO TBT Agreement, Article 2.2.

Table 7-1. *Policy Objectives and Coverage of Standards-Related Measures*

Agreements	Policy objective	Compatibility and equivalence	Right to establish level of protection
Customs unions			
MERCOSUR (Treaty of Asunción; GMC resolutions)	Harmonize	No	No
Andean Community (Decision 419: Modification of Decision 376) (Andean System of Standardization, Accreditation, Testing, Certification, Technical Regulations and Metrology)	Harmonize	No	No
Central American Common Market (Guatemala Protocol and the Reglamento Centro-americano de medidas de Normalización, Metrología y Procedimientos de Autorización)	Harmonize	No	No
CARICOM (Treaty of Chaguaramas/Protocol III: Industrial Policy–Protocol Amending the Treaty Establishing the Caribbean Community)	Harmonize	No	No
Free trade agreements			
NAFTA (Part Three: Technical Barriers to Trade, Chapter 9: Standards-Related Measures)	Make compatible	Yes	Yes
Group of Three (Mexico, Colombia, Venezuela) (Chapter XIV: Technical Standards)	Make compatible	Yes	Yes
Bolivia-Mexico (Chapter XIII: Standards Measures)	Make compatible	Yes	No
Chile-Mexico (Chapter 8: Standards-Related Measures)	Make compatible	Compatibility	Yes
Costa Rica-Mexico (Chapter XI: Standards Measures)	Make compatible	Yes	Yes
Mexico-Nicaragua (Chapter XIV: Standards-Related Measures)	Make compatible	Yes	Yes
Mexico-Northern Triangle (Chapter XV: Standards-Related Measures)	Make compatible	Yes	Yes
Canada-Chile	. . .	. . .	. . .
Central America-Chile (Chapter 9: Standards Measures, Metrology and Authorization Procedures)	Make compatible	Yes	No
Central America-Dominican Republic (Chapter XII: Technical Barriers to Trade)	Make compatible	Yes	No
CARICOM-Dominican Republic (Appendix VI to Annex I: Technical Barriers to Trade)	Make compatible	Yes	No

Note: The Canada-Chile agreement does not address technical barriers to trade.

the technical regulations that are identified as barriers.[15] MERCOSUR is the only agreement that explicitly aims to identify offending technical regulations and to eliminate the obstacles they create through regional harmonization. In its associative agreements with Bolivia and Chile, MERCOSUR aims for coordination and compatibility, aiming for harmonization only in sanitary and phytosanitary measures with Chile. The Andean Community's objective is to "initiate a gradual harmonization process," which is to be achieved as the community seeks to "coordinate, develop and harmonize at a subregional level, the activities of standardization, testing, accreditation, certification, technical regulations and metrology within the priorities of the integration process."[16]

In Central America countries are to harmonize their respective standards-related measures, authorization procedures, and metrology measures without lowering the level of security or protection of health or life.[17] CARICOM also aims to harmonize standards-related measures. Its program on standards and technical regulations is to include "harmonization of standards and technical regulations, and transparency in the development and promulgation of standards and technical regulations."[18]

The free trade agreements take a different approach. NAFTA introduces the use of the phrase *make compatible* to the standards lexicon, defining this as bringing different standards-related measures that have the same scope to a level such that they are identical, equivalent, or permit goods or services to be used in each other's place to fulfill the same purpose.[19] NAFTA's objective is "to the greatest extent practicable, [to] *make compatible* their respective standards-related measures,"[20] and to seek "through appropriate measures, to promote the compatibility of a specific standard or conformity assessment procedure that is maintained in its territory or with [those] maintained in the territory of the other Party."[21] A clear demonstration that NAFTA does not aim for harmonization is the provision stipulating that, in pursuing its legitimate objectives, each country may establish the level of protection it considers appropriate so that countries are able to

15. MERCOSUR, GMC Resolution 61/97.
16. Andean Community Decision 419: Modification of Decision 376 (Andean System of Standardization, Accreditation, Testing, Certification, Technical Regulations and Metrology).
17. Article 9 of the CACM regime on standardization, metrology, and authorization procedures.
18. CARICOM, Article 47, Protocol III.
19. NAFTA, Article 906.
20. NAFTA, Article 906.2.
21. NAFTA, Article 906.3.

express their different levels of tolerance for risk.[22] The WTO includes no such stated provision, although it is implicitly present in the TBT Agreement. NAFTA explicitly states that countries may adopt standards-related measures, as long as they are in accordance with the agreement, even if they prohibit the importation of goods or services from other NAFTA countries if the approval procedures are not completed or measures are not in compliance.

The Group of Three agreement replicates this approach, as do the Costa Rica-Mexico, Chile-Mexico, and the Mexico-Northern Triangle bilateral agreements. The other free trade agreements also aim for compatibility but do not include language on setting the level of protection. The MERCOSUR associate agreements with Bolivia and Chile follow the free trade agreements in agreeing to compatibility in their standards and technical regulations but leave open the possibility for future deeper integration by agreeing to coordinate some activities.

Scope and Coverage

Provisions on standards in the regional arrangements among countries in the Western Hemisphere differ somewhat from the WTO in their coverage, mainly with respect to services and the inclusion of sanitary and phytosanitary measures in the same chapter or section as technical barriers to trade. Additionally, many regional trade arrangements in the hemisphere also contain specific provisions on metrology.

As table 7-2 shows, all of the customs unions cover services in their standards disciplines. MERCOSUR refers to the need to "harmonize standards in order to eliminate nontariff barriers that are linked to quality requirements for goods and services" and that otherwise might interfere with the free flow of goods and services in the region.[23] The Andean Community covers standards-related activities for "all the products and services made or traded in the subregion."[24] The Central American regime covers standards-related measures, authorization procedures, and metrology measures that may affect, directly or indirectly, trade in goods and services. In CARICOM one of the objectives of standards disciplines is "enhanced efficiency in the production and delivery of goods and services."[25]

22. NAFTA, Article 904(2).
23. MERCOSUR, GMC Resolution 05/92.
24. Article 4, Andean Community Decision 419: Modification of Decision 376 (Andean System of Standardization, Accreditation, Testing, Certification, Technical Regulations and Metrology).
25. CARICOM, Protocol III, Article 47.

Table 7-2. *Scope and Coverage of Standards-Related Measures*

Agreement	Services	SPS	Measures included							Separate provision on	
			S	TR	A, T, C	CAP	AP	M	MRAs	Labeling	Protection of environment
Customs unions											
MERCOSUR	Yes	Yes	Yes	Yes	No	Yes	No	Yes	Yes	No	No
Andean Community	Yes	No	Yes	Yes	Yes	No	No	Yes	No	No	No
CACM[a]	Yes	No	Yes	Yes	No	Yes	No	Yes	Yes	No	No
CARICOM	Yes	No	Yes	Yes	No	Yes	No	Yes	Yes	No	No
Free trade agreements											
NAFTA	Yes	No	Yes	Yes	No	Yes	Yes	No	Yes	No	No
Group of Three (G-3)	Yes	No	Yes	Yes	No	Yes	Yes	Yes	Yes	Yes	No
Bolivia-Mexico	Yes	No	Yes	Yes	No	Yes	Yes	Yes	Yes	Yes	No
Chile-Mexico[a]	Yes	No	Yes	Yes	No	Yes	Yes	No	Yes	No	No
Costa Rica-Mexico	Yes	No	Yes	Yes	No	Yes	Yes	Yes	Yes	Yes	No
Mexico-Nicaragua	Yes	No	Yes	Yes	No	Yes	Yes	Yes	Yes	Yes	Yes
Mexico-Northern Triangle	Yes	No	Yes	Yes	No	No	No	No	No	Yes	No
Canada-Chile	No	No	No	No	No	Yes	Yes	Yes	No	No	No
Central America-Chile[a]	Yes	No	Yes	Yes	No	Yes	No	Yes	Yes	No	No
Central America-Dominican Republic	Yes	No	Yes	Yes	No	Yes	No	Yes	Yes	Yes	Yes
CARICOM-Dominican Republic	Yes	No	Yes	Yes	No	Yes	No	Yes	No	Yes	Yes

S=Standards; SPS=Sanitary, phytosanitary measures; TR=Technical Regulations; CAP=Conformity Assessment Procedures; A=Accreditation; C=Certification; T=Testing; M=Metrology; AP= Approval Procedures; MRAs=mutual recognition agreements.

a. Measures include authorization procedures.

The majority of the free trade agreements also cover services in some form. In NAFTA the definition of services is limited to land transportation services and telecommunications services. The Group of Three and the Bolivia-Mexico agreements exclude financial services. The Costa Rica-Mexico agreement excludes services related to air transport; financial services; any loan or subsidy authorized by a party of the state, including loans and insurance supported by the government; and government services. The Chile-Mexico agreement includes information and connected services and any other subsectors agreed upon by the Committee on Standardization.

The second divergence in coverage involves MERCOSUR's treatment of sanitary and phytosanitary standards: MERCOSUR itself as well as the MERCOSUR associative arrangements with Bolivia and with Chile include standards, technical regulations, sanitary and phytosanitary measures, and other measures in a single chapter. All other agreements that specify coverage follow the WTO norm and specifically separate sanitary and phytosanitary standards from TBT provisions.

A third difference in coverage concerns metrology, which the WTO does not specifically address, although it figures implicitly in the standards disciplines. Neither NAFTA nor the Chile-Mexico bilateral agreement contains sections on metrology. This is one element, however, on which the other post-NAFTA free trade agreements diverge from NAFTA. The Group of Three and all other Mexico bilateral agreements contain metrology measures, as do the Central America-Chile, Central America-Dominican Republic, and CARICOM-Dominican Republic agreements. Generally, these provisions invoke use of the International System of Units as a basis for metrology measures and urge members to ensure the traceability of metrological standards back to international measures. Several contain recommendations for cooperation and coordination in metrological infrastructure.

Additionally, several of the bilateral free trade agreements among Latin American and Caribbean countries incorporate separate provisions on labeling into their agreements. In both the WTO and NAFTA, labeling is included in the definition of standard and technical regulation. The Group of Three and Mexico's agreements with Bolivia, Costa Rica, Nicaragua, and the Northern Triangle (El Salvador, Guatemala, and Honduras) all contain provisions that aim toward a common system of symbols for use in labels among the members and set up committees to work toward this goal. The Central America-Dominican Republic agreement aims toward harmonization of labeling procedures and the CARICOM-Dominican Republic agreement aims to develop agreed standards.

Finally, three relatively recent free trade agreements—Mexico-Nicaragua, Central America-Dominican Republic, and CARICOM-Dominican Republic—include specific provisions on environmental protection. Although environmental protection is included as part of the legitimate objectives for which countries may develop or implement technical regulations in all arrangements in some format, these agreements go further and specifically set down the right to preserve and protect the environment, invoking United Nations Environment Program recommendations and other international agreements. The Mexico-Nicaragua agreement also acknowledges a country's right to regulate the transport or exchange of hazardous or radioactive materials according to its national regulations.

Standards and Technical Regulations

MERCOSUR, the Andean Community, and CARICOM all aim to develop common subregional standards. MERCOSUR has been very active in this regard: forming a common regime for technical standards in order to eliminate technical barriers to trade and to facilitate the free circulation of goods and regional integration between the parties. Within this framework, the Working Group on Technical Standards has set up a hierarchy of standards: international, regional, subregional, national.

Within the Andean Community, gradual harmonization of national standards is to lead to the development of a set of official Andean standards. Standards should be adopted that are "of subregional interest."[26] In the development and adoption of standards, member countries are urged to refer to international, regional, or national standards from other countries, and standards are to be "based on the results of science, technology, and experience and should obtain optimum benefits for the community." A provision does exist that permits countries, "without prejudice" to the previous exhortations on harmonization, "to elaborate standards which are of national interest."[27] Members are encouraged to gradually harmonize technical regulations already in force, but are allowed to maintain their own technical regulations that protect the environment as well as animal, human, and plant life or safety.[28] Technical regulations on design and

26. Article 10, Andean Community Decision 419.
27. Article 12, Andean Community Decision 419: Modification of Decision 376 (Andean System of Standardization, Accreditation, Testing, Certification, Technical Regulations and Metrology).
28. Article 25, Andean Community Decision 419: Modification of Decision 376 (Andean System of Standardization, Accreditation, Testing, Certification, Technical Regulations and Metrology).

descriptive characteristics may be developed as long as these are connected to usage.

Under the CARICOM agreement regional standards have been developed for seventy-two products to date. There is talk of regional infrastructure development and shared international obligations. In the Central American regime harmonization is not obligatory, but members may enter into agreements to harmonize their standards-related measures and standard procedures. Members are obliged to use international standards as a basis for the elaboration or application of their standards-related measures, and in the absence of international standards, the members are encouraged to use standards adopted in other regional integration arrangements, in third countries or in internationally recognized private organizations.

NAFTA encourages members to utilize international standards except where they would be an ineffective or inappropriate means to fulfill legitimate objectives. An international standard might be deemed ineffective, for example because of fundamental climatic, geographical, technological, or infrastructural factors; scientific justification; or the level of protection that the party considers appropriate. NAFTA Article 906 (4) provides for reciprocal recognition of technical standards if the exporting party can demonstrate satisfactorily to the importing party that its technical regulations adequately fulfill the importing party's legitimate objectives.

The bilateral agreements generally exhort members to make their measures compatible as far as possible and encourage equivalency. Nearly all agreements urge their members to refer to international standards, where possible or appropriate, as a basis for their technical regulations and standards.

Conformity Assessment Procedures

The WTO agreement on technical trade barriers aims to keep conformity assessment procedures from becoming obstacles to trade by obliging such procedures to be no stricter than necessary to ensure that a good conforms. Procedures should be expeditious and undertaken in nondiscriminatory order. Obligations are set for processing of applications, requests for information, treatment of confidential or proprietary information, imposition of fees, location of facilities, and treatment of samples.

One vehicle that has been used to avoid duplication and burdensome costs of conformity assessment procedures is the use of mutual recognition agreements. Under these agreements "two independent parties agree to recognize either the inspection results, test reports, and/or certificates of conformity issued by agreed and accredited bodies located in the territory of the other party. . . ."[29] Nearly all of the subregional agreements include provisions encouraging their members to consider mutual recognition agreements. Other means toward lessening the costs to trade include reciprocal recognition arrangements, third-party certification, and suppliers' declaration of conformity.

MERCOSUR encourages increased compatibility of national conformity assessment systems, structures, and activities, with the objective of achieving mutual recognition within the region.[30] Under the Andean Community system, members are encouraged to use internationally recognized certification systems and to harmonize the application of such certification systems. The general secretariat of the Andean Community is mandated to set up a register of certifying bodies, accredited by national accreditation bodies. The Central American framework does not include a regional exhortation for mutual recognition agreements but does allow two or more members to enter into such agreements, which should be open to participation by other members. CARICOM aims for the recognition of conformity assessment procedures through mutual recognition or other means.

NAFTA contains detailed requirements on conformity assessment that are similar to those elaborated in the WTO, although differently worded, and without a requirement that the procedure include a complaint review process. NAFTA provides that the requirements that apply to conformity assessment procedures also apply to approval procedures. Wherever possible, a member is required to accept the results of a conformity assessment procedure conducted in another NAFTA country if satisfied that the procedure ensures that the good complies with the objectives of its own technical regulation. NAFTA Article 1304 further encourages parties to accept test results from laboratories of testing facilities in another party in the area of telecommunications.

The bilateral free trade agreements generally promote the principle of compatibility and urge members to seek mutual recognition, when possible, of certification systems, testing laboratories, and conformity assessment results.

---

29. Stephenson (1999).
30. MERCOSUR, GMC Resolution 61/97.

Reference to the WTO Agreement

Nearly all of the agreements signed after the WTO was established reference its provisions on technical barriers to trade.[31] MERCOSUR states that "in the process of preparing and reviewing technical regulations, MERCOSUR must use as a basis the general principles and guidelines established in the World Trade Organization Agreement on Technical Barriers to Trade particularly with respect to transparency, information and notification" (GMC Resolution 152/96). The agreements between MERCOSUR and Bolivia and Chile both refer to obligations in the WTO agreements on technical barriers and on sanitary and phytosanitary standards. Many of the subregional and bilateral arrangements explicitly include nondiscrimination provisions—national treatment and most-favored-nation treatment—the basic principles of the WTO.

Transparency and Information Systems

In the WTO, countries are required to establish enquiry points, or centers of information that can answer questions and provide relevant documentation in a timely fashion and at an equitable price. Most of the regional agreements in the Americas also establish or urge the use of such a center of information and provide for the countries to notify each other about their standards-related measures (table 7-3).

MERCOSUR sets out procedures to allow transparency for internal and international notification and provides a mechanism to facilitate the identification of technical barriers to trade.[32] The Andean Community includes provisions on notifications of new and intended technical regulations, standards, conformity evaluation procedures, and other obligatory measures within ninety days. The Center for Information and Registry of the Andean Community was established as an enquiry point. Within CARICOM, national standards bureaus were set up and used as points of enquiry, and in Protocol III a regional standardizing body is envisaged.

Under NAFTA members must set up inquiry points. Public notice must be given prior to the adoption or modification of standards or standards-related measures that may affect trade within the free trade area. This

31. NAFTA and the Group of Three refer to the General Agreement on Tariffs and Trade because at the time of their signature, the Tokyo Round provisions were in effect.
32. MERCOSUR GMC Resolution 61/97.

Table 7-3. *Transparency, Information, and Institutional Issues*

Agreement	Establish-ment of inquiry points	Standards committees/ bodies	Coopera-tion among national bodies	Dispute settle-ment and alternative settlement mechanisms
Customs unions				
MERCOSUR	Yes	Yes	Yes	No
Andean Community	Yes	Yes	Yes	Yes
Central American Common Market	Yes	Yes	Yes	No
CARICOM	No	Yes	Yes	No
Free trade agreements				
NAFTA	Yes	Yes	Yes	Yes
Group of Three	Yes	Yes	Yes	Yes
Bolivia-Mexico	Yes	Yes	Yes	Yes
Chile-Mexico	Yes	Yes	Yes	Yes
Costa Rica-Mexico	Yes	Yes	Yes	Yes
Mexico-Nicaragua	Yes	Yes	Yes	Yes
Mexico-Northern Triangle	Yes	Yes	Yes	Yes
Central America-Chile	Yes	Yes	Yes	Yes
Central America-Dominican Republic	Yes	Yes	Yes	Yes
CARICOM-Dominican Republic	Yes	No	Yes	No

notice must identify the good or service to be covered, set out the objectives of and reason for the measure, and provide opportunity for comment. Similar provisions exist in the Mexico free trade agreements. The Chile agreements include methods for the notification and exchange of information between signatory countries in good time when adopting or modifying standardization measures.

Degree of Institutionalization

Generally, the agreements establish an overseeing body to aid in the implementation of the agreements and, in some cases, to aid in resolving disputes among members. The degree of institutionalization tends to correlate with the desired degree of integration. Appropriately, the Andean Community has the most institutionalized agreement. A subregional committee, accredited before the community's general secretariat was set up, is composed of two nationals from each country. In turn, the committee oversees the Andean Standardization Network, made up of the national standardization bodies in all the member countries, the Andean Network of National Accreditation Bodies, the Andean Network of Testing Laboratories, and the Andean Network of Accredited Certification Bodies. An Information and Registration Center for standards, technical regulations, and conformity assessment procedures serves as an inquiry point.

The MERCOSUR Standardization Committee guides the harmonization process under this agreement. A committee was set up to facilitate conformity assessment structures and systems.

A Central American committee on standards-related measures, authorization procedures, and metrology oversees the implementation of the Central American standards regime. Its duties are to facilitate the harmonization of standards-related measures, authorization procedures, and metrology measures and to communicate with international and regional organizations, identify and promote mechanisms for technical cooperation, and propose modifications to the regime. In CARICOM, a regional standardizing body is foreseen although not yet operational.

In NAFTA, a Committee for Standards-Related Measures was created, along with subcommittees on standards for telecommunications, land transportation, and textile and apparel labels. The Group of Three includes a Committee for Standards-Related Measures and a Subcommittee on Health Standards Harmonization. The bilateral agreements tend to have established committees to oversee the implementation of the agreements, in addition to subcommittees on topical issues such as health, labeling, packaging, wrapping, and consumer information, and telecommunications.

Dispute Settlement

In the WTO, any disagreements with regard to the working of the TBT Agreement take place under the WTO dispute settlement body procedures (see table 7-3). Many of the regional arrangements have their own dispute resolution mechanisms and also allow for consultations through the standardization committees set up under the agreements that are discussed above. For example, the NAFTA Committee on Standards-Related Measures was set up to monitor the implementation and administration of the provisions in the TBT Agreement; to facilitate the attainment of compatibility; to enhance cooperation on developing, applying, and enforcing standards-related measures; and to facilitate consultations regarding disputes in this area. The Group of Three agreement provides for technical consultations, and under the bilateral agreements between Mexico and Costa Rica and Mexico and Bolivia, disputes on standards-related measures may be taken to the Working Group on Standardization Measures or to the dispute settlement mechanism.

Standards and TBT in the FTAA: Future Steps in the Americas

The Western Hemisphere is still a long way from having a common regional approach toward standards issues that can affect trade. Many of the countries in the Americas are relatively new to this issue, having incorporated provisions on standards and technical barriers to trade into their subregional arrangements only in the 1990s; many experienced multilateral disciplines on the issue for the first time upon joining the WTO in 1995 or later. Nevertheless, there is much activity in the standards area, whether in the creation of new provisions within new trade agreements, in resolving trade disputes with neighbors, or in collaboration with regional and international standardizing organizations.

Increasingly, a common base for hemispheric regulation of standards-related measures at the multilateral level is emerging, in fact as well as in word. Implementation of TBT obligations among countries of the Western Hemisphere is increasing. To date, fourteen of the thirty-four FTAA countries have submitted their Statement of Implementation (Article 15.2); twenty-eight have established an enquiry point (of these, six are enquiry points for sanitary and phytosanitary standards only); and twenty-one have accepted the Code of Good Practice.[33] There has been a marked improvement in implementation. A study published in 1997 found that only seven FTAA countries had submitted a Statement of Implementation, fourteen had established enquiry points, and eight had accepted the Code of Good Practice.[34] Today many of the FTAA countries are participating actively in the triennial reviews of the TBT Agreement and in international standardizing organizations; several are participating in working groups on the elaboration of international standards, and as of 2001 Brazil will hold the presidency of the International Organization on Standardization.

In the Ministerial Declaration of San José, the countries negotiating the FTAA pledged to "eliminate and prevent unnecessary technical barriers

33. Figures based on Londoño (1999), updated to February 2000 from WTO information (www.wto.org).
34. Stephenson (1997).

to trade in the FTAA." A challenge to the FTAA negotiators will be to determine where a hemispheric agreement could go beyond existing multi- lateral disciplines and to build the most effective mechanisms possible to ensure that inevitable differences in national standards and technical regu- lations do not constitute barriers to trade among FTAA countries.

References

Croome, John. 1996. *Reshaping the World Trading System: A History of the Uruguay Round.* Boston: Kluwer Law International.

Hufbauer, Gary, Barbara Kotschwar, and John S. Wilson. 2000. "Trade, Standards and Development Perspectives for Central America." Paper presented at the Workshop on Trade Facilitation, Regulation, and Standards: The Development Challenge in Central America, June 27-29. Available at (www.worldbank.org/research/trade/conference/ WBI_OAS_papers.htm).

Londoño, Carmiña. 1999. *Free Trade Area of the Americas (FTAA) Conformity Assessment Structure.* NIST Special Publication 941. U.S. Department of Commerce, Washington, D.C. Also available at (www.ts.NIST.gov).

Organization for Economic Cooperation and Development. 1996. *Proceedings from the Conference on Consumer Product Safety Standards and Conformity Assessment: Their Effect on International Trade.* Paris.

Otsuki, Tsunehiro, John S. Wilson, and Mirvat Sewadeh. 2000. "Saving Two in a Billion: A Case Study to Quantify the Trade Effect of European Food Safety Standards on African Exports." World Bank Draft Working Paper, October 2000.

Stephenson, Sherry. 1997. "Standards and Conformity Assessment as Nontariff Barriers to Trade." Working Paper 1826. World Bank, Development Research Group, Washington, D.C. September.

———. 1999. "Mutual Recognition and Its Role in Trade Facilitation." *Journal of World Trade* 33 (2):141–76.

SHERRY M. STEPHENSON

8 | *Services*

A strong wind of liberalization has blown over trade in services in the Western Hemisphere. It began in 1994, when the North American Free Trade Agreement (NAFTA) entered into force, followed in 1995 by the first multilateral disciplines on services to become effective under the World Trade Organization. Since then countries in the hemisphere have concluded no fewer than fourteen subregional arrangements on trade in services, involving all of the participants in the Free Trade Area of the Americas (FTAA). These agreements represent not only concrete proof of a heightened interest in the services area, but also a recognition of the importance of efficient service sectors to economic growth and development. The pacts also show a desire to liberalize markets in services, a sector that has traditionally been closed to international trade and competition. This liberalization at the subregional level has, in turn, promoted interest and active participation in services negotiations at the hemispheric level within the FTAA process and in the second round of services negotiations at the multilateral level under the WTO.

The author is grateful to Soonhwa Yi for providing valuable research assistance.

163

Approaches to Liberalization of Services Trade

Two major approaches toward the liberalization of trade in services have been manifest within the Western Hemisphere, as elsewhere in the multilateral trading system: the "positive list," or "bottom-up," approach; and the "negative list," or "top-down," approach. All fourteen subregional agreements that encompass services have used one or the other of these two modalities to liberalize trade in services. The positive list approach emphasizes progressive liberalization of services trade through the undertaking of commitments regarding market access, the treatment of foreign service suppliers in specific service sectors, or both. Additional liberalization in sectors where commitments are not initially undertaken is to be carried out through periodic rounds of negotiations. The positive list, bottom-up approach is the one that was agreed and carried forward during the Uruguay Round of Multilateral Trade Negotiations and is now in place at the multilateral level under the WTO General Agreement on Trade in Services, or GATS, in effect since January 1995. A second round of services negotiations at the multilateral level began in January 2000.

Within the Western Hemisphere, members of MERCOSUR (Common Market of the South) have chosen to follow a variant of the positive list approach, one that sets a specific goal of achieving a common market in services within a specific timeframe. Much like the GATS approach, the Protocol of Montevideo on Trade in Services of MERCOSUR, signed in December 1997, stipulates that services liberalization is to be progressive among members and is to be carried out through annual rounds of negotiations. In contrast to the GATS preamble, which states the desirability of "the early achievement of progressively higher levels of liberalization of trade in services through successive rounds of multilateral negotiations aimed at promoting the interests of all participants on a mutually advantageous basis. . . ," MERCOSUR members have agreed that the ultimate result of their progressive liberalization process will be the complete elimination of all restrictions affecting either services trade or service suppliers in all sectors. This common market in services is to be achieved within a ten-year period, beginning with the implementation of the protocol (which had not taken effect as of December 2000).

Members of the Andean Community have adopted the same objective as MERCOSUR but set a different timetable, namely, the complete elimination of barriers to intraregional trade in services within a five-year period. Decision 439 on Trade in Services, adopted in June 1998, specifies that this process is to begin when comprehensive national inventories of measures affecting trade in services for all members of the Andean Community are finalized. Discriminatory restrictions identified in these inventories are to be lifted gradually through a series of negotiations, ultimately resulting in a common market free of barriers to services trade. A process to harmonize national regulatory regimes in key service sectors is to be conducted in parallel.

The negative list, top-down approach has been incorporated into a large majority of the subregional agreements in the Western Hemisphere encompassing services. These agreements oblige their parties to liberalize all forms of discriminatory treatment in all service sectors except for sectors or measures included in lists of reservations accompanying the agreement. These reservations exclude specific sectors and measures either temporarily or permanently. In certain agreements, however, these reservations are to be liberalized over time through periodic negotiations. Canada, Mexico, and the United States pioneered this approach in NAFTA. Since NAFTA took effect in January 1994, Mexico has played a pivotal role in extending this liberalization approach and similar types of disciplines to other subregional agreements it has signed with countries in South and Central America. These include the Group of Three agreement, negotiated between Mexico, Colombia, and Venezuela, and bilateral free trade agreements Mexico has concluded with Bolivia, Chile, Costa Rica, Nicaragua, and the Northern Triangle group, consisting of El Salvador, Guatemala, and Honduras. Chile has concluded similar agreements with Canada (in effect since July 5, 1997), and Central America as a whole (signed in October 1999); the Dominican Republic has negotiated NAFTA-type agreements with Central America as a whole, which had not taken effect as of December 2000, and with the Caribbean Community and Common Market (CARICOM) in August 1998.

CARICOM members finalized Protocol II on Establishment, Services, and Capital covering trade in services and investment in July 1997. It entered into force provisionally in July 1998. The protocol itself does not specify an approach to services liberalization but envisages removing all existing restrictions on trade in services in the region through a program to be established upon entry into force of the protocol.

The fourteen subregional arrangements constitute a set of occasionally overlapping agreements containing various levels of disciplines and obligations. All of these agreements, however, are distinguished by their ambitious objectives that in most cases go well beyond those defined at the multilateral level. Although the GATS rules and disciplines provide the least common denominator for trade in services in the hemisphere, all of the subregional agreements posit much freer services trade and stronger disciplines than does GATS.[1] This may be either with respect to the type of disciplines they contain, to the wider scope of liberalization they envisage, to the ultimate objectives they embrace, or to a combination of these factors. In services, it may safely be said that subregional efforts at liberalization are giving multilateral liberalization a strong push forward.

Convergence and Divergence

A large number of the subregional agreements on trade in services in the Western Hemisphere, particularly those that have followed the NAFTA model, have numerous similarities. This section analyzes the major points of convergence and divergence apparent in the approaches to liberalization that these agreements take regarding six criteria: principles; rules and disciplines; market access; negotiating modality; exclusions; and special sectoral treatment.

Principles on Trade in Services

All fourteen subregional agreements contain basic obligations regarding national treatment, and all but the CARICOM Protocol II carry obligations regarding most-favored-nation (MFN) treatment.[2] These two principles constitute two of the most basic building blocks to any agreement on services, just as they do in the goods area. MERCOSUR and the Andean Community set out these two principles in an unqualified form, which means that there can be no deviation from the application of the MFN or national treatment principles among members. Under GATS, in

1. The content of these agreements is summarized in OAS Trade Unit (1999). In contrast to these comprehensive trade agreements, a number of sectoral agreements on services have also been signed, sometimes as formal agreements and other times as more informal cooperation agreements. Some of these subregional and bilateral sectoral agreements on services carry with them rules and disciplines, while others are limited to specifying good intentions or cooperative action. Such sectoral stand-alone agreements, by their nature, cannot be considered in the same way as those integration arrangements that contain comprehensive provisions and rules covering all services. See OAS Trade Unit (1998) for information on these stand-alone agreements.

2. The fact that the CARICOM protocol does not contain a provision on MFN treatment means that no CARICOM member is obliged to accord MFN treatment to other CARICOM members for any trade concession granted to nonmembers.

contrast, national treatment is not a general obligation but rather the result of specific commitments by each WTO member, and MFN, although a general obligation, can be qualified through time-bound exemptions.[3]

The free trade agreements that have followed the NAFTA model set out both MFN and national treatment as unconditional principles. Country-specific exceptions (also known as reservations or nonconforming measures) to either of these principles may be taken for services sectors on either a temporary or a permanent basis, however. These exceptions should be specified at the federal, state, or provincial level either at the time the agreement comes into force or within a specified period of time thereafter and are set out in the lists of reservations to a given agreement. Besides these two fundamental principles, a basic discipline also exists in the NAFTA-type agreements not to impose a local presence requirement on a service provider from another member or in other words, not to require the establishment of a representative office or branch in a member country's territory as a condition for the cross-border provision of a service. This is referred to as the "right of nonestablishment."

All subregional arrangements covering trade in services in the Western Hemisphere adhere to the principle of transparency and contain an article to this effect. All agreements (with the exception of CARICOM Protocol II) stipulate an obligation to publish relevant measures affecting trade in services, and most agreements go further to require notification as well. Upon entry into force, the CARICOM protocol requires notification of existing restrictions on the provision of services and right of establishment by each member to the CARICOM Council for Trade and Economic Development.[4] As under GATS, MERCOSUR, the Andean Community, NAFTA, and all NAFTA-type agreements oblige the prompt publication

---

3. Under Article II of GATS, the MFN principle can be the object of temporary exceptions with respect to specific service sectors. An annex to GATS Article II specifies the procedures under which such exemptions may be sought and the time period for such exemptions (in principle not more than ten years). The annex subjects MFN exemptions to periodic review and future negotiation. The GATS definition of MFN does not necessarily imply liberal or restrictive conditions of market access; it simply requires that the most favorable treatment given to any service supplier be accorded to all foreign service suppliers equally, in all sectors, and for all modes of supply. National treatment is a principle of a specific nature under GATS resulting from the negotiating process and applies only to those sectors and modes of supply that participants incorporate specifically into their national schedules of commitments.

4. Protocol II of CARICOM defines right of establishment as the right to engage in any non-wage-earning activities of a commercial, industrial, professional, or artisanal nature and to create and manage economic enterprises within the region.

Table 8-1. *Summary of Principles Relevant to Trade in Services*

Agreement	MFN treatment[a]	National treatment	Transparency	No local presence
GATS	Yes	Yes	Yes	No
MERCOSUR	Yes	Yes	Yes	No
CARICOM	No	Yes	Yes	No
Andean Community	Yes	Yes	Yes	No
NAFTA	Yes	Yes	Yes	Yes
Group of Three	Yes	Yes	Yes	Yes
Bolivia-Mexico	Yes	Yes	Yes	Yes
Costa Rica-Mexico	Yes	Yes	Yes	Yes
Canada-Chile	Yes	Yes	Yes	Yes
Chile-Mexico	Yes	Yes	Yes	Yes
Central America-Dominican Republic	Yes	Yes	Yes	Yes
CARICOM-Dominican Republic	Yes	Yes	Yes	Yes
Mexico-Nicaragua	Yes	Yes	Yes	Yes
Central America-Chile	Yes	Yes	Yes	Yes
Mexico-Northern Triangle	Yes	Yes	Yes	Yes

a. With exemptions to MFN treatment allowed under the Annex to the GATS and subject to a list of reservations for all other arrangements, as in the case of national treatment, except for those of MERCOSUR and the Andean Community.

of measures affecting trade in services and service providers at the national level. Again similar to GATS, MERCOSUR, NAFTA, and the NAFTA-type agreements also require notification of changes in existing laws and any new laws, regulations, and administrative procedures affecting trade in services. In an innovative step, NAFTA and some NAFTA-type agreements also contain the right for parties to comment on proposed changes, to the extent possible. Like GATS, NAFTA and all NAFTA-type agreements as well as MERCOSUR further require parties to establish contact points or information centers and to provide information on measures affecting services trade upon request (see table 8-1 for a summary of basic principles of the subregional agreements).

Rules and Disciplines: Areas of Convergence

Several of the rules and disciplines for trade in services contained in the subregional agreements of the Western Hemisphere are very similar,

Table 8-2. *Rules and Disciplines on Trade in Services: Areas of Convergence*

Agreement	Domestic regulations	Recognition	Quantitative restrictions	Subsidy disciplines	Denial of benefits
GATS	Yes	Yes	Yes[a]	Future	Yes
MERCOSUR	Yes	Yes	Yes[a]	Future	Yes
CARICOM	Yes[b]	Yes	Not specified	No	Yes
Andean Community	Yes[b]	Yes	Yes	No	Yes
NAFTA	Yes[b]	Yes	Yes	No	Yes
Group of Three	Yes[b]	Yes	Yes	No	Yes
Bolivia-Mexico	Yes[b]	Yes	Yes	No	Yes
Costa Rica-Mexico	Yes[b]	Yes	Yes	No	Yes
Canada-Chile	Yes[b]	Yes	Yes	No	Yes
Chile-Mexico	Yes[b]	Yes	Yes	No	Yes
Mexico-Nicaragua	Yes[b]	Yes	Yes	No	Yes
Central America-Dominican Republic	Yes[b]	Yes	Yes	No	Yes
CARICOM-Dominican Republic	Yes[b]	Reference: (GATS)	Yes	No	Yes
Central America-Chile	Yes[b]	Yes	Yes	No	Yes
Mexico-Northern Triangle	Yes[b]	Yes	Yes	No	Yes

a. Disciplines on quantitative restrictions only apply to those sectors where specific commitments are made.

b. Rules on domestic regulations in these agreements are set out in a more narrowly focused manner and apply only to the licensing and certification of professional service suppliers.

notwithstanding the different approaches to liberalization chosen by the members to the agreements. These include, among others, domestic regulation, recognition of licenses or certifications obtained in a member country, quantitative restrictions, subsidies, denial of benefits, and general exceptions (see table 8-2 for a summary of areas of convergence on key rules and provisions).[5]

DOMESTIC REGULATION. GATS recognizes the right of WTO members to regulate services within their territories in order to meet national policy

5. GATS includes references to avoid double taxation. NAFTA-type agreements also include such a provision in their chapter on general exceptions.

objectives. National laws and regulations, however, must be transparent, administered with due process, and changed or adapted in a predictable manner. Further, such laws and regulations should not be more trade restrictive than is necessary to fulfill a legitimate objective (necessity test). Members must explain the specific objectives intended by their regulations upon request, provide an opportunity for trading partners to comment upon proposed regulations, and give consideration to such comments.

Although MERCOSUR envisages a similar provision on domestic regulations, neither NAFTA nor the NAFTA-type agreements contain an article on domestic regulation per se in their chapter on trade in services. Rather, the equivalent of the GATS discipline is contained in a more narrowly focused article related to the licensing and certification of professionals. These requirements are meant to ensure that any measure on licensing or certification of nationals of another member country (professional service suppliers only) does not constitute an unnecessary barrier to trade. However, where the GATS article states that the measure in question should not restrict the supply of a service under any mode, the NAFTA-type agreements narrow this requirement to the cross-border supply of a service.[6]

The Andean Community agreement on services likewise does not contain disciplines on domestic regulation per se but partially addresses the issue through an article that binds members not to establish new measures that would increase the degree of nonconformity or fail to comply with the liberalizing commitments contained in the agreement.

RECOGNITION. GATS contains an article to encourage the recognition of the education, licenses, or certifications of service suppliers in general, with the possibility of allowing other WTO members to negotiate their accession to such arrangements. In the subregional agreements on services of the Western Hemisphere, such recognition is more narrowly targeted to providers of professional services. Like GATS, such recognition is encouraged in the agreements of the hemisphere but is not mandated.

All the subregional agreements also contain an obligation to develop a

---

6. NAFTA-type agreements are structured so that the disciplines of the services chapter cover only cross-border trade in services (modes 1 and 2 of service supply, according to the GATS definition), while commercial presence for services (mode 3 of service supply) is covered in a separate chapter on investment that encompasses disciplines relevant to both goods and services, and the movement of natural persons (mode 4 of service supply) is covered in a separate chapter on the temporary entry for business persons. A business person means "a citizen of a Party who is engaged in trade in goods, the provision of services or the conduct of investment activities" (see NAFTA, Article 1608).

generic blueprint aimed at defining procedures for assisting service professions to achieve mutual recognition of licenses and certifications. The NAFTA-type agreements contain an obligation to abolish nationality or permanent residency requirements in effect for the recognition of diplomas and the granting of licenses for the providers of professional services from other parties within two years of entry into force of the respective agreements. If the deadline is not met, the other party does not need to respect the obligation. Parties to these agreements are also to consult periodically on the feasibility of such objectives. The agreement between the Dominican Republic and CARICOM does not have a provision on recognition but specifies that matters not covered in the agreement shall be governed by the relevant provisions of GATS. Parties to this agreement are endeavoring to develop a separate chapter on professional services that would achieve mutual recognition of licenses and certifications.

The MERCOSUR agreement on services contains a provision on the recognition of professionals through the development of mutually acceptable criteria to determine the equivalence of licenses, certifications, professional degrees, and accreditations granted by another member country. The agreement also encourages the elaboration of mutually acceptable standards and criteria for the exercise of professional services that would later be adopted by the various member governments. Members of the Andean Community are in the process of drafting criteria to permit the mutual recognition of licenses, certifications, professional degrees, and accreditations granted in the various member states.

QUANTITATIVE RESTRICTIONS. All the subregional agreements covering services contain an article on nondiscriminatory quantitative restrictions, but the focus of the agreements differs. The MERCOSUR agreement prohibits the introduction of new nondiscriminatory quantitative measures on any scheduled commitment and sector. This prohibition mirrors a similar requirement of GATS.

The approach adopted in NAFTA and the NAFTA-type agreements requires a listing of quantitative restrictions on services in annexes, separating those that are discriminatory from those that are not, with subsequent notification to other parties of a given agreement of any new nondiscriminatory quantitative restriction that a party may adopt. To promote further liberalization, these top-down agreements request the parties to consult periodically with each other and endeavor to negotiate the liberalization or removal of such restrictions.

SUBSIDY DISCIPLINES. GATS does not set out any actual disciplines governing the use of subsidies for service activities but specifies that future discussions will take place to develop multilateral disciplines with the aim of avoiding the trade-distorting effects of such subsidies and to address the appropriateness of countervailing procedures. Such negotiations have not yet come to any agreement in this area. NAFTA and the NAFTA-type agreements, the Andean Community, and CARICOM do not contain provisions on subsidies. MERCOSUR specifies that general subsidy disciplines, once elaborated, will apply to services.

DENIAL OF BENEFITS. GATS allows a member to deny the benefits of the agreement to the supply of a service and to a service supplier from or in the territory of a nonmember of the WTO. Under the WTO, a service supplier that is a juridical person is defined as any legal entity subject to majority ownership, effective control, and affiliation with another person. All subregional agreements in the hemisphere (with the exception of MERCOSUR) go further than GATS to define a service supplier not only as a legal entity under majority ownership or effective control, but also as one that must conduct substantial business activities or operations in the territory of any of the member countries in order to benefit from a given agreement.

Rules and Disciplines: Areas of Divergence

Major rules and disciplines in which the subregional agreements diverge from each other include standard of treatment, treatment of investment, monopoly disciplines, general safeguards, and modification of schedules (see table 8-3 for a summary).

STANDARD OF TREATMENT. Many of the NAFTA-type agreements include a "standard of treatment" clause that requires each party to accord service providers of any other party the more favorable of any treatment provided under the principles of MFN and national treatment. The provision appears in NAFTA and in the bilateral agreements Chile has entered into with Canada, Mexico, and Central America. None of the other subregional agreements contain such a provision.

Unlike the other subregional agreements, NAFTA and all NAFTA-type agreements also contain a ratchet mechanism that ensures that all future liberalization eliminating restrictions on a service sector or discriminatory

Table 8-3. *Rules and Disciplines on Trade in Services: Areas of Divergence*

Agreement	Standard of treatment	Treatment of investment	Monopoly disciplines	General safeguards	Modification of schedules
GATS	No	Within GATS	Yes	Future	Yes
MERCOSUR	No	Separate protocols	Separate protocol	No	Yes
CARICOM	No	Within Protocol II	Separate protocol	Yes	Not specified
Andean Community	No	Decisions 439 and 291[a]	Separate decision	No	...
NAFTA	Yes	Separate chapter	Yes	No	...
Group of Three	No	Separate chapter	Yes	No	...
Bolivia–Mexico	No	Separate chapter	No	Future	...
Costa Rica–Mexico	No	Separate chapter	Future	Future	...
Canada–Chile	Yes	Separate chapter	Yes	No	...
Chile–Mexico	Yes	Separate chapter	Yes	No	...
Mexico–Nicaragua	No	Separate chapter	Future	Future	...
Central America–Dominican Republic	No	Separate chapter	Yes	Future	...
CARICOM–Dominican Republic	No	Separate chapter	Yes	No	...
Central America–Chile	Yes	Bilateral agreement	Yes	No	...
Mexico–Northern Triangle	No	Separate chapter	No	Future	...

. . . = Not relevant.

a. For more on Decision 291 on investment, see chapters 3 and 9.

treatment affecting a service supplier from another party is automatically bound in the agreement.

TREATMENT OF INVESTMENT. One important difference between the approaches to services liberalization by countries in the Western Hemisphere relates to the interplay between services and investment. At the multilateral level, GATS does not contain a comprehensive body of disciplines to protect investment, but it does incorporate investment in services as one of the four modes of service delivery (mode 3, or commercial presence). Within the hemisphere this approach has been followed by MERCOSUR members, which also have agreed to separate protocols on investment.[7]

In contrast, NAFTA and the NAFTA-type agreements (with the exception of the Central America-Chile agreement) set out investment rules and disciplines for both goods and services in a separate chapter. These agreements guarantee the free entry of investments of other parties, albeit with country-specific reservations. The Central America-Chile agreement incorporates, in its investment chapter, the bilateral investment treaties each Central American country signed with Chile. The parties may at any time decide to broaden the coverage of the investment rules in the bilateral investment treaties (and must analyze the possibility within two years after the agreement enters into force). CARICOM includes commercial presence as an integral part of the agreement. The Andean Community also includes commercial presence as part of its services agreement. It also has an agreement on investment (Decision 291), signed in 1991 (see chapters 3 and 9).

MONOPOLY DISCIPLINES. Unlike GATT, GATS contains very general disciplines over monopoly practices and exclusive service suppliers. These disciplines aim to ensure that monopoly suppliers do not abuse their market position or act in a way inconsistent with the specific commitments undertaken by a WTO member. In the Western Hemisphere some agreements contain disciplines on monopoly service providers and others do not.[8] NAFTA, the Group of Three, and several of the bilateral agreements set out disciplines on monopoly practices with respect to both goods and services and extend those disciplines to state-owned enterprises as well.

7. Before concluding a Protocol on Services, MERCOSUR members elaborated two protocols containing comprehensive disciplines on investment: the Protocol of Colonia for the Reciprocal Promotion and Mutual Protection of Investment was signed on January 17, 1994, and the Protocol of Buenos Aires for the Promotion and Protection of Investments of Third States was signed on August 5, 1994. These two protocols, like the one on services, have not yet been brought into effect.
8. See also chapter 11 in this volume on competition policy.

The agreement between the Dominican Republic and CARICOM not only contains a provision on monopoly and exclusive services suppliers, but also envisages the future elaboration of a provision on anticompetitive business practices. The Andean Community has a separate agreement on competition (Decision 285), as does CARICOM (Protocol VIII). The other agreements of the hemisphere neither contain nor envisage anticompetition provisions, although MERCOSUR members are in the process of developing separate protocols on competition policy.

GENERAL SAFEGUARDS. GATS contains an article pertinent to general safeguard action, inspired by a similar article in GATT.[9] In the Western Hemisphere, only the CARICOM agreement includes an operational safeguard article at the time of this writing. Several of the subregional agreements, including NAFTA and MERCOSUR, do not contain a general safeguard article for services trade, while other agreements specify that general safeguards may be applied once future disciplines are developed on the subject.[10]

MODIFICATION OF SCHEDULES. GATS foresees the possibility of modifying schedules (that is, withdrawing concessions). Any WTO member may modify or withdraw a commitment contained in its services schedule after a period of three years, subject to negotiating appropriate compensation. Modification of national schedules is also possible under the MERCOSUR agreement, subject to similar conditions. This is not the case for any of the top-down or NAFTA-type agreements because they do not contain schedules of commitments.

Market Access

Because services do not face trade barriers in the form of border tariffs or taxes, countries restrict market access for service providers through discriminatory treatment contained in laws, decrees, and national regulations. Thus the liberalization of trade in services implies modifications of national laws and regulations, which make services negotiations both more

9. Article X of GATS allows members to modify or withdraw a specific commitment one year after the commitment enters into force. The country doing so must show the Council on Trade in Services that the modification or withdrawal cannot await the lapse of the three-year period provided for in Article XX of GATS.

10. The NAFTA agreement, the Group of Three, and the bilateral agreements that Chile has signed with Canada, Central America, and Mexico do not contain a general safeguard article, but they do contain an article on safeguards for balance of payments difficulties, in the case of disequilibrium in the current account.

Table 8-4. *Market Access for Service Providers*

Agreement	Coverage of sectors	Coverage of modes	Government procurement
GATS	Selective	All	Future
MERCOSUR[a]	Universal	All[b]	Future, separate protocol
CARICOM	Undetermined	All[b]	No
Andean Community[a]	Universal	All[b]	Future, separate decision
NAFTA	Universal[c]	All[b]	Included
Group of Three	Universal[c]	All[b]	Included
Bolivia-Mexico	Universal[c]	All[b]	Included
Costa Rica-Mexico	Universal[c]	All[b]	Included
Canada-Chile	Universal[c]	All[b]	No
Chile-Mexico	Universal[c]	All[b]	No
Mexico-Nicaragua	Universal[c]	All[b]	Included
Central America-Dominican Republic	Universal[c]	All[b]	Included
CARICOM-Dominican Republic	Universal[c]	All[b]	Future
Central America-Chile	Universal[c]	All[b]	Included
Mexico-Northern Triangle	Universal[c]	All[b]	No

a. The Montevideo Protocol of MERCOSUR specifies the full liberalization of services with respect to all sectors and measures within a ten-year period. The Andean Community Decision 439 sets out the same objective, to be achieved over a five-year period.

b. Mode 4 is covered partially.

c. Air transport is excluded.

difficult and more sensitive for governments as well as a long-term process. Table 8-4 summarizes the following market access components of services trade agreements in the hemisphere: sectoral coverage; coverage of modes of supply; and government procurement.

Under the bottom-up approach, market access, like national treatment, is the object of commitments that specify the conditions under which foreign service suppliers can enter a given market. These commitments are taken for each service sector or activity and, once listed, are considered to be binding. GATS lists six types of limitations or restrictions that may be placed on market access commitments undertaken by WTO members; other forms of restrictions are not allowed.[11] Under the

11. The six types of limitations to market access specified in GATS are limitations on the number of service suppliers; the total value of service transactions or assets; the total number of service operations or on the total quantity of service output; the total number of natural persons that may be employed in a particular service sector or that a service supplier may employ and who are necessary

top-down, NAFTA-type approach, the concept of "market access" does not appear as a separate article in the services chapter but is addressed under disciplines related to nondiscriminatory quantitative restrictions as well as through a guaranteed national treatment provision applying to discriminatory measures. In both areas, the NAFTA-type agreements follow a "list or lose" approach, listing any measure not in conformity with these disciplines, thus ensuring transparency.

GATS includes four modes for the delivery of services within its scope of application: cross-border delivery; consumption abroad; commercial presence; and movement of natural persons. In the latter two cases the factors of production—capital and labor—move to provide the service in a foreign location. As shown in table 8-4, all four modes of service supply are included within the scope of the subregional agreements in the hemisphere, but the treatment of the last mode of service supply, movement of natural persons, varies considerably. In the MERCOSUR agreement, as in GATS, the ability of service suppliers to move within the region on a temporary basis is dependent upon scheduled commitments (at least during the ten-year transition period). The Andean Community agreement requests members to facilitate the free movement and temporary presence of natural or physical persons for the provision of services. CARICOM provides for the temporary movement of persons as service providers solely in conjunction with the establishment of foreign-owned business activities, including management, supervision, and technical staff and their spouses. NAFTA and the NAFTA-type agreements contain obligations that are limited to the temporary movement of business service providers only rather than the movement of natural persons in general, so this mode of service delivery is only partially covered in several agreements.

Because of the large number of contracts tendered, government procurement is an important component of market access in services.[12] It has been included within GATS, but during and subsequent to the Uruguay Round no agreement was reached on how services procurement should be treated. The intention, stated in GATS, is for WTO members to negotiate future disciplines in this area. At the subregional level, NAFTA broke new ground by including government procurement for services within the scope of the chapter on government procurement, requiring all federal agencies and several state enterprises to open public contracts to service providers in

---

for, and directly related to, the supply of a specific service; measures that restrict or require specific types of legal entity or joint venture; and the participation of foreign capital.

12. See also chapter 12 in this volume on government procurement.

the three NAFTA member countries (under a positive list approach for entity coverage and a negative list approach for services coverage). Similar provisions are included in the Group of Three and in certain of the bilateral free trade agreements (see table 8-4).

The Andean Community agreement on services includes government procurement within its scope of application, although it establishes no disciplines. If a separate instrument is not finalized before January 2002, then members will be required to apply the national treatment principle for government procurement to the services sector. The MERCOSUR protocol does not include government procurement within its scope, but negotiations are ongoing to develop a separate instrument in this area. CARICOM does not include government procurement, nor is there a separate protocol envisaged as yet in this area.

Negotiating Modality

As explained earlier in this chapter, the bottom-up negotiating modality is based upon positive listing, whereby members to an agreement list national treatment and market access commitments specifying the type of access or treatment offered to services or service suppliers in scheduled sectors. This modality was adopted by MERCOSUR to carry out its liberalization of services trade during a ten-year transition period. Annual rounds of negotiations based on the scheduling of increasing numbers of commitments in all sectors (with no exclusions) are to result in the elimination of all restrictions to services trade among members, once the protocol enters into force.

The alternative top-down negotiating modality is based upon negative listing, whereby all sectors and measures are to be liberalized unless otherwise specified in annexes containing reservations, or nonconforming measures. This is the so-called list-or-lose technique. Any exception to sectoral coverage and to nondiscriminatory treatment must be specified in the annexes. Nonconforming measures in the annexes are to be liberalized through consultations or periodic negotiations. Once again, this is the approach pioneered by NAFTA and followed by all subsequent NAFTA-type agreements since then.

NAFTA represents a status quo agreement regarding services, in the sense that no mechanism for the future liberalization of reservations or nonconforming measures was incorporated into the agreement and no timetable specified for ongoing liberalization efforts. Certain of the free trade agreements negotiated after NAFTA go further in their commitment to ongoing liberalization of trade in services. All of the agreements signed by Mexico (although not the subsequent agreements negotiated by Chile) contain an article stipulating "future liberalization," whereby parties are to negotiate the liberalization and removal of nonconforming measures listed in the annexes; the articles thereby introduce a marked element of dynamism into these agreements.

Andean Community members have chosen a negotiating modality that is based on negative listing but that is to be carried out over a transition period and that places heightened emphasis on transparency during the liberalization process. Decision 439 sets a goal of eliminating all restrictions on services trade and service providers among members to the agreement within a five-year period (beginning in the year 2000 or shortly thereafter). This is to begin with an exchange of national inventories of measures affecting trade in services, containing the universe of both discriminatory and nondiscriminatory measures. Negotiations are to result in the removal of all discriminatory measures, and a parallel process is to be undertaken to harmonize measures that do not discriminate against foreign services but nonetheless impede foreign access. The CARICOM protocol seeks the full removal of all restrictions on trade in services and service providers. Members are in the process of establishing a timetable and selecting a negotiating modality for this purpose.

Table 8-5 summarizes the negotiating modality adopted by the fourteen subregional agreements and indicates the relative focus of service negotiators in each case. Services negotiations carried out under the positive listing modality are focused on the inclusion of commitments in national schedules and on the need to determine their broad equivalency for the purpose of reciprocity. This is much more difficult to do for services than for goods, because barriers to foreign service providers are not quantifiable border measures such as tariffs and quotas, but rather discriminatory elements contained in national laws, decrees, and regulations. Under the negative listing modality, negotiations focus on the content of the lists of reservations, or nonconforming measures, to ensure that these do not excessively compromise the liberalizing objective of the agreement.

In reality neither of the two negotiating modalities guarantees full liberalization and is not presumed to do so unless this objective is explicitly set out by members to any given integration agreement. The top-down agreements provide a great deal of information in a transparent form on the existing barriers to trade in services (nonconforming measures), thus giv-

Table 8-5. *Negotiating Modality for Services*

Agreement	Modality	Focus of negotiations
GATS	Positive list	Included commitments
MERCOSUR	Positive list	Included commitments
CARICOM	Not yet defined	Not yet defined
Andean Community	Negative list	Content of inventories of measures
NAFTA	Negative list	List of reservations
Group of Three	Negative list	List of reservations
Bolivia-Mexico	Negative list	List of reservations
Costa Rica-Mexico	Negative list	List of reservations
Canada-Chile	Negative list	List of reservations
Chile-Mexico	Negative list	List of reservations
Central America-Dominican Republic	Negative list	List of reservations
CARICOM-Dominican Republic	Negative list	List of reservations
Mexico-Nicaragua	Negative list	List of reservations
Central America-Chile	Negative list	List of reservations
Mexico-Northern Triangle	Negative list	List of reservations

ing national service providers knowledge of foreign markets. In the bottom-up agreements the sectoral coverage of commitments may vary significantly between the parties. Moreover, the type of conditions and limitations on market access and national treatment in national schedules are often listed as ceilings on or minimum levels of treatment and thus do not necessarily reflect actual practice. This possibility results in less transparency for service providers and less legal and economic certainty regarding market access.

Exclusions

Certain service sectors have been excluded both from GATS and from the subregional arrangements. One example is the air transport sector, where traffic rights or routing agreements are excluded from GATS as they are from all of the subregional arrangements. Likewise, GATS and all the subregional agreements exclude government when they are provided on a non-commercial basis and are not in competition with one or more service suppliers, services such as educational or health services provided exclusively by the government.

Nearly all of the subregional agreements exclude subsidies from their coverage (MERCOSUR is the exception), and about half of the agreements exclude government procurement for services. Financial services are excluded from the agreement between Mexico and Costa Rica, and cross-border financial services are excluded from the agreements signed by Chile with Canada, Mexico, and Central America.

It is important for service providers to be able to know which sectors in the top-down agreements have been either excluded from the liberalizing scope of the agreement or qualified by reservations or nonconforming measures. In the case of some agreements such reservations have been finalized at the time of signature and published in annexes. This is the case for NAFTA, for the Canada-Chile and the Chile-Mexico free trade agreements, and for the Costa Rica-Chile component of the Chile-Central America agreement. In these agreements one or more parties have listed reservations to air, land, and water transport services; communications services; construction services; cultural services; financial services; energy services; professional services; social services; recreation and sport services; and business services.

For the other NAFTA-type agreements such lists of reservations have not been published along with the agreement. They have either been subsequently finalized and published in national sources (the Group of Three and the Costa Rica-Mexico agreements), or have not yet been finalized (Bolivia-Mexico, Mexico-Nicaragua, Central America-Dominican Republic, CARICOM-Dominican Republic, and the other countries of Central America-Chile). The inability to access such critical information removes a vital element of transparency from these latter agreements and makes them much less valuable to service providers.

Special Sectoral Treatment

Given the wide-ranging nature and complexity of the many sectors included within the services area, various sectors have often received special attention. These sectors have been the subject either of separate chapters in various subregional integration agreements or of annexes to a chapter or protocol. Such individual chapters or annexes spell out with greater precision the rules and disciplines governing the sector in question, the form of acceptable regulatory intervention, or the definition of the scope of liberalization.

Table 8-6 sets out the different service sectors that have received special attention in the fourteen subregional agreements of the Western Hemisphere. The temporary entry for business persons (actually not a sector but a mode of service supply), professional services, and telecommunications are the three sectors that appear the most frequently.

As noted earlier, mode four has been defined narrowly in most of the subregional agreements as "temporary entry for business persons," whereas under GATS it refers more broadly to the "movement of natural persons." Thus, with the exception of MERCOSUR and the Andean Community, only the business component of labor mobility has been incorporated within the hemispheric agreements. Professional services are highlighted in the majority of the subregional agreements, with the objective of promoting the recognition of licensing and qualification requirements, through the elaboration of an agreed set of criteria for the equivalency of diplomas and titles, for the various professions among members to an agreement.

Services in the FTAA Negotiations

The following objectives for services negotiations within the Free Trade Association of the Americas were set out in the San José Declaration of March 1998: to establish disciplines to progressively liberalize trade in services so as to permit the achievement of a hemispheric free trade area under conditions of certainty and transparency; and to ensure the integration of smaller economies into the FTAA process. Vice ministers subsequently defined the mandate of the FTAA Negotiating Group on Services (NGSV) to be the development of a framework incorporating comprehensive rights and obligations in services and the identification of appropriate supplementary sector-specific standards.

During the first phase of the negotiations (June 1998-November 1999), members of the NGSV discussed in depth the scope of a future agreement on services and six elements of consensus that had been agreed at the end of the preparatory phase of the FTAA process (March 1995 to March 1998). These six elements include sectoral coverage, most-favored-nation treatment, national treatment, market access, transparency, and denial of benefits. Discussion has centered on the treatment to be granted to these elements in a future chapter on services. The meetings of the negotiating group have benefited from an exchange of views in these areas that have

Table 8-6. *Provisions for Specific Service Sectors in the Subregional Integration Agreements*

Agreement	Trade in services	Temporary entry of business persons	Professional services	Telecommunications	Financial services	Air transport	Land transport
MERCOSUR	Protocol of Montevideo	Annex to the protocol	...	...	Annex to the protocol	Annex to the protocol	Annex to the protocol
Andean Community	Decision 439	...	...	Decision 462	...	...	...
CARICOM	Protocol II	...	1995 and 1996 policy decisions[a]	...	...	Multilateral agreement[b]	...
NAFTA	Chapter 12	Chapter 16	Annex to chapter 12	Chapter 13	Chapter 14	...	Annex to chapter 12
Group of Three	Chapter 10	Chapter 13	Annex to chapter 10	Chapter 11	Chapter 12	Annex to chapter 10	...
Bolivia-Mexico	Chapter 9	Chapter 11	Annex to chapter 9	Chapter 10	Chapter 12	...	...
Costa Rica-Mexico	Chapter 9	Chapter 10	Annex to chapter 9	...	...	...	
Canada-Chile	Chapter H	Chapter K	Annex to chapter H	Chapter I	...	...	
Chile-Mexico	Chapter 10	Chapter 13	Annex to chapter 10	Chapter 12	...	Chapter 11	
Mexico-Nicaragua	Chapter 10	Chapter 12	Annex to chapter 10	Chapter 11	Chapter 13	...	Annex to chapter 10
Mexico-Central America-Dominican Republic	Chapter 10	Chapter 11	Annex to chapter 10	...	...	...	...
CARICOM-Dominican Republic	Annex II	Annex on temporary entry of business persons	Future	...	...	...	...
Central America-Chile	Chapter 11	Chapter 14	Annex to chapter 11	Chapter 13	...	Chapter 12	...
Mexico-Northern Triangle	Chapter 10	Chapter 13	Annex to chapter 10	Chapter 12	Chapter 11	...	Annex to chapter 10

a. These decisions allow for the free movement of skilled persons who have university degrees as well as artists, sports persons, musicians, and media workers, among the CARICOM countries.

b. The CARICOM Multilateral Air Services agreement governs the operation of air services within the Caribbean Community.

drawn both from the rules and disciplines contained in GATS as well as
those contained in the subregional agreements of the hemisphere. At the
meetings during the year 2000, the negotiating group moved toward fulfilling the mandate given by trade ministers at the Toronto Ministerial
Meeting in December 1999 and began to prepare a draft text of a services
agreement. At the end of 2000, the negotiating group finalized a draft text
containing proposed language for the six issues of consensus and for other
issues that the participating delegations felt were related.

As in other FTAA negotiating groups and bodies, the NGSV has benefited from the expertise and analytical support of the Tripartite Committee, in particular the Organization of American States, as well as from
background studies prepared upon request by that committee. These include, among others, a compendium on "Provisions on Trade in Services
in Trade and Integration Agreements of the Western Hemisphere," which
sets out in a comparable format the provisions relating to services as they
appear in the various subregional agreements. Another such study is entitled "Sectoral Agreements on Services in the Western Hemisphere."[13] The
Tripartite Committee has also provided technical assistance to the members of the negotiating group in four specific areas: subregional workshops
conducted to facilitate the completion by FTAA participants of national
"Inventories of Measures Affecting Trade in Services"; the elaboration of a
work program on statistics for international trade in services; the preparation of a glossary of terms for trade in services to facilitate the negotiations;
and the elaboration of the "Manual for Completing the Questionnaire on
Measures Affecting Services Trade in the Hemisphere."

Challenges for the Future

Three critical issues in the services area were outstanding at the end of
the second FTAA negotiating phase (January 2000–March 2001) that must
be resolved before a services chapter can be finalized and market access
negotiations can begin in the services area.

The first is to decide upon a modality for liberalizing trade in services,
namely, whether to adopt a positive list, bottom-up approach to services
liberalization or a negative list, top-down approach, or some modified form
of either. Resolution of this critical question is necessary before further

13. Both studies are regularly updated and are available on the official FTAA website (www.ftaa-alca.org).

progress can be made on the rules and disciplines to be included in the services chapter, because the form of many of these obligations is dependent on the given liberalizing modality. A second issue is whether the commitments made by countries will reflect the status quo and how far and in what way they will go beyond current market openness for service suppliers. The third issue is the relationship between services and investment. Given the importance of investment to services trade, it will be important to identify this interrelationship clearly and to ensure that the modalities negotiated by the Negotiating Groups on Services and Investment are compatible. The question of how to deal with the elaboration of specific sectoral disciplines for services will need to be tackled once these three issues are resolved.

References

OAS Trade Unit. 1998. *Sectoral Agreements on Services in the Western Hemisphere*. Washington, D.C.: Organization of American States. April (www.ftaa-alca.org).

———. 1999. *Provisions on Trade in Services in Trade and Integration Agreements of the Western Hemisphere*. Washington, D.C.: Organization of American States. October (www.ftaa-alca.org).

MARYSE ROBERT

9 | *Investment*

T rade rules governing foreign investment in the Americas have begun to converge in the 1990s. After years of imposing controls excluding or restricting the entry of foreign firms, Latin American and Caribbean countries embarked on a series of ambitious economic reforms in the mid-1980s and early 1990s. They abandoned the import-substitution model and undertook to liberalize trade and ease restrictions on foreign investment. At the beginning of the twenty-first century, most countries in the Western Hemisphere are now seeking to attract investment from abroad both to foster economic growth and development and to stimulate transfer of technology and competition. In 1999 foreign direct investment (FDI) in Latin America and the Caribbean reached a new record. The total of $90 billion in inflows was a twelve-fold increase over the annual average from 1984 to 1989. The region has become as attractive to investors as developing Asia, which received $106 billion in FDI inflows in 1999.[1] Market-oriented policies, including privatization programs, have played a significant role in the investment surge experienced by the region in the 1990s.

1. Several Latin American countries experienced a significant increase in foreign direct investment (FDI) inflows in 1999. Overseas investment into Brazil totaled $31 billion, while FDI flows into Argentina jumped more than three-fold to $23 billion, due in large part to the $13 billion takeover of

Approaches to Investment: Protection and Liberalization

In addition to laws and regulations that are more investment friendly, governments of the Western Hemisphere have entered into binding obligations to improve their investment climate. Traditionally, investment agreements have set standards for the treatment and protection of the investment and investor; have included an admission clause, which refers to the laws and regulations of the host state for the admission of investments; and have provided an effective dispute settlement mechanism between the investor and the host state. In the 1990s a growing number of countries in the Americas concluded agreements that go beyond this traditional approach. These new agreements include a right of establishment (right to establish a new business or to acquire an existing one) with no admission provision but with a list of country-specific exceptions; these agreements therefore add a "market access" component to the "protection element" of a traditional investment agreement. Investment agreements do not themselves attract investment, but they complement the main determinants of FDI flows. Countries that have locked in the liberalization achieved at the domestic level have gained from the signaling effects of such binding agreements.

Bilateral Investment Treaties and Regional Trade Agreements

Since the early 1990s more than sixty bilateral investment treaties (BITs) have been signed between countries of the hemisphere. Although the first BITs originated in Europe in the late 1950s, it took more than thirty years before countries of the Americas started negotiating bilateral investment treaties among themselves. The first BIT concluded within the region was between the United States and Panama in 1982. During the 1980s only the United States was active in entering into bilateral investment treaties with other countries of the region, signing a BIT with Haiti in 1983 and one with Grenada in 1986. An overwhelming majority of the countries in the Americas have now signed at least one bilateral investment treaty. In fact, only two countries (the Commonwealth of the Bahamas and St. Kitts and Nevis) have not yet done so, while twenty-four have concluded at least one

YPF, Argentina's largest oil company, by the Spanish-based company Repsol. Mexico ($11 billion), Chile ($9 billion), and Peru ($2 billion) also saw higher inward investment in 1999. However, Venezuela ($2.6 billion) and Colombia ($1.3 billion) suffered a decrease. See UNCTAD (2000) and *Financial Times*, "Latin America Sees Investment Surge," February 2, 2000, p. 7.

BIT with another country of the region. Of all these bilateral investment treaties, those signed by the United States and Canada include a right of establishment and a list of reservations.[2] At the regional level the North American Free Trade Agreement (NAFTA), the free trade agreement among members of the Group of Three (Colombia, Mexico, and Venezuela), and the bilateral free trade agreements signed by Mexico with Bolivia, Chile, Costa Rica, Nicaragua, and the Northern Triangle (El Salvador, Guatemala, and Honduras), and by Chile with Canada embrace this new approach. They incorporate a protection element and a market access component. The investment chapter of the free trade agreement between the Central American countries and the Dominican Republic includes an additional element, an admission clause, which suggests that the entry of investors and investments of one party into the territory of another party is subject to the laws of that other party. The Colonia Protocol for MERCOSUR (Common Market of the South) also includes an admission clause. The Buenos Aires Protocol for non-MERCOSUR members follows the traditional approach adopted in bilateral investment treaties, and so does the investment agreement between the Caribbean Community and Common Market (CARICOM) and the Dominican Republic. Other arrangements such as the Andean Community Decision 291 and CARICOM Protocol II contain a few investment provisions. Protocol II establishes that members shall not introduce in their territories any new restrictions relating to the right of establishment of nationals of other member states except as otherwise provided in the agreement.[3] Finally, the bilateral investment treaties signed by each Central American country with Chile are incorporated as an integral part of the chapter on investment in the free trade agreement between Chile and these countries.[4]

2. In contrast to a general exception, which has the effect of exempting a party from the whole set of obligations contained in the agreement, a reservation is applicable only in relation to specific provisions. States usually take reservations regarding national treatment, most-favored-nation treatment, performance requirements, and senior management and boards of directors. A reservation identifies the sector in which the reservation is taken and the obligation against which the reservation is taken, and it often also refers to the specific measure (laws, regulations, or other measures) for which the reservation is taken.

3. The Protocol of Colonia for the Reciprocal Promotion and Protection of Investment in MERCOSUR was signed on January 17, 1994. MERCOSUR's Protocol for the Promotion and Protection of Investment of Third States (Buenos Aires Protocol) was signed on August 5, 1994. Protocol II of CARICOM entered into force provisionally on July 4, 1998. Decision 291 of the Andean Community was signed in Lima on March 21, 1991.

4. Article 10.02 of the free trade agreement between Chile and Central American countries, signed on October 18, 1999, states that parties may at any time decide—and must within two years of the entry into force of the agreement analyze the possibility—to broaden the coverage of the investment rules in the bilateral investment treaties between Chile and each Central American country.

Investment at the WTO

Several agreements resulting from the Uruguay Round include investment provisions, but there is no comprehensive agreement on investment. The WTO Agreement on Trade-Related Investment Measures (TRIMs) addresses the issue of performance requirements for goods, whereas the General Agreement on Trade in Services (GATS), as explained in chapter 8, covers investment in two of its four modes of supply—commercial presence (mode 3) and movement of natural persons (mode 4). The TRIMs Agreement establishes an illustrative list of prohibited performance requirements, those contrary to the principle of national treatment (Article III of GATT 1994), such as local content and trade-balancing requirements, and those inconsistent with the general obligation of eliminating quantitative restrictions (Article XI of GATT 1994), such as trade and foreign exchange–balancing restrictions and domestic sales requirements. Member countries had ninety days from the date of entry into force of the WTO agreement to report all inconsistent TRIMs to the Council for Trade in Goods. Developed countries had to eliminate their performance requirements within two years of the date of entry into force of the WTO agreement. Developing countries had a deadline of five years (January 1, 2000), and least-developed countries had seven years. The Council for Trade in Goods may extend the transition period for developing and least-developed countries, and a few countries have requested extension of their deadline.

The GATS provisions regarding national treatment (Article XVII) and market access (Article XVI) are conditional, a clear departure from common practice in investment agreements with respect to the national treatment provision.[5] They are granted according to specific commitments listed in members' schedules indicating to which sectors and modes of supply these provisions apply. GATS thus makes use of what is known as a "positive list" by identifying those sectors that are covered by the agreement. More specifically, this approach means that new discriminatory measures are allowed in sectors not included in a member's schedule. Moreover, in sectors where commitments have been made, existing measures inconsistent with the agreement do not have to be eliminated as long as they are listed in a member's schedule.[6] In fact, once a sector is listed in a member's schedule, it is bound in full by the market access and national treatment obligations for the four modes of supply, unless a limitation to this treatment (the

5. WTO (1996, p. 71).
6. Sauvé (1994).

negative list approach) is specified for one or several modes in the columns entitled "limitations on market access" and "limitations on national treatment." Schedules include a number of "unbound" entries for each mode of supply, which means that a WTO member is not bound by any commitment in GATS for a particular mode in a particular sector with respect to either national treatment or market access. When commitments are unbound, countries are not obliged to maintain the same level of openness or to liberalize further. Commercial presence is the mode with the lowest percentage of unbound commitments; it has been scheduled for full liberalization by about 20 percent of WTO members. Liberalization of mode 4, movement of natural persons, was much less common, with full liberalization by less than 1 percent of WTO members.

Unlike the NAFTA-type agreements, GATS does not contain a right of nonestablishment promoting services trade along lines of comparative advantage. Such right ensures that no party may require a service provider of another party to establish or maintain a representative office or any form of enterprise, or to be resident, in its territory as a condition for the cross-border provision of a service. A right of nonestablishment prohibits regulators from requiring establishment as a condition for delivery of a service.

The Agreement on Trade-Related Aspects of Intellectual Property Rights (TRIPS) is the first ever comprehensive multilateral agreement to set minimum standards protecting all areas of intellectual property rights (copyright and related rights, trademarks, geographical indications, industrial designs, patents, layout designs of integrated circuits, and trade secrets), to include domestic enforcement measures, and to be covered by a dispute settlement mechanism. Its impact on investment issues, although indirect, is nonetheless significant. The TRIPS Agreement contributes to strengthening the protection afforded to foreign investment by reinforcing the protection of intellectual property rights, one of the key elements often listed in the definition of investment found in most recent BITs and free trade agreements currently in force worldwide.

The Agreement on Subsidies and Countervailing Measures (ASCM) contains disciplines covering investment-related issues. Some examples of investment incentives (fiscal, financial, or indirect) fall under the meaning of subsidy, as defined in the ASCM. Except as provided in the Agreement on Agriculture, such investment incentives are prohibited if they are conditioned upon export performance or use of domestic over imported goods (Article 3). Other incentives that may not be prohibited but that are found to cause adverse effects are subject to compensation. However, as noted by the WTO, "the underlying concepts of the ASCM are oriented toward trade in goods, and as such may not in all cases be easily applied to investment incentives." For example, an investment incentive is usually granted *before* any production begins, which means that "neither a recommendation to withdraw or modify a subsidy, nor a countervailing duty applied to the exported goods, will be able to 'undo' or to change an investment that already has been made."[7]

Convergence and Divergence

The 1990s have seen the emergence of a new consensus in the Americas over the rules governing foreign investment. On issues that once seemed controversial, common approaches have been adopted in investment agreements signed between countries negotiating the Free Trade Area of the Americas (FTAA). This section analyzes the convergence and divergence on the following issues: scope and coverage (including definitions of *investment* and *investor*); general standards of treatment; performance requirements; key personnel; compensation for losses; transfers; expropriation; and dispute settlement.

Scope and Coverage

The scope of an investment agreement has three essential components (table 9-1). The substantive scope consists of the disciplines and the definition of key terms such as *investment* and *investor*. The territorial scope refers to the territory of the parties that falls under the agreement, including the application of the provisions at the subnational level. In free trade agreements, this issue is generally dealt with in an article that covers the whole agreement. The temporal scope informs on whether the agreement applies to investments made, and disputes that arose, before the agreement entered into force. The provision on scope may also include economic activities reserved to the state that parties choose to exclude from the agreement. This is the case for the NAFTA-type agreements.

DEFINITION OF INVESTMENT. With the exception of CARICOM's Protocol II, which does not define investment, and Decision 291 of the Andean Community, which covers only FDI, all investment agreements in the

7. WTO (1996, pp. 72–73).

Table 9-1. *Scope and Coverage of Investment Agreements*

Agreement	Definition of investment	Definition of investor	Temporal scope
MERCOSUR			
Colonia	Yes	Yes	Yes
Buenos Aires	Yes	Yes	Yes
CARICOM			
Protocol II	No	Yes	No
Andean Community			
Decision 291	Yes, FDI only	Yes	No
NAFTA	Yes	Yes	Yes
Group of Three	Yes	Yes	Yes
Bolivia-Mexico	Yes	Yes	Yes
Costa Rica-Mexico	Yes	Yes	Yes
Mexico-Nicaragua	Yes	Yes	Yes
Mexico-Northern Triangle	Yes	Yes	Yes
Canada-Chile	Yes	Yes	Yes
Chile-Mexico	Yes	Yes	Yes
Central America-Dominican Republic	Yes	Yes	Yes
CARICOM-Dominican Republic	Yes	Yes	No

Americas have adopted a broad, open-ended, asset-based definition of the term *investment*. Such definition is more encompassing than the traditional definition of foreign direct investment because it also includes portfolio investment and intangible assets such as intellectual property rights. Modern definitions typically use phrases such as "every kind of asset," "any kind of asset," or "every kind of investment," accompanied by an illustrative but nonexhaustive list of examples. The list commonly includes the following five components: movable and immovable property and any related property rights, such as mortgages, liens, or pledges; shares, stock, bonds, debentures, or any other form of participation in a company, business enterprise, or joint venture; money, claims to money, claims to performance under contract having a financial value, and loans directly related to a specific investment; intellectual property rights; and rights conferred by law (such as concessions) or under contract.

Although the objective of using such a comprehensive definition is to guarantee protection to as many forms of investment as possible, there has been an attempt to avoid coverage of purely monetary or speculative flows

not related to an investment. Thus, recent agreements include qualifications of their coverage. For example, a few recent agreements exclude "real
estate or other property, tangible or intangible, not acquired in the expectation or used for the purpose of economic benefit or other business purposes" from the definition of covered investment. This exception is built
into the definition of investment in NAFTA, the Group of Three, and the
Canada-Chile, Mexico-Nicaragua, and Mexico-Northern Triangle free trade
agreements. Their "asset-based" definition covers a broad list of assets that
are expressly linked with the activities of an enterprise. It excludes, for example, those transactions that might occur in capital or money markets
with no connection to a specific investment and claims to money that arise
solely from commercial contracts.

DEFINITION OF INVESTOR. The definition of *investor* covers natural and juridical persons (or other legal entities). In most investment instruments
citizenship is the only criterion used to determine whether a natural person
should be considered an investor under the agreement. In a few agreements—for example, those signed by Canada—the definition is broadened to include permanent residents. Residency is also sometimes used to
exclude natural persons from coverage of the agreements.

With respect to juridical persons, three different criteria have been commonly used to define the nationality of a company or legal entity: incorporation, seat, and control. Countries with common law tradition, such as
Canada, the United States, and the CARICOM members, use the place of
incorporation of a company to determine its nationality. Other investment
instruments such as NAFTA and the Canada-Chile free trade agreement
follow the same approach. Under NAFTA, to be an "investor of a Party" an
enterprise (and a branch of an enterprise) must be constituted or organized
under the law of that party. There is no requirement that the enterprise be
controlled by nationals of a NAFTA country. If the enterprise is controlled
by investors of a nonparty, however, benefits can be denied if the enterprise
has no substantial business activities in the territory of the party under
whose laws it is constituted. The denial-of-benefits clause also provides
that the host state may deny benefits of the agreement if it does not maintain diplomatic relations with the nonparty or if it adopts or maintains
measures with respect to the nonparty that prohibit transactions with the
enterprise.

The incorporation criterion has also been used between countries with
civil law traditions (Group of Three, and the free trade agreements signed

by Mexico with Bolivia, Chile, Costa Rica, Nicaragua, and the Northern Triangle). But civil law countries have traditionally relied instead on the place where the management or seat of the company is located. The two MERCOSUR protocols on investment have elected that criterion. In the case of BITs signed between Latin American countries, this criterion is often combined with the place of incorporation and, in some cases, with the requirement that the company actually must have effective economic activities in the home country. In other cases, BITs use the control of the company by nationals of a party as the sole criterion to determine its nationality. This is the case of the Colombia-Peru BIT. Finally, some agreements combine the above criteria or use them as alternatives. In general, it can be said that the combination of different criteria is used in those cases where governments are interested in restricting the benefits of the agreement to those legal entities that effectively have ties with the home country. In contrast, when the objective is to broaden the scope of application, agreements provide for the possibility of applying alternative criteria.

TEMPORAL SCOPE. All investment agreements that address this issue make clear that all investments, including those made before the investment agreement has entered into force, are covered by the agreement. In a few cases, for example, the Costa Rica-Mexico and the Central America-Dominican Republic free trade agreements, the agreement stipulates that it does not apply to disputes that arose before the entry into force of the agreement.

General Standards of Treatment

There is a broad consensus in the region on the treatment that applies to investments once they have been made by an investor of a party in the territory of another party. States have incorporated a number of standards of treatment in their investment agreements, including fair and equitable treatment, national treatment, and most-favored-nation (MFN) treatment (table 9-2).

FAIR AND EQUITABLE TREATMENT. Fair and equitable treatment is a general concept without a precise definition. It provides a basic standard unrelated to the host state's domestic law and serves as an additional element in the interpretation of the provisions of an investment agreement. Almost all agreements incorporate a provision on fair and equitable treatment. Notable exceptions include the free trade agreements concluded by Mexico

Table 9-2. *General Standards of Treatment in Investment Agreements*

Agreement	Fair and equitable treatment	National treatment	Most-favored-nation treatment
MERCOSUR			
Colonia	Yes	Yes	Yes
Buenos Aires	Yes	Yes	Yes
CARICOM	No	Right of	No
Protocol II		establishment	
Andean Community			
Decision 291	No	Yes	No
NAFTA	Yes	Yes	Yes
Group of Three	Yes	Yes	Yes
Bolivia-Mexico	No	Yes	Yes
Costa Rica-Mexico	No	Yes	Yes
Mexico-Nicaragua	No	Yes	Yes
Mexico-Northern Triangle	Yes	Yes	Yes
Canada-Chile	Yes	Yes	Yes
Chile-Mexico	Yes	Yes	Yes
Central America-Domincan Republic	Yes	Yes	Yes
CARICOM-Dominican Republic	Yes	Yes	Yes

with Bolivia, Costa Rica, and Nicaragua. This standard is generally combined with the principle of full protection and security or that of nondiscrimination. Full protection and security traces its origins in the modern Friendship, Commerce, and Navigation treaties signed by the United States until the 1960s. Although it does not create any liability for the host state, full protection and security "serves to amplify the obligations that the parties have otherwise taken upon themselves" and provides a general standard for the host state "to exercise due diligence in the protection of foreign investment."[8] In a few cases, these three standards are combined together. In other cases, it is clear that fair and equitable treatment shall be in accordance with the principles of international law. Most treaties also require some form of protection, albeit not necessarily full protection and security.

8. Dolzer and Stevens (1995, p. 61). These treaties provided for "the most constant protection and security."

NATIONAL TREATMENT AND MFN TREATMENT. Two different approaches have been adopted with respect to the entry of investments and investors of a party into the territory of another party. Newer instruments such as NAFTA, the Group of Three, and the bilateral free trade agreements concluded by Mexico with Bolivia, Chile, Costa Rica, Nicaragua, and the Northern Triangle and by Chile with Canada create a right of establishment for investors and investments of the other party. In fact, these instruments have been designed with the purpose of assuring the free entry of such investments—albeit with country-specific reservations—into the territory of the host country. They require national treatment and most-favored-nation treatment and prohibit specific performance requirements as a condition for establishment. They indicate that such treatment shall be for investments made in "like circumstances." As mentioned at the beginning of this chapter, the Central America-Dominican Republic agreement adds an admission clause, which refers to the laws of each party. The Colonia Protocol for the MERCOSUR countries also includes an admission clause but does not refer to the laws and regulations of the parties. Other agreements require that the national treatment and MFN standards be applied to investments of investors *after* admission of these investments.

National treatment is a relative standard that prohibits discriminatory treatment. The intent is to avoid cases in which investments—and investors—of other parties cannot compete on equivalent terms with those of the host state. All investment agreements in the Americas provide that once the investment has been made, the host state must accord national treatment to investments or investors of other parties, that is, treatment no less favorable than that granted to its investments and investors. The Andean Community Decision 291 stipulates that national treatment can be regulated according to the national laws of each member. Although the CARICOM Protocol II does not include a national treatment provision per se, as mentioned earlier, it does establish that members shall not introduce in their territories any new restrictions relating to the right of establishment of nationals of other member states except as otherwise provided in the agreement.

With respect to MFN treatment, most investment agreements in the region require that, once the investment is established, each party must grant investments of investors of other parties treatment no less favorable than that it accords to investments of investors of third countries. The Andean Community and CARICOM do not include an MFN provision. Therefore, members of these two arrangements are not required to extend to the other members more favorable treatment granted to nonmembers. It is also worth noting that the NAFTA-type agreements require that the investment and investor of another party be granted the better of national treatment and MFN treatment.

National treatment and MFN treatment are rarely accorded without limitations. The agreements that follow the NAFTA model and the CARICOM-Dominican Republic agreement state that these two standards must be granted in "like circumstances." U.S. and Canadian BITs refer to "like situations" or "like circumstances." The NAFTA-type agreements, which provide for a right of establishment, include a list of reservations to national treatment and MFN treatment. This list includes nonconforming measures at the federal and subfederal levels. The Colonia Protocol for MERCOSUR members includes a list of temporary sectoral reservations.

A few investment agreements incorporate an exception to the MFN treatment in the case of the privileges deriving from membership or association in a free trade agreement, customs union, common market, or regional agreement. The two MERCOSUR protocols on investment, the free trade agreements concluded by Mexico with Bolivia, Costa Rica, Nicaragua, and the Northern Triangle, as well as those signed by the Dominican Republic with Central America and CARICOM do include such provision. The two MERCOSUR protocols, the Group of Three, and the CARICOM-Dominican Republic agreement also stipulate that the MFN treatment does not apply to preferences or privileges resulting from an international agreement relating wholly or mainly to taxation. The NAFTA and the free trade agreements concluded by Chile with Canada and Mexico have a general exception for taxation treaties that covers not only the investment chapter but the entire agreement.

Performance Requirements

The majority of bilateral investment treaties signed between developing countries in the Americas do not address performance requirements. The exceptions are the BITs between the Dominican Republic and Ecuador and between El Salvador and Peru. Free trade agreements do include provisions on performance requirements, however. Whereas those signed by the Dominican Republic with Central America and CARICOM refer to the WTO TRIMs Agreement, the others (NAFTA; those signed by Mexico with Bolivia, Chile, Costa Rica, Nicaragua, and the Northern Triangle; and the Canada-Chile agreement) go further, as does the Colonia

Protocol of MERCOSUR. The TRIMs Agreement only covers goods and clearly states that no member shall apply any TRIM that is inconsistent with the provisions of Article III (principle of national treatment) or Article XI (general obligation of eliminating quantitative restrictions) of GATT 1994.

The NAFTA-type agreements prohibit specific performance requirements for both goods *and* services. For example, NAFTA and the Chilean free trade agreements with Canada and Mexico require that performance requirements to achieve a particular level or percentage of local content, to purchase local goods and services, to impose trade- or foreign exchange–balancing requirements, to restrict domestic sales of goods or services, to export a given level or percentage of goods or services, to transfer technology, and to act as exclusive supplier of goods and services be prohibited as a condition of the establishment, acquisition, expansion, management, conduct, or operation of a covered investment. The first four requirements are also prohibited as a condition for receiving an advantage (that is, a subsidy or an investment incentive). There is, however, no such limitation on requirements to locate production, provide a service, train or employ workers, construct or expand particular facilities, or carry out research and development. Moreover, there are some exceptions to the performance requirement prohibition. For instance, NAFTA Article 1106 (6) provides that requirements to achieve given levels of domestic content or to purchase local goods and services are allowed, provided that they are not applied in an arbitrary or unjustifiable manner or do not constitute a disguised restriction, if these measures are necessary to secure compliance with laws and regulations that are not inconsistent with the provisions of the agreement; to protect human, animal or plant life or health; or to conserve exhaustible natural resources. Finally, the prohibition on performance requirements does not apply to some of the above requirements with respect to export promotion and foreign aid programs, procurement by a state enterprise, and the content of goods necessary for an importing party to qualify for preferential tariffs or tariff quotas.

The Andean Community, in contrast, establishes particular provisions for the performance of contracts for the license of technology, technical assistance, and technical services and for other technological contracts under the national laws of each member.

Key Personnel

Most free trade agreements and a few bilateral investment treaties (essentially those signed by the United States and Canada) in the Americas provide for the temporary entry of managers and other key personnel relating to an investment. Some agreements allow investors of another party to hire top managerial personnel of their choice, regardless of nationality. Other agreements state that a party may not require that an enterprise of that party appoint to senior management positions individuals of any particular nationality. These agreements also mention that a party may require that a majority of the board of directors of an enterprise that is an investment under the agreement be of a particular nationality, provided that the requirement does not materially impair the ability of the investor to exercise control over its investment.

Moreover, most free trade agreements grant temporary entry to a business person to establish, develop, administer, or provide advice or key technical services to the operation of an investment as long as the business person or his enterprise has committed, or is in the process of committing, a substantial amount of capital. The business person must comply with existing immigration and labor laws and work as a supervisor or executive or in a job that involves essential skills.

Compensation for Losses

No investment agreement requires compensation for losses due to war or other armed conflict, civil disturbances, or other *force majeure* (including natural disasters, as mentioned in the Costa Rica-Mexico agreement). Most agreements, however, provide for national treatment and MFN treatment in respect to any measure a party adopts or maintains related to those losses. This issue is either covered in a specific provision on compensation for losses or by the national treatment and MFN provisions. It is worth noting that the CARICOM-Dominican Republic free trade agreement grants only the MFN treatment in such cases (table 9-3).

Transfers

All investment agreements state that the host country must guarantee the free transfer of funds related to investments to investors of the other party. Most include an illustrative list of types of payments that are guaranteed such as returns (profits, interests, dividends, and other current incomes); repayments of loans; and proceeds of the total or partial liquidation of an investment. In addition, other types of payments are often listed; these include additional contributions to capital for the maintenance or development of an investment, bonuses and honoraria, wages and other

Table 9-3. *Investment Protection and Dispute Settlement Provisions*

Agreement	Compensation for losses	Transfers	Expropriation	Dispute settlement
MERCOSUR				
Colonia	Yes	Yes	Yes	Yes
Buenos Aires	Yes	Yes	Yes	Yes
CARICOM	Yes, under			Yes, other
Protocol II	national treatment	Yes	No	protocol
Andean Community	Yes	Yes	No	Yes, Andean
Decision 291				Court
NAFTA	Yes	Yes	Yes	Yes
Group of Three	Yes	Yes	Yes	Yes
Bolivia-Mexico	Yes	Yes	Yes	Yes
Costa Rica-Mexico	Yes	Yes	Yes	Yes
Mexico-Nicaragua	Yes	Yes	Yes	Yes
Mexico-Northern Triangle	Yes	Yes	Yes	Yes
Canada-Chile	Yes	Yes	Yes	Yes
Chile-Mexico	Yes	Yes	Yes	Yes
Central America-Dominican				
Republic	Yes	Yes	Yes	Yes
CARICOM-Dominican				
Republic	Yes, only MFN	Yes	Yes	Yes

remuneration accruing to a citizen of the other party, compensation or indemnification, and payments arising out of an investment dispute (see table 9-3).

Most agreements stipulate that the transfer shall be made without delay in a freely convertible currency or freely usable currency at the normal exchange rate applicable on the date of the transfer.[9] Some agreements allow for limitations or exceptions to transfers, such as balance of payments difficulties and prudential measures, as long as these restrictions are exercised for a limited period of time in an equitable way, in good faith, and in a nondiscriminatory manner. Chile reserves the right to maintain requirements and adopt measures for the purpose of preserving the stability of its currency.[10]

9. There are five currencies, as defined by the International Monetary Fund, as freely usable: U.S. dollar, yen, deutsche mark, French franc, and pound sterling.

10. These measures are explained in Annex G-09.1 of the Canada-Chile free trade agreement. In BITs signed by Chile, transfers of capital are restricted for a period of one year.

Expropriation

An important concern of foreign investors is to ensure that their interests are protected in the event that the host country expropriates their investment. Investment agreements generally refer to either expropriation or nationalization (or both) without differentiating between these terms. In fact, the language is broad enough to allow for coverage of "indirect" or "creeping" expropriations, that is, measures having equivalent effects to expropriation or nationalization. Under customary international law, states are allowed to expropriate foreign investment as long as it is done on a nondiscriminatory basis (that is, under principles of national treatment and MFN treatment), for a public purpose,[11] under due process of law, and with compensation. With the exception of the Andean Community Decision 291 and CARICOM Protocol II, which do not cover this issue, all investment agreements discussed in this chapter prohibit the expropriation of investments except when these conditions are met.

Most agreements use the Hull formula, which stipulates that compensation should be "prompt, adequate, and effective."[12] Only in a very few cases is the more general expression "just compensation" used. In relation to the value of the expropriated investment, most agreements use the term "market value" or "fair market value," while others use expressions such as "genuine value," immediately before the expropriatory action was taken or became known, thus protecting the investor from any reduction in value that may result as a consequence of the expropriation. Agreements also stipulate that compensation shall include interest and, in most cases, specify that it should be calculated at a normal commercial rate from the date of expropriation. In general, payments must be fully realizable, freely transferable, and made without delay. In some instances, payments must be transferable at the prevailing market rate of exchange on the date of expropriation. In most cases, however, exchange rates are not dealt with in the context of expropriation. Instead, general transfer provisions are applicable (see table 9-3).

11. Some treaties add expressions such as "national interest," "public use," "public interest," "public benefit," "social interest," or "national security." Notwithstanding the fact that "public purpose" is difficult to define in precise terms, there is a general consensus that a sate can adopt expropriatory measures only when there is a collective interest that justifies it.

12. This standard was formulated by U.S. Secretary of State Cordell Hull, who declared in 1938, in correspondence to the Government of Mexico, that "under every rule of law and equity, no government is entitled to expropriate private property, for whatever purpose without provisions for prompt, adequate and effective payment thereof." See Dolzer (1981).

Dispute Settlement

Following traditional treaty practice, provisions for the settlement of disputes between parties are included in both bilateral investment treaties and in regional trade arrangements containing provisions on investment. In the free trade agreements, investment disputes between parties fall under the general dispute settlement mechanism included in these agreements. This mechanism is based on consultation and, failing resolution through consultation, panel review. In the Andean Community, state-to-state disputes are referred to the Andean Court of Justice. MERCOSUR's Colonia protocol provides for disputes concerning its interpretation or application to be resolved through the dispute settlement procedures established in the Brasilia Protocol of December 17, 1991. When disputes involve a third state, the Buenos Aires Protocol refers them to ad hoc arbitration. Protocol IX of CARICOM addresses the issue of disputes among members. In Central America there is no regional agreement on investment, but there is a new state-to-state dispute settlement agreement approved on September 27, 2000, which means that should members of the Central American Common Market (CACM) sign an investment agreement, their state-to-state investment disputes would most likely be covered by this new agreement.

Almost all investment instruments include separate provisions for the settlement of investor-state disputes. This constitutes a departure from traditional practice in this field where no such mechanism was provided. Thus, a foreign investor was limited to bringing claim against the host state in a domestic court or having its home state assume his claim against the host state (diplomatic protection). Investment agreements include a reference to a specific institutional arbitration mechanism. They normally refer to arbitration under the Convention on the Settlement of Investment Disputes between States and Nationals of Other States (ICSID Convention) or under ICSID Additional Facility Rules where either the host or home state of the foreign investor is not an ICSID contracting party.[13] Following an increasingly common practice in modern investment agreements, most agreements include alternative forms of arbitration such as UNCITRAL (United Nations Commission on International Trade Law) rules.[14] These

13. The ICSID Convention came into force in 1966. On the ICSID Convention, see ICSID (1985); on the ICSID Additional Facility Rules, see ICSID (1979).

14. Only in the case of the Haiti–United States BIT is a reference made to arbitration under the International Chamber of Commerce. On UNCITRAL, see United Nations Commission on International Trade Law (1976).

might prove particularly relevant where ICSID arbitration is unavailable due to jurisdictional constraints.

Most agreements require that the investor and the host state seek to solve the dispute amicably through consultations and negotiations before taking it to arbitration. In some cases, a certain period of time has to elapse before the dispute can be submitted to arbitration. Evidently, investors also have the right to bring disputes to local courts of the host state, although agreements differ in the way recourse to local remedies is treated. The most common approach is to allow the investor to choose between referring the dispute to local courts or resorting to arbitration. When following this approach, a number of BITs signed between Latin American countries as well as the Colonia Protocol state that election by the investor of either international arbitration or domestic remedies "shall be final." Other agreements provide for arbitration only when the case has previously been submitted to local courts *and* a certain period of time (usually eighteen months) has elapsed without a final decision being made or the decision is inconsistent with the agreement or the decision is "manifestly unjust." A different approach is taken in recent U.S. BITs. To avoid inconsistent decisions in different forums, the agreements do not allow recourse to international arbitration if the investor has already submitted the dispute to local courts or administrative tribunals (see table 9-3).

Other Issues

Other issues are also covered in some investment agreements. Two are mentioned here: general exceptions, and environmental concerns.

GENERAL EXCEPTIONS AND OTHER DEROGATIONS. General exceptions allow countries to exempt from the obligations of an agreement all actions related to such exceptions; that is, they often—but not always—apply to all obligations and also to all parties to an agreement. They are generally invoked for reasons of maintenance of national security, international peace and security, and public order. In the Americas, the free trade agreements, U.S. BITs, and the Peruvian bilateral investment treaties with Bolivia, Paraguay, and Venezuela permit such general exceptions. Other exceptions to treaty obligations include a carve-out for taxation matters found in almost all investment agreements; exceptions to the MFN principle when a party is a member of a preferential trade agreement; country-specific reservations with respect to national treatment, MFN treatment, performance requirements, and senior management and boards of directors; temporary derogation in case of balance of payments problems; and prudential measures to protect the rights of creditors and the stability of the financial system.

ENVIRONMENTAL CONCERNS. The free trade agreements and most post-NAFTA BITs signed by Canada mention that nothing is to be construed so as to prevent a party from adopting, maintaining, or enforcing any measure otherwise consistent with the agreement that it considers appropriate to ensure that investment activity in its territory is undertaken in a manner sensitive to domestic health, safety, and environmental concerns. The parties recognize that it is inappropriate to encourage investment by relaxing domestic health, safety, or environmental measures. Accordingly, a party should not waive or otherwise derogate from, or offer to waive or otherwise derogate from, such measures as an encouragement for the establishment, acquisition, expansion, or retention in its territory of an investment of an investor. If a party considers that another party has offered such an encouragement, it may request consultations with the other party and the two parties shall consult with a view to avoiding any such encouragement.

Investment in the FTAA Negotiations

In March 1998 in the San José Declaration, trade ministers agreed upon the objective of the new Negotiating Group on Investment (NGIN): to establish a fair and transparent legal framework to promote investment through the creation of a stable and predictable environment that protects the investor, the investment, and related flows without creating obstacles to investments from outside the hemisphere. A few months later, in June 1998, the Trade Negotiations Committee defined the mandate of the Negotiating Group on Investment as being the development of a framework incorporating comprehensive rights and obligations on investment, taking into consideration the substantive areas already identified by the FTAA Working Group on Investment, and the development of a methodology to consider potential reservations and exceptions to the obligations.

During the first phase of the negotiations, the negotiating group discussed twelve issues identified by the working group as possible elements for inclusion in an investment chapter. The discussions have focused on basic definitions of investment and investor; scope; national treatment; most-favored-nation treatment; fair and equitable treatment; expropriation and compensation; compensation for losses; key personnel; transfers;

performance requirements; general exceptions and reservations; and dispute settlement. During the second phase of the FTAA negotiations in 2000, the negotiating group began to prepare a draft investment chapter, as instructed by trade ministers at their Fifth Ministerial Meeting held in Toronto in November 1999.

The Tripartite Committee, particularly through the Organization of American States, is providing expertise and analytical support to the NGIN. The Negotiating Group on Investment requested the Tripartite Committee to update the two compendiums that were prepared under the guidance of the working group: the Organization of American States's "Investment Agreements in the Western Hemisphere: A Compendium," and the Inter-American Development Bank's "Foreign Investment Regimes in the Americas: A Comparative Study." The Negotiating Group has also discussed the statistical studies prepared by the UN Economic Commission for Latin America and the Caribbean on investment flows in the region.[15]

Challenges for the Future

A first challenge is to determine how a hemispheric investment agreement would be a commitment to go beyond the status quo. Most countries of the region have either accepted the notion of a right of establishment accompanied by a list of reservations or have substantially liberalized their investment regime. Bound commitments that minimally reflect the status quo would help the Western Hemisphere gain in credibility and confidence. A related issue is whether the FTAA investment chapter would go beyond a standstill commitment and aim at progressive liberalization with, for instance, a built-in agenda and a ratchet mechanism, which would ensure that all liberalization that occurs is automatically bound in the agreement.

A second challenge is the linkages with services. One of the four modes of supply defined in GATS—commercial presence—is entirely about investment, which means that the negotiating modality of both the FTAA investment and services chapters must be compatible.

But the central question is the role the FTAA investment chapter should have. Should it aim at providing for nondiscrimination treatment and investment protection with an effective dispute settlement mechanism and also at locking in the status quo, and how should it ensure progressive liberalization?

15. These studies are available on the official FTAA home page (www.ftaa-alca.org).

References

Dolzer, Rudolph. 1981. "New Foundations of the Law of Expropriation of Alien Property." *American Journal of International Law* 75: 553.

Dolzer, Rudolph, and Margrete Stevens. 1995. *Bilateral Investment Treaties*. Boston: Martinus Nijhoff Publishers.

ICSID (International Centre for the Settlement of Investment Disputes). 1979. "ICSID Additional Facility." Washington, D.C.

——. 1985. "ICSID Basic Documents." Washington, D.C.

Sauvé, Pierre. 1994. "A First Look at Investment in the Final Act of the Uruguay Round." *Journal of World Trade* 28 (October): 12.

United Nations Commission on International Trade Law. 1976. "Decision on UNCITRAL Rules." UN doc. A/CN.9/IX/CRP.4/Add.1, amended by UN doc. A/CN.9/SR. 198.

UNCTAD (United Nations Conference on Trade and Development). 2000. *World Investment Report 2000*. Geneva.

WTO (World Trade Organization). 1996. *Annual Report, Special Topic: Trade and Foreign Investment*. Geneva.

CÉSAR PARGA

10 | *Intellectual Property Rights*

A n impressive wave of change in intellectual property regimes took place in the Western Hemisphere in the 1990s. Membership in the World Trade Organization (WTO) and adherence to its Agreement on Trade-Related Aspects of Intellectual Property Rights (TRIPS) by all but one of the thirty-four countries participating in negotiations on the Free Trade Area of the Americas (FTAA) represent a firm commitment to setting minimum standards to protect intellectual property rights.[1] Countries in the Americas have modified or adopted new legislation in all areas of intellectual property and have joined the most important international conventions governing such issues as trademarks, copyrights, and patents.[2] Moreover, countries have devoted enormous efforts and resources to adopting regulations and strengthening administrative and judicial institutions and procedures to guarantee adequate

1. The Bahamas—the thirty-fourth country—is actively considering membership in the WTO.
2. For a listing of the countries and areas where substantial improvement in protecting intellectual property has been achieved and for a description of those laws, see Correa (1997). See also the section on intellectual property in SICE (OAS Foreign Trade Information System) (www.sice.oas.org) for a list and texts of national intellectual property legislation in the thirty-four FTAA countries. All the FTAA countries are now members of both the Paris and the Berne conventions. See WIPO ratification situation (www.wipo.int/eng/ratific/doc/d-paris.doc [September 20, 2000]) and (www.wipo.int/eng/ratific/doc/e-berne.doc [September 20, 2000]).

protection and effective enforcement of intellectual property rights. Some countries have also taken steps toward greater and better protection through bilateral and subregional arrangements.

No single factor explains all of the new intellectual property regimes in the Americas. Shifts in economic policies or strategies, the need to attract foreign investment, changes in technology and information systems, and evolving views on intellectual property in the region have significantly contributed to bring about change in these regimes. The North American Free Trade Agreement (NAFTA) and the WTO TRIPS Agreement, the first trade agreements involving countries of the hemisphere that include comprehensive provisions on intellectual property rights, have also significantly influenced the new approaches adopted in the region, serving as blueprints for reform. Their provisions are mirrored in several trade agreements signed between FTAA countries.

TRIPS Agreement: Intellectual Property in Trade Negotiations

The TRIPS Agreement represents not only the most comprehensive international agreement on intellectual property protection to date, but also the most ambitious international intellectual property convention ever attempted.[3] The agreement grew out of the Uruguay Round of Multilateral Trade Negotiations, where the initial focus was on preventing the widespread production and trade of counterfeited goods. The scope of the TRIPS Agreement now extends to each of the main categories of intellectual property rights: copyright and related rights, trademarks, geographical indications, industrial designs, patents, layout designs (topographies) of integrated circuits, protection of undisclosed information, and control of anticompetitive practices in contractual licenses. The agreement establishes standards of protection as well as rules on enforcement and provides for the application of the WTO Dispute Settlement Understanding (DSU) to resolve disputes between member states.

The results of the Uruguay Round have had a direct impact on the intellectual property laws of WTO members because all these laws must comply with TRIPS. The TRIPS Agreement also innovated in establishing the protection of intellectual property as an integral part of the multilateral trading system. Together with trade in goods and services, intellectual property is now one of the three pillars of the WTO regime.[4] TRIPS's influence

3. Otten and Wager (1996, p. 393); Reichman (1996, p. 366).
4. Otten and Wager (1996, p. 393).

has also reached beyond trade negotiations to serve as a basis for further development of international rules on intellectual property, and it has facilitated the negotiations of agreements under the framework of the World Intellectual Property Organization (WIPO).[5] In fact, activities related to all areas of intellectual property rights have increased considerably since 1994. Based on the work of standing committees on the Law of Patents, Trademarks, and Copyright, WIPO members have held diplomatic conferences and approved new intellectual property conventions, several of which are substantive in nature. For example, the Final Act of the Trademark Law Treaty, designed to streamline formalities in trademark registration, was opened for signature in 1994 and entered into force in 1996.[6] In December 1996 a diplomatic conference adopted the so-called WIPO Internet treaties on Copyright (WCT) and on Performances and Phonograms (WPPT). These treaties include provisions that attempt to meet the challenges of digital technology, particularly the Internet. The WCT, a special agreement under Article 2 of the Berne Convention, constitutes the first update of that convention since 1972.

Diplomatic conferences convened by WIPO adopted the New Act of the Hague Agreement Concerning the International Deposit of Industrial Designs in July 1999 and the Patent Law Treaty (PLT) in June 2000. A third diplomatic conference dealt with substantive provisions of an instrument on the protection of audiovisual performances in December 2000.[7]

5. The two major conventions administered by WIPO—the Paris Convention for the Protection of Industrial Property and the Berne Convention for the Protection of Literary and Artistic Works—date back to the late nineteenth century. Their latest revisions were agreed upon in 1967 and 1971, respectively. For the next twenty-five years every effort to update or upgrade existing international conventions failed, and until the TRIPS Agreement was negotiated, there was no substantive multilateral agreement on intellectual property. The Paris Convention, the principal international treaty governing patents, trademarks, and unfair competition, was concluded in 1883 and was the first international effort to standardize and simplify the protection of intellectual property rights in member states. This treaty has been subsequently amended several times, the last amendment occurring in Stockholm in 1967. The Paris Convention for the Protection of Industrial Property, opened for signature March 20, 1883, as amended at Stockholm, July 14, 1967, 21 U.S.T. 1630, 828 U.N.T.S. 305. The Berne Convention for the Protection of Literary and Artistic Works of Sept. 9, 1886, in force July 14, 1967, 331 U.N.T.S. 217.

6. The Trademark Law Treaty, which opened for signature on October 28, 1994 and entered into force on August 1, 1996, seeks procedural harmonization by setting forth a list of maximum requirements that members may impose for various actions. The treaty also prohibits the imposition of additional formalities. For additional information, see Leaffer (1998).

7. The Patent Law Treaty aims at streamlining and harmonizing national patent formalities set by national or regional patent offices for the filing of national or regional patent applications, the maintenance of patents, and certain additional requirements related to patents or patent applications. For information on the Diplomatic Conference on the Protection of Audiovisual Performances, see (www.wipo.org/end/meetings/2000/iavp/index_2.htm).

Table 10-1. *Number of Accessions to the Paris and Berne Conventions before and after TRIPS*

Time frame	Paris Convention		Berne Convention	
	Worldwide	*FTAA*	*Worldwide*	*FTAA*
Before 1970	76	9	59	5
1970–1990	22	3	20	9
1990–2000	59	22	64	20

Source: WIPO Ratification Situation (www.wipo.org/treaties/index.html).

Also worth mentioning are the Joint Recommendations Concerning Provisions on the Protection of Well-Known Marks, aimed at the improvement of the international protection of well-known trademarks, adopted in September 1999, and the Joint Recommendation Concerning Trademark Licenses in September 2000, where countries sought simplification and harmonization of formalities concerning the recording of licenses.

Work in other areas and new agreements are under discussion. On copyright and related rights the international protection of broadcasting organizations is being updated, and consideration is being given to extending international protection to databases, which currently do not qualify for protection under copyright law. Countries are studying the legal implications of the use of trademarks on the Internet and are identifying areas where international cooperation appears to be necessary and achievable.

New subjects are also being discussed, including topics of interest to developing countries such as intellectual property issues that arise in the context of access to genetic resources, protection of traditional knowledge, and expressions of folklore. Other issues related to the new technologies are the relationships of trademarks and international nonproprietary names for pharmaceutical substances, Internet domain names, and intellectual property and biotechnology.

The changes in international protection motivated by TRIPS have also enhanced participation in multilateral treaties and intellectual property conventions. From 1970 to 1990 accession to major intellectual property conventions remained stagnant. Since TRIPS was negotiated, however, the number of countries, especially developing nations, signing onto intellectual property conventions has increased noticeably. For example, the number of states acceding to the Berne Convention on copyrights and the Paris Convention on industrial property more than doubled after TRIPS was signed (table 10-1). Among countries of the Western Hemisphere the increased participation is even more noticeable. With Nicaragua's accession to the Berne Convention on August 23, 2000, all FTAA countries were members of both conventions, which means that more than half of the thirty-four FTAA countries became parties to these agreements, directly or indirectly, as a result of TRIPS.

Approaches to Intellectual Property in Trade and Integration Arrangements

Trade and integration agreements have provided another alternative to harmonizing and strengthening intellectual property standards in the Americas. Almost all the existing arrangements deal with the subject, but not all of them include comprehensive provisions or a separate chapter on intellectual property rights. The coverage and approaches vary, but most of the agreements have been greatly influenced by NAFTA and TRIPS.

The structure and scope of any agreement is a key element in determining the type of intellectual property provisions that can be negotiated at the regional and subregional level. In the case of the free trade agreements, most countries have been able to negotiate standards of protection to be implemented according to the characteristics of their national legal systems. NAFTA led the way, with its chapter 17, which establishes standards for the protection of intellectual property and the enforcement of intellectual property rights in the three NAFTA countries. The agreement requires each government to apply the substantive provisions of the world's most important intellectual property conventions, supplement those conventions with substantial additional protections, and ensure that enforcement procedures are available in each country. Although NAFTA closely follows several of the provisions in TRIPS, one of NAFTA's major contributions was its timing and influence on the results of the WTO TRIPS negotiations, which were still in progress at the time NAFTA was signed.

All the bilateral free trade agreements signed by Mexico with Colombia and Venezuela (Group of Three), Bolivia, Chile, Costa Rica, Nicaragua, and the Northern Triangle (El Salvador, Guatemala, and Honduras) include a comprehensive chapter on intellectual property. These agreements differ somewhat with respect to the substantive areas they cover, but most of the provisions follow the structure of chapter 17 of NAFTA.

The chapter on intellectual property in the free trade agreement between Central America and the Dominican Republic confirms the rights and obligations of the parties under TRIPS and provides for the creation of an Intellectual Property Commission.

The Canada-Chile and the Central America-Chile free trade agreements do not have an intellectual property chapter. Nevertheless, the Canada-Chile agreement includes some provisions related to intellectual property rights and references to the TRIPS Agreement. For example, Article C-11 states that, "taking into account the TRIPS Agreement, the Parties shall protect the geographical indications for the products" specified in an annex. Under Article G-40, the definition of investment includes "intangible property." Similarly, Article D-16 provides for payments made as "considerations for the use or right to use any copyright, literary, artistic, or scientific work, patent, trademark, design, model, plan, secret formula or process" to be considered within the definition of "royalties."

Countries party to arrangements such as the Andean Community, the Central American Common Market (CACM), and MERCOSUR (Common Market of the South) have pursued provisions that seek to harmonize the intellectual property rights in each member country's national laws or that provide regulations directly applicable to all members where the level of detail is comparable to drafting a national law. These efforts have been generally concentrated on specific intellectual property issues, with comprehensive provisions and detailed rules.

The current intellectual property regime for all five countries of the Andean Community is found in four decisions issued by the Andean Commission, the community's highest governing body. Decisions automatically become the law in each of the countries belonging to the community. Matters not covered by commission decisions are regulated according to the domestic legislation of member countries. The countries can also provide for more extensive protection where appropriate. The recently approved Decision 486, Common Regime on Industrial Property, contains rules to protect patents, utility models, industrial designs, trademarks, geographical indications and appellations of origin, layout designs of integrated circuits, undisclosed information, and unfair competition. It also includes rules on enforcement of the aforementioned rights. In addition to industrial property, the Andean Community also has adopted common regimes on copyrights and related rights (Decision 351), access to genetic resources (Decision 391), and protections for plant breeders' rights (Decision 345).[8]

8. Decision 486, Regimen Común sobre Propiedad Industrial, September 14, 2000, entered into force on December 1, 2000. Published in the Official Gazette of the Cartagena Agreement, Septem-

Even though MERCOSUR's Asunción Treaty did not explicitly provide a framework for an intellectual property regime, members signed a Protocol for the Harmonization of Intellectual Property Rules With Respect to Trademarks and Geographical Indications on August 5, 1995.[9] The protocol establishes rules for the effective protection of trademarks and geographical indications and is seen as a first step toward harmonization of trademark rules in the region.[10] The four MERCOSUR members, however, have not yet ratified the document, which is currently under revision. Therefore, there is no binding agreement in force in MERCOSUR regarding the protection of intellectual property rights.[11]

The only CACM instrument on intellectual property is the 1968 "Central American Convention for the Protection of Industrial Property," addressing the issues of trademarks, trade names, advertising slogans or signs, appellations of origin, and geographical indications. The convention also included provisions related to unfair competition. Although a protocol improving the convention was signed in 1994, the convention was repealed on January 1, 2000. It will continue to be regarded as national law in the member countries until new domestic legislation on trademarks is enacted.

The Caribbean Community and Common Market (CARICOM) has no regional legislation or regulations protecting intellectual property rights, since these matters are dealt with exclusively by the domestic laws of each member state. In their free trade agreement CARICOM and the Dominican Republic agreed to develop and adopt an agreement on intellectual property rights, taking into account the rights and obligations provided for in the TRIPS Agreement and other relevant agreements to which all the member states of CARICOM and the Dominican Republic are signatories.

Some free trade agreements recently signed by countries of the Americas with countries outside the Western Hemisphere have adopted interesting approaches to intellectual property. The Mexico-European Union free

---

ber 19, 2000 (vol. 7, no. 600). Decision 486 replaced Decision 344, Common Provisions on Industrial Property (January 1, 1994), Decision 351, Regimen Común sobre Derecho de Autor y Derechos Conexos, December 17, 1993. Decision 345, Regimen Común de Protección a los Derechos de Obtentores de Variedades Vegetales, Oct. 21, 1993. Decision 391, Regimen Común sobre Acceso a los Recursos Genéticos, July 2, 1996.

9. See MERCOSUR Trademark Protocol available at ⟨www.mercosur.org.uy/espanol/snor/normativa/decisiones/DEC895.htm [September 20, 2000]⟩.

10. Hicks and Holbein (1997).

11. Paraguay ratified the protocol in 1996; see Official Gazette, no. 89 BIS, law 912 (August 7, 1996). Uruguay also ratified the protocol but has not yet deposited the corresponding instrument. Brazil has ratified the protocol only in part.

trade agreement includes provisions on intellectual property that are not comprehensive in nature but that provide for the creation of a Consultation Mechanism for Intellectual Property Matters. Pursuant to Article 40 of Decision 2/2000 of the EC/Mexico Joint Council, a special committee, made up of representatives of the parties, will try to reach mutually satisfactory solutions to difficulties arising in the protection of intellectual property.[12] On the substantive front, under Article 36 of Decision 1/2000 the agreement confirmed obligations arising under major intellectual property conventions.[13] Additionally, parties agreed to accede or complete the necessary procedures for their accession to the Nice Agreement on registration of marks (by the entry into force of the free trade agreement), the Budapest Treaty dealing with patents for microorganisms (within three years), and the WIPO Internet Treaties (at the earliest possible opportunity).[14]

The U.S.-Jordan free trade agreement, signed on October 24, 2000, includes detailed provisions addressing intellectual property rights protection, although it is not as comprehensive as NAFTA, and nor is it an iteration of the TRIPS Agreement.[15] This agreement nonetheless includes some innovative features. For instance, it provides that parties shall give effect to the Joint Recommendations Concerning Provisions on the Protection of Well-Known Marks (1999) and selected articles from the WIPO Copyright Treaty, the WIPO Performances and Phonograms Treaty, and the 1991 International Convention for the Protection of New Varieties of Plants (UPOV Convention). Additionally, the U.S.-Jordan agreement establishes a best-efforts clause to ratify or accede to the Patent Cooperation Treaty and the Protocol to the Madrid Agreement, dealing with trademark registration.[16] The free trade agreement includes substantive provisions on trademarks and geographical indications, copyright and related rights, patents, and enforcement and strengthens protection for undisclosed test and other data. Like TRIPS, there are "transition periods" but with shorter time lim-

12. See the European Union-Mexico free trade agreement, signed on March 23, 2000, and entered into force July 1, 2000. Available at (www.secofi-snci.gob.mx).

13. TRIPS, Paris, Berne, and Rome conventions, the Patent Cooperation Treaty, and the International Convention for the Protection of New Varieties of Plants (UPOV Convention).

14. Patent Cooperation Treaty (Washington 1970, amended in 1979 and modified in 1984); UPOV Convention; Nice Agreement Concerning the International Classification of Goods and Services for the purposes of the Registration of Marks (Geneva, 1977 and amended in 1979); and Budapest Treaty of the International Recognition of the Deposit of Microorganisms for the Purposes of Patent Procedure (1977, modified in 1980).

15. U.S.-Jordan Free Trade Agreement, available at (www.ustr.gov).

16. Protocol Relating to the Madrid Agreement Concerning the International Registration of Marks (1989).

its for parties to comply with specific obligations arising from the agreement, including the obligation for Jordan to ratify or accede to the WIPO Internet treaties and the 1991 UPOV Convention in one and two years, respectively. The two countries also agreed on a Memorandum of Understanding on issues related to the protection of intellectual property. This memorandum clarified certain issues, such as setting the amount of criminal penalties considered sufficiently high to deter future acts of infringement in Jordan and stipulating that "Jordan shall take all steps necessary to clarify that the exclusion from patent protection of mathematical methods does not include such methods as business methods or computer related inventions."

Convergences and Divergences

The main issues covered in the provisions on intellectual property in the trade arrangements in the hemisphere include the following: general provisions and basic principles; patents, trademarks, and geographical indications; industrial designs; utility models; copyright and related rights; encrypted program-carrying satellite signals; layout designs of integrated circuits; protection of undisclosed information; and enforcement of intellectual property rights (table 10-2).

General Provisions and Basic Principles

A general clause on protection of intellectual property, more extensive protection, national treatment, most-favored-nation (MFN) treatment, intellectual property conventions, control of anticompetitive practices, cooperation and technical assistance, and transfer of technology are all included in TRIPS, but most free trade agreements in the Americas follow chapter 17 of NAFTA, albeit with some differences in language and scope (table 10-3). Because of its supranational and unique characteristics, the Andean Community follows a different model, which covers only the basic obligations regarding national treatment and MFN treatment.

The free trade agreements signed by Mexico with Bolivia, Costa Rica, Chile, Nicaragua, the Northern Triangle, and the Group of Three establish that each party shall provide "adequate and effective protection and enforcement of intellectual property rights, while ensuring that measures to enforce intellectual property rights do not themselves become barriers to legitimate trade." NAFTA subscribes to the same principle but under the

Table 10-2. *Scope and Coverage of Trade Agreements with Intellectual Property Provisions*

Agreement	Copyright, related rights	Trademarks	Geographical indications	Patents	Industrial designs	Utility models	Plant varieties	Layout designs of integrated circuits	Undisclosed information	Satellite signals	Control of anticompetitive practices[a]	Enforcement
TRIPS	Yes	Yes	Yes	Yes	Yes	No	Yes	Yes	Yes	No	Yes	Yes
NAFTA	Yes	Yes	Yes	Yes	Yes	No	Yes	Yes	Yes	Yes	Yes	Yes
Andean Community	Yes	Yes	Yes	Yes	Yes	Yes	Yes	Yes	Yes	No	No	Yes
Bolivia-Mexico	Yes	Yes	Yes	Yes	Yes	Yes	Yes	No	Yes	Yes	Yes	Yes
Costa Rica-Mexico	Yes	Yes	Yes	No	No	No	No	No	Yes	Yes	Yes	Yes
Chile-Mexico	Yes	Yes	Yes	No	No	No	No	No	No	Yes	Yes	Yes
Group of Three	Yes	Yes	Yes	No	No	No	Yes	No	Yes	Yes	Yes	Yes
Mexico-Nicaragua	Yes	Yes	Yes	No	No	No	Yes	No	Yes	Yes	Yes	Yes
Mexico-Northern Triangle	Yes	Yes	Yes	Yes	Yes	Yes	Yes	No	Yes	Yes	Yes	Yes

Note: MERCOSUR and the CACM cover trademarks and geographical indications in their agreements.

a. This control extends only to contractual licenses.

Table 10-3. *General Provisions and Basic Principles*

Agreement	Intellectual property protection Preamble	More extensive protection Article 1	National treatment Article 3	MFN Article 4	Intellectual property conventions	Cooperation, technical assistance Article 67 and Article 69	Control of anti-competitive practices Article 40	Transfer of technology Article 7
TRIPS	Preamble	Article 1	Article 3	Article 4	Incorporated by reference; multiple articles	Article 67 and Article 69	Article 40	Article 7
Andean Community	No	No	Yes	Yes	No	No	No	No
NAFTA	Yes	Yes	Yes	No	Yes	Yes	Yes	No
Group of Three	Yes	Yes	Yes	Yes	Yes	No	Yes	Yes
Bolivia-Mexico	Yes	Yes	Yes	Yes	Yes	Yes	Yes	Yes
Costa Rica-Mexico	Yes	Yes	Yes	Yes	Yes	Yes	Yes	No
Chile-Mexico	Yes	Yes	Yes	Yes	Yes	Yes	Yes	No
Nicaragua-Mexico	Yes	Yes	Yes	Yes	Yes	Yes	Yes	No
Mexico-Northern Triangle	Yes	Yes	Yes	Yes	Yes	Yes	Yes	No

heading "Nature and Scope of Obligations." This provision, which has no equivalent in TRIPS, closely resembles the mandate from the Uruguay Round and mirrors the first part of the mandate given to the FTAA Negotiating Group on Intellectual Property (see below).

The TRIPS Agreement sets minimum standards, but Article 1 allows members to provide "more extensive protection" than required by the agreement. A similar provision exists in all the free trade agreements, including NAFTA, that Mexico has signed with countries in the hemisphere. In addition, Mexico's agreements with Costa Rica, Nicaragua, and the Northern Triangle borrow from TRIPS, giving each country the freedom to determine the appropriate method of implementing the provisions within their own legal system and practice.

NAFTA and the other free trade agreements Mexico has signed in the hemisphere all impose a broad national treatment obligation with only relatively minor exceptions, which are specifically set out in every agreement. The Andean Community's Decision 351 on Copyright and Related Rights also grants national treatment but does not include exceptions. Traditionally, national treatment has been an across-the-board obligation in the main intellectual property conventions. All these clauses mirror TRIPS Article 3.

The Andean Community also includes a national treatment obligation in its common regime on industrial property, but Decision 486, Article 1 appears to be broader than the provisions referred to in the previous paragraph, granting "treatment no less favorable than that it accords to its own nationals" not only to members of the Andean Community but also to "Members of the WTO and the Paris Convention." The inclusion of articles on national treatment and MFN treatment is one of the distinctive features of this recently approved Decision 486 compared with the Andean regime previously in force.

Traditionally MFN treatment was not included in the intellectual property conventions. It was incorporated into the TRIPS Agreement, however, to ensure that the "better than national" treatment, granted by some countries to the nationals of one or more of their trading partners as a result of bilateral agreements, would be extended to the nationals of all TRIPS members.[17] NAFTA includes no reference to the MFN principle. All the NAFTA-

---

17. It was nonetheless recognized that the circumstances in which a country would give better treatment to foreign nationals than it granted to its own nationals were likely to arise relatively infrequently. This issue was therefore viewed as significant but not critical.

like agreements signed by Mexico incorporate the MFN clause with exceptions equivalent to those set forth in Article 4 of TRIPS.

Like its national treatment, the Andean Community's MFN treatment
is broader than that in the free trade agreements. Under Decision 486,
Article 2, "any advantage, favour, privilege or immunity granted by a Member to the nationals of any other Member of the Andean Community shall
be accorded to the nationals of any Member of the WTO or the Paris
Convention." The language of the clause suggests that more than granting
MFN to the members of the Andean Community, this article is confirming that it will extend such treatment to WTO members arising out of an
existing obligation under the TRIPS Agreement.

The TRIPS Agreement incorporates, by reference, substantive provisions of the Paris and Berne conventions and the Treaty on Intellectual
Property in Respect of Integrated Circuits.[18] The free trade agreements follow a different approach, providing that parties shall give effect to the substantive provisions or ratify or accede to numerous "international intellectual
property conventions." The number of conventions and the transition periods to accede to or ratify those treaties varies depending on the countries
involved (table 10-4). The Andean Community does not address this issue.

All the free trade agreements between Mexico and countries in the
hemisphere, including NAFTA, allow parties to adopt or maintain measures to control "anticompetitive practices in contractual licenses" and prohibit certain licensing practices that adversely affect competition. Following
Article 40 of TRIPS, the Chile-Mexico agreement is the only one that provides specific examples of cases that may constitute abuse of intellectual
property (such as exclusive grant-back clauses, and conditions preventing
challenges to validity and coercive package licensing). The Bolivia-Mexico
and the Group of Three agreements each include a provision highlighting
the importance of promoting technological innovation and the transfer
and dissemination of technology.

Patents

The Andean Community, NAFTA, and the Bolivia-Mexico and
Mexico-Northern Triangle free trade agreements are the only agreements
in the hemisphere that include patent provisions. Other than minor changes

18. Treaty on Intellectual Property in Respect of Integrated Circuits, Washington, D.C., May 26,
1989.

Table 10-4. *Intellectual Property Conventions Incorporated in Free Trade Agreements*

Convention	NAFTA	Group of Three	Bolivia-Mexico	Costa Rica-Mexico	Chile-Mexico	Nicaragua-Mexico	Mexico-Northern Triangle
Paris	Yes	Yes	Yes	Yes	Yes	Yes	Yes
Berne	Yes	Yes	Yes	Yes	Yes	Yes	Yes
Rome	No	Yes	Yes	Yes	Yes	Yes	Yes
Geneva	Yes	Yes	Yes	Yes	Yes	Yes	Yes
UPOV	Yes	No	No	No	No	No	No
Brussels	No	No	Yes	No	No	Yes	No
Lisbon	No	No	Yes	Yes	No	No	No
UCC	No	Yes	No	No	No	No	No

Paris Convention: International Convention for the Protection of Industrial Property, March 20, 1883.

Berne Convention: Convention for the Protection of Literary and Artistic Works, September 9, 1886.

Rome Convention: International Convention for the Protection of Performers, Producers of Phonograms and Broadcasting Organizations, October 26, 1961.

Geneva Convention: Convention for the Protection of Producers of Phonograms against Unauthorized Duplication of their Phonograms, Geneva, October 29, 1971.

UPOV Convention: International Convention for the Protection of New Varieties of Plants, 1961, revised in Geneva (1972, 1978, and 1991).

Brussels Convention: Convention Relating to the Distribution of Programme-Carrying Signals Transmitted by Satellite, Brussels, May 21, 1974.

Lisbon Agreement: Agreement for the Protection of Appellations of Origin and Their International Registration, October 31, 1958, revised at Stockholm on July 14, 1967, and amended 1979.

UCC: Universal Copyright Convention, adopted at Geneva (1952), revised at Paris (1971).

in order and wording, Mexico's agreements with Bolivia and the Northern Triangle mirror the TRIPS's section on patents. The main provisions, also included in Decision 486 of the Andean Community, are that parties shall make patent protection available for any inventions, in all fields of technology, if they are new, involve an inventive step, and are capable of industrial application; countries may exclude particular inventions from patentability only in a few, narrowly defined cases; patents must include the right to exclude others from making, using, offering for sale, selling, or importing infringing products; use without authorization of the right holder is allowed in certain limited circumstances; and the patent term must be at least twenty years from the filing of the application. NAFTA provides similar standards of protection but with slight differences in some provisions. For example, NAFTA established an obligation (the so-called "pipeline protection") for any country that did not offer product patent protection for pharmaceutical or agricultural chemical products before the dates specified in the agreement to provide such protection, upon request, to any such product if it has been patented by another NAFTA government and is being marketed in that country for the first time. On the rights conferred to the right holder, NAFTA did not include the right to exclude others from offering for sale or importing infringing products. The patent term also varies, extending at least twenty years from the date of filing or seventeen years from the date of grant.

The section on patents in Decision 486 of the Andean Community is much more detailed than the provisions included in the free trade agreements. It implements the substantive standards of TRIPS and in its sixty-six articles addresses issues generally reserved for domestic legislation. It covers matters affecting the availability, scope, maintenance (including administrative procedures), rights conferred and limitations, and enforcement of patent rights. A new provision not included in the previous decision is Article 3, which covers biological and genetic resources as well as traditional knowledge. Patents on inventions based on material obtained from biological and genetic resources or traditional knowledge are granted subject to the acquisition of such material in conformity with the national, regional, and international legal regimes. In those cases a copy of the license or authorization granting access to the biological and genetic resources or traditional knowledge must be presented when filing a patent application. There are also some changes on the exclusions from patentability. For example, no mention is made of the inventions relating to pharmaceutical products from the World Health Organization's List of Essential Drugs.

Decision 486 also provides detailed rules on disclosure and best mode of carrying out the invention and on the characteristics of patent claims.

Trademarks and Geographical Indications

NAFTA and the agreements signed by Mexico include a chapter on trademarks and geographical indications. The substantive elements and the general structure are comparable to the corresponding section in the TRIPS Agreement with a few exceptions. All these agreements grant trademark owners certain basic rights and include provisions on protectable subject matter, registration, and licensing and assignment.

Trademarks under NAFTA, and Mexico's agreements with Bolivia, Costa Rica, and Nicaragua include service marks and collective marks. In a similar provision, the Group of Three and the Mexico-Northern Triangle free trade agreements refer only to collective marks. NAFTA and the Mexico-Nicaragua agreements also incorporate certification marks as well, whereas TRIPS makes no reference to collective or certification marks. TRIPS establishes a term of not less than seven years for initial trademark registration, and registration must be renewable indefinitely. NAFTA and the other free trade agreements with trademark chapters require those periods to last for at least ten years. Only the Chile-Mexico agreement includes a provision similar to TRIPS stipulating that where signs are not inherently capable of distinguishing the relevant goods or services, parties may register them based on distinctiveness acquired through use.

Mirroring TRIPS, all the free trade agreements, including NAFTA, establish that the nature of the goods or services shall in no case form an obstacle to registration.

The NAFTA-type free trade agreements signed by Mexico include more-detailed paragraphs on the protection of well-known marks than do either NAFTA and TRIPS. Nonetheless all the agreements provide rules that follow Article 6bis of the Paris Convention.

Under NAFTA and the Bolivia-Mexico agreement, registration of a trademark may be canceled if the mark is not used for at least two years, unless valid reasons are shown by the trademark owner. TRIPS and Mexico's free trade agreements with Costa Rica, Chile, the Northern Triangle, and the Group of Three establish a period of three years. The Mexico-Nicaragua agreement provides for a period of no more than five years. The Group of Three and the Bolivia-Mexico agreements provide additional rules on concurrent use of trademarks and cancellation and revocation of registration.

Under all free trade agreements incorporating trademark rules, parties are prohibited from adopting compulsory licensing measures or from imposing special requirements, such as use with another trademark that could impair a trademark's role as a source indicator for a product or service. Only the Bolivia-Mexico agreement includes an article to facilitate establishing franchises.

In the same way as TRIPS, NAFTA and all the NAFTA-type agreements that Mexico has signed require parties to protect geographical indications according to their domestic law and prevent any use that constitutes an act of unfair competition within the meaning of Article 10bis of the Paris Convention. They also do not allow the registration of marks that are deceptively misdescriptive of geographic origin regardless of whether the marks have acquired distinctiveness. The Costa Rica-Mexico and Mexico-Nicaragua agreements include definitions of appellation of origin and geographical indication. The Chile-Mexico free trade agreement contains an annex that includes a list identifying the geographical indications to be recognized by the parties. It is worth noting that countries of the Western Hemisphere are very active in the ongoing negotiations conducted under TRIPS to establish a multilateral system of notification and registration of geographical indications for wines and spirits.

Decision 486 of the Andean Community devotes 102 articles to trademarks and geographical indications. Many of the provisions are based on Decision 344 and on the obligations arising out of TRIPS, and these provisions are as comprehensive as domestic legislation. They cover protectable subject matter, exclusions, rights conferred, transfer and registration, termination, and enforcement. Decision 486 contains more-detailed rules on scope, availability, and exclusions from trademark protection than the previous decision did, and it includes a new chapter on certification marks and a new title on special rights for well-known signs.

Industrial Designs

The only free trade agreements addressing the issue of industrial designs are NAFTA, and the agreements Mexico has entered with Bolivia and the Northern Triangle. These three agreements provide protection, in terms very similar to those in the TRIPS Agreement, for industrial designs that are independently created and are new or original. A term of protection of at least ten years must be granted. Decision 486 of the Andean Community includes the same basic TRIPS obligations in the section on industrial designs. Additionally, it provides detailed rules on the requirements and procedures for registration.

Utility Models

Two free trade agreements, the Bolivia-Mexico and Mexico-Northern Triangle agreements, address the issue of utility models—those inventions that do not rise to the level of patentable inventions but that nonetheless are deemed to deserve some period of protection. The Bolivia-Mexico agreement covers protectable subject matter and specifies a minimum term of protection of ten years from the date of filing. The Mexico-Northern Triangle agreement refers the issue to the domestic legislation of each party. The Andean Community also considers utility models within the intellectual property rights covered under Decision 486.

Copyright and Related Rights

This subject is covered in Decision 351 of the Andean Community, NAFTA, and all of the NAFTA-type agreements Mexico has signed. TRIPS addresses copyrights in a slightly different manner by incorporating by reference Articles 1 through 21 of the Berne Convention and the appendix thereto, with the exception of Article 6bis on moral rights.

There are no significant differences in how all these agreements establish the term of protection for copyright and related rights. They also all provide protection for computer programs and copyrightable compilations of data. TRIPS and the Chile-Mexico agreement establish that computer programs must be protected *as* literary works, whereas under NAFTA computer programs *are* considered literary works within the meaning of the Berne Convention.

Unlike TRIPS, NAFTA and Mexico's agreements with Costa Rica, Nicaragua, and the Northern Triangle enumerate the rights of authors and their successors in interests to authorize or prohibit certain acts involving their works, such as importation, communication to the public, and first public distribution. A more limited list can also be found in the Bolivia-Mexico and Group of Three agreements. The Chile-Mexico agreement refers to the rights conferred and exceptions and limitations of the Berne Convention.

As is the case in TRIPS, the Chile-Mexico agreement provides for the so-called "rental right" for computer software and cinematographic works in certain circumstances. There is a similar provision in NAFTA and Mexico's free trade agreements with Bolivia, Costa Rica, Nicaragua, and the Northern Triangle, but it is limited to computer programs only. Additionally, NAFTA and the Bolivia-Mexico agreement have a limitation on granting translation and reproduction licenses where legitimate needs in that party's territory for copies or translations could be met by the right holder's voluntary actions.

Decision 351 of the Andean Community establishes comprehensive provisions on scope of protection, moral and economic rights, and exceptions and limitations.[19]

In the area of "related or neighboring rights," the Andean Community, NAFTA, and all the free trade agreements signed by Mexico provide protection to producers of phonograms. In addition to the right to authorize or prohibit the direct or indirect reproduction of phonograms as in TRIPS, all the other free trade agreements, including NAFTA, and the Andean Community add the right for producers of phonograms to authorize or prohibit the importation, commercial rental, and first public distribution of their phonograms. The Chile-Mexico agreement has an article on producers of phonograms but refers to the rights and obligations of the Rome and Geneva Conventions.

The Andean Community and all the free trade agreements with chapters on copyright protection, except NAFTA, include provisions on rights for performers. NAFTA and the Bolivia-Mexico and Chile-Mexico agreements are the only ones that do not cover the rights of broadcasting organizations. The Andean Community also includes rules on collective administration of rights, performing rights societies, and some specific provisions on enforcement of copyright and related rights.

Encrypted Program-Carrying Satellite Signals

The protection of encrypted program-carrying satellite signals is one of the subjects not covered by TRIPS. It is included in NAFTA and the NAFTA-type agreements signed by Mexico. These agreements are substantively the

---

19. Civil law countries generally protect both the moral rights of authors and their economic rights. Moral rights are inalienable rights that preserve the integrity of an author's work, give the author the right to be known as the author and the right to determine in what form the work will be made public. Because moral rights are usually not transferable, they may impede the economic rights associated with a given work since the owner of these rights may not be the author. NAFTA requires parties to apply the substantive provisions of the Berne Convention for the Protection of Literary and Artistic Works (1971) but does not impose any obligations on the United States to give effect to Article 6bis on moral rights, pursuant to NAFTA Annex 1701.3 (2).

same—they all provide civil and criminal sanctions for unauthorized use of program-carrying signals. However, the location of the article varies. Some agreements provide a basic definition of satellite signals and include the provision as an enforcement measure (Bolivia-Mexico and Mexico-Nicaragua). NAFTA has it as a separate heading. The Group of Three includes this issue as one of the rights of broadcasting organizations (related right), and in Mexico's agreements with Chile, Costa Rica and the Northern Triangle, it is under copyright and related rights.

Layout Designs of Integrated Circuits

NAFTA and Decision 486 of the Andean Community are the only agreements establishing rules on protection of layout designs (topographies) of integrated circuits based on certain provisions of the Treaty on Intellectual Property Rights in Respect of Integrated Circuits and TRIPS. Countries must protect products incorporating a protected layout design and provide a minimum term of protection of ten years.

Protection of Undisclosed Information

The Andean Community's Decision 486, NAFTA, and all the free trade agreements signed by Mexico except its agreement with Chile require the protection of undisclosed information (or trade secrets) if the information is secret, has commercial value, and has been subject to reasonable steps to keep it secret. All these agreements follow TRIPS Article 39, including the protection for undisclosed test or other data, submitted as a condition of approving the marketing of pharmaceutical or of agricultural chemical products.

Enforcement of Intellectual Property Rights

As TRIPS does, the Andean Community, NAFTA, and the NAFTA-type agreements Mexico has signed establish extensive procedures to ensure that intellectual property rights are enforced at, and within, each member country's borders. Each government must provide fair and transparent enforcement procedures and access to right holders to effective judicial proceedings for the enforcement of rights, including a range of civil and administrative remedies, prompt and effective provisional measures, and criminal procedures and penalties. Also required are effective procedures allowing for seizures of pirated and counterfeited goods at the border, subject to certain safeguards. In the Andean Community, these provisions on enforcement are included only in Decision 486 and are thus available only for those issues of industrial property covered by the decision. In industrial property and other areas, enforcement measures are also covered in the national legislation of each Andean country.

Intellectual Property in the FTAA Negotiations

The Working Group on Intellectual Property Rights was one of twelve working groups created in 1996 by the trade ministers of the thirty-four countries participating in the FTAA negotiations. These groups concentrated their efforts on gathering and compiling information on the status of specific trade issues in the hemisphere. The Organization of American States Trade Unit assisted the group in preparing compilations on national legislation, regional agreements, and international conventions in subjects such as patents, copyrights, trademarks, trade secrets, industrial designs, layout designs of integrated circuits, geographical indications, encrypted program-carrying satellite signals, utility models, and plant varieties. The working group prepared the groundwork for the negotiations and served as a mechanism for information exchange and cooperation among the different countries in the hemisphere. The Negotiating Group on Intellectual Property Rights (NGIP) was created in 1998 with the mandate to "reduce distortions in trade in the Hemisphere and promote and ensure adequate and effective protection to intellectual property rights. Changes in technology must be considered." The NGIP prepared a draft chapter on intellectual property rights to comply with the Toronto Ministerial mandate during the second cycle of negotiations.

The Tripartite Committee through the OAS Trade Unit has continued to provide technical and analytical support to the NGIP. As background information and to increase transparency, the group agreed to update the inventories prepared by the OAS during the preparatory phase and to create a web site containing the complete text of intellectual property rights laws and regulations of the countries of the hemisphere, a directory of national authorities, and links to Internet sites of national offices on intellectual property matters.[20]

---

20. This website can be reached at (www.sice.oas.org/int_prop.asp).

Challenges for the Future

Since the TRIPS negotiations concluded in 1994, intellectual property has evolved, particularly because of changes in technology and information systems. New questions and areas, such as Internet-related issues, were unforeseen at the time. Developing countries have also brought to relevant international forums areas related to intellectual property of particular interest to them such as protection of folklore and traditional knowledge and access to genetic resources and geographical indications.

Furthermore, the level of protection of intellectual property rights in the Western Hemisphere is radically different from that afforded at the end of the Uruguay Round and the start of the FTAA negotiations. As of January 1, 2000, all FTAA countries but Haiti, due to its status as a least-developed country, had to be in compliance with the TRIPS Agreement. Although some countries are still facing the challenges of complying with their new international obligations, most of them have completely updated their legislation. The fact that the thirty-four FTAA countries share common minimum standards of protection and understanding of intellectual property provides a solid base for hemispheric negotiations in this area.

Against this backdrop, the FTAA negotiations on intellectual property rights have to address a series of challenges if they are to comply with their objective and goals.

First is the challenge of negotiating a package that is responsive to the new developments in intellectual property in a way that accounts for the interests of all participants. There are elements that would seem to allow for such an outcome. Intellectual property issues that arise in the context of domain names, biotechnology, traditional knowledge and folklore, copyright and related rights in digital networks, protection of databases, and access to genetic resources are all areas omitted from TRIPS that might find a place in a balanced package as a result of the negotiations.

Second, negotiations will face a series of challenges derived from the need to define the relationship of the FTAA provisions on intellectual property to international regimes that are already in place, that are in the process of being negotiated, or that are still not binding on all FTAA countries. Linked to this are questions concerning the most appropriate forum for addressing certain issues and the advisability of beginning to define their treatment at the regional level (either in parallel with or before such efforts are undertaken in international forums). The relationship to TRIPS is particularly critical in this context and suggests the possibility, for example, of identifying certain provisions where clarification could be sought, elements that could be further developed, or other issues that could be addressed. It seems that all these questions might need to be considered on a case-by-case basis, because the answer could be different depending on the nature and special characteristics of the intellectual property issue involved.

Third, challenges are associated with the need to take into account the needs and concerns of the smaller economies participating in the FTAA negotiations. Some of these countries recognize not only the importance of an adequate and effective protection of intellectual property rights, but also that these protections are linked to their development processes as a whole.

Finally, there is the overall challenge of ensuring that the final package resulting from the FTAA negotiations reflects in a balanced way the interests of all participants. Only by ensuring an appropriate balance in all areas—including market access, services, agriculture, investment, and so forth—will it be possible to achieve progress in specific areas, such as intellectual property rights, and to ensure that the final result will be accepted by all as a "single undertaking."

References

Correa, Carlos M. 1997. "Implementation of the TRIPS Agreement in Latin America and the Caribbean." *European Intellectual Property Review* 8: 435, 439–442.

Hicks, Laurinda L., and James R. Holbein. 1997. "Convergence of National Intellectual Property Norms in International Trading Agreements." *American University Journal of International Law and Policy* 12: 769.

Leaffer, Marshall A. 1998. "The New World of International Trademark Law." *Marquette Intellectual Property Law Review* 2: 1.

Otten, A., and H. Wager. 1996. "Compliance with TRIPS: The Emerging World View." *Vanderbilt Journal of Transnational Law* 29: 391.

Reichman, J. H. 1996. "Compliance with the TRIPS Agreement: Introduction to a Scholarly Debate." *Vanderbilt Journal of Transnational Law* 29: 363.

JOSÉ TAVARES DE ARAUJO JR.

11 | *Competition Policy*

W ith the exception of the United States, competition policy is a relatively new subject everywhere.
Some countries such as Canada, Australia, and New Zealand have had
antitrust laws since the turn of the twentieth century, but their role as public policy instruments became relevant only in recent decades. In most industrialized countries these laws were enacted for the first time after the
Second World War. However, in the United Kingdom, for instance, the
annual workload of the Monopolies Commission until 1965 seldom included more than two investigations, while merger review procedures were
introduced in the European Union only in 1990. In 1989 only 31 countries
had competition laws, and by 1997 about half of the members of the World
Trade Organization had yet to pass such laws in their territories.[1]

In contrast with the infant stage of antitrust institutions in most countries, technical progress engendered a pervasive trend toward global competition during the second half of the twentieth century. As a result of these
uneven developments, a defining feature of the current multilateral trading

The author wishes to acknowledge the research assistance provided by Jorge Mario Martínez.
1. WTO (1997).

230

system is the lack of mechanisms for checking global mergers, international cartels, and anticompetitive practices of transnational corporations. According to the U.S. International Competition Policy Advisory Committee, "in 1999 global mergers and acquisitions were at an all-time high, with approximately $3.4 trillion in activity announced worldwide"; moreover, "approximately 25 percent of the more than 625 criminal antitrust cases filed by the Department of Justice since fiscal year 1990 were international in scope."[2] In 1998 the European Commission examined twenty merger cases in which the relevant geographic market was the world economy.

In the Western Hemisphere, besides the United States and Canada, only five countries had competition laws in 1990: Argentina (first law passed in 1919), Brazil (1962), Chile (1959), Colombia (1959), and Mexico (1934). Between 1991 and 1996 new laws were approved in Costa Rica (1994), Jamaica (1993), Panama (1996), Peru (1991), and Venezuela (1991). Moreover, draft laws have been discussed recently in Bolivia, El Salvador, Guatemala, Nicaragua, Dominican Republic, and Trinidad and Tobago. However, even though antitrust is becoming a relevant issue in a growing number of Latin American and Caribbean countries, one major challenge to be faced by the Free Trade Area of the Americas (FTAA) initiative is the enforcement of competition rules in the domestic markets of the member countries, as twenty-two of them still do not have such institutions.

Because of the lack of a multilateral framework, regional provisions on competition policy play a crucial role in contemporary trade agreements for three main reasons. First, such provisions stimulate the coherence of domestic policies, as the goals of promoting efficiency and consumer welfare become priority topics on the negotiating agenda. Second, they provide the conditions for a balanced treatment of foreign direct investment, whereby the discussion about market access and other investor's rights is complemented by a set of mechanisms for controlling competitive business practices. Third, they establish the institutional background for regulatory reform of monopolistic industries, particularly in the area of public services, thus facilitating trade liberalization in this area.

Approaches to Competition Policy in the Western Hemisphere

Table 11-1 summarizes the main characteristics of the competition policy provisions within the regional trade agreements of the Western Hemi-

---

2. ICPAC (2000, pp. 3, 167).

Table 11-1. *Regional Competition Policy Provisions in the Western Hemisphere*

Agreement	National law	Regional provisions	Scope of existing provisions	Mergers and acquisitions
Andean Community	3 out of 5 members	Yes	Supranational treatment of cases with regional dimension	No
CACM	1 out of 5 members	No	. . .	. . .
CARICOM	1 out of 15 members	Yes	Supranational treatment of cases with regional dimension	Yes
MERCOSUR	2 out of 4 members	Yes	Building up a common regional policy	Yes
NAFTA	All members	Yes	Strengthening of national agencies and cooperation among agencies	Yes
Central America-Chile	2 out of 6 members	Yes	Endeavor to adopt common provisions	No
Central America–Dominican Republic	1 out of 6 members	Yes	Endeavor to adopt common provisions	No
Canada-Chile	Both members	Yes	Cooperation between authorities	No
Chile-Mexico	Both members	Yes	Cooperation between authorities	No
Group of Three	All members	Limited provisions	Policy guidelines on state enterprises	No
Bolivia-Mexico	1 member	No	. . .	. . .
Costa Rica-Mexico	Both members	No	. . .	. . .
Mexico-Nicaragua	1 member	No	. . .	. . .

. . . = Not applicable.

sphere. The top tier includes the comprehensive agreements, namely, the Andean Community, Central American Common Market (CACM), CARICOM (Caribbean Community and Common Market), MERCOSUR (Common Market of the South), and NAFTA (North American Free Trade Agreement); and the bottom tier includes bilateral and other agreements such as the Group of Three, signed by Colombia, Mexico, and Venezuela, and the one between Central America and the Dominican Republic. The table provides four categories of information: the existence of national competition laws in member countries; the presence of provisions on this subject in the agreements; the scope of existing provisions; and treatment regarding mergers and acquisitions. As the table illustrates, countries in the region have taken three different approaches in dealing with international competition issues. The first is based on supranational institutions, the second gives priority to the harmonization of national laws, and the third focuses on strengthening national agencies and cooperation among them.

The Supranational Approach: Andean Community and CARICOM

The Andean Community, by Decision 285 in 1991, and CARICOM, by Protocol VIII in March 2000, adopted the supranational approach. Decision 285 is the first effort to address competition issues at a subregional level in the Western Hemisphere. Its substantive provisions and enforcement mechanisms, like those of the CARICOM protocol, are modeled after European Union (EU) competition rules. Therefore, supranationality principles applied by community bodies govern both systems. It should be noted that when these provisions were enacted, Colombia and Jamaica were the only members of either agreement that already had competition laws. Although Decision 285 was seen as a model for policy harmonization in the Andean Community, its components and scope fall short compared to what was developed in each country later on. Nonetheless, due to the supranational principles, Decision 285 prevails over domestic law in cases of subregional dimension. CARICOM's provisions are more comprehensive and do not contradict the Jamaican law.

Decision 285 has a limited scope. It deals with restrictive practices resulting either from collusive agreements or from abuses of dominant position so long as they affect competition in more than one country of the subregion. If the practice does not have extraterritorial implications, then national law applies. Concerted actions prohibited by the decision include price-fixing; restraints on output, distribution, technical development and investments; market allocation; discrimination; and tying arrangements. Abuses of dominant position include, in addition to the practices noted above, refusals to deal, withholding of input to competing firms, and discriminatory treatments. Decision 285, however, does not address some important practices affecting competition in integrated markets such as vertical restraints and mergers.

The enforcement of Decision 285 is the responsibility of the Andean Community secretariat, which conducts investigations and proceedings at the request of countries or affected firms. In this regard the decision does not follow the EU model but instead provides the Andean Community secretariat with a rule of reason standard. In what looks more like an anti-dumping analysis than a competition policy one, joint consideration must be given to the evidence on the practice, threat of injury or actual injury to a subregional industry, and the cause-effect relationship between the practice and the injury using a rule of reason standard. Proceedings must be completed within two months after investigations are initiated. If the secretariat determines that the practice restricts competition, it may issue a cease-and-desist order and it may also authorize the affected country to impose corrective measures, that is, lower tariffs to the products exported by means of restrictive practices.

Policy Harmonization: The MERCOSUR Approach

In December 1996 MERCOSUR countries signed the Fortaleza Protocol, which set guidelines for a common competition policy in the region. The implementation of this protocol implies, among other institutional innovations, that all member countries will have an autonomous competition agency in the near future, that the national law will cover the whole economy, that the competition agency will be strong enough to challenge other public policies whenever necessary, and that the member countries will share a common view about the interplay between competition policy and other governmental actions. Following the usual MERCOSUR rules, the Fortaleza Protocol does not create supranational organisms, and the effectiveness of the regional disciplines will rely on the enforcement power of the national agencies.

The goals of the Fortaleza Protocol are threefold. First, it provides mechanisms to control firms' anticompetitive practices with MERCOSUR dimension. Second, it calls for convergent domestic laws to ensure similar conditions of competition and independence among firms regarding the formation of prices and other market variables. Third, it provides an agenda for surveying public policies that distort competition conditions and affect trade among the member countries. Thus, the MERCOSUR competition policy is an instrument for abolishing obstacles to the enlargement of the regional market. From this viewpoint, this protocol cannot be seen just as a set of rules to be applied to anticompetitive practices with extraterritorial implications. It is more far-reaching because it deals with both government and firms' interference with the competition process.

Regarding the first goal, the protocol seeks to prevent any concerted practice between competing firms or individual abuse of dominant position aimed at limiting competition in the MERCOSUR market. Its provisions apply to acts performed by any person, be it natural or legal, private or public, including state enterprises and natural monopolies, so long as such practices have extraterritorial effects. The list includes price-fixing, restraints, reduction or destruction of input and output, market division, restriction of market access, bid-rigging, exclusionary practices, tying arrangements, refusal to deal, resale price maintenance, market division, predatory practices, price discrimination, and exclusive dealings.

The protocol is enforced by the MERCOSUR Trade Commission, which has adjudicative functions, and the Committee for the Defense of Competition, which is responsible for the investigation and evaluation of cases. Modeled after the Brazilian law, the proceedings and adjudication of cases are conducted on a three-stage basis. Proceedings are initiated before the competition authority of each country at the request of an interested party. The competition agency, after a preliminary determination on whether the practice has MERCOSUR implications, may submit the case to the committee for the Defense of Competition for a second determination. Both evaluations must follow a rule of reason analysis in which a definition of the relevant market and evidence of the conduct and the economic effects must be provided. Based on this evaluation, the committee must decide whether the practice violates the protocol and recommend that sanctions and other measures be imposed. The committee's ruling is submitted to the MERCOSUR Trade Commission for final adjudication by means of a directive. As part of these procedures, the protocols establish provisions for preventive measures and undertakings of cessation. The monitoring of these measures and the enforcement of the sanctions fall on the national competition authorities.

Cooperation among National Authorities: The NAFTA Approach

Chapter 15 of NAFTA presents five main topics for addressing international issues related to competition, namely: focus on domestic law enforcement; a strengthening of national agencies through mutual regional assistance; priority attention to the conduct of firms, instead of the attributes of industry structure; no formal commitments to the harmonization of competition policy with other policies at a regional level; and gradual and pragmatic advance toward joint commitments for dealing with international competition policy cases.

Article 1501 indicates that NAFTA countries should take measures to proscribe anticompetitive business conduct, but it does not establish any standards to be incorporated into the domestic laws. It also recognizes the importance of cooperation: the parties shall cooperate on issues of competition law enforcement policy, including mutual legal assistance, notification, consultation, and exchange of information relating to the enforcement of competition laws and policies in the free trade area.

NAFTA negotiations have had a marked influence on the recent modernization of Mexican competition policy institutions. On December 24, 1992, a new law replaced the old 1934 legislation and established the Federal Competition Commission as an autonomous agency. This commission has had an active role in the national process of regulatory reform, particularly in the areas of energy, transportation, and telecommunications, and it has followed a busy international agenda that includes regular meetings with NAFTA and FTAA working groups, the Asia-Pacific Economic Cooperation Forum, the Organization for Economic Cooperation and Development, the UN Conference on Trade and Development, and the European Union. In March 1998 the commission enacted a series of regulations, including guidelines for mergers and acquisitions that are similar to those of Canada and the United States in all relevant aspects.

The NAFTA approach to competition was clearly influenced by the previous bilateral experience between the United States and the European Union. In 1991 they signed an agreement that has had several consequences. Besides paving the way for other bilateral initiatives, such as the ones the United States signed with Canada in 1995 and with Brazil and Mexico in 1999, the U.S.-EU agreement proved to be an effective mechanism for dealing with international antitrust cases and generated a new flow of data that kept the subject of competition policy alive on the international agenda. That agreement included the following procedures:

—The parties must notify each other of enforcement activities that may affect the interests of the other country, including both anticompetitive practices and mergers. Notifications shall be sufficiently detailed to enable the notified party to make an initial evaluation of the effect of the enforcement activity on its own interests and shall include the nature of the activities under investigation and the legal provisions concerned. Where possible, notifications must include the names and locations of the persons involved.

—Officials of either competition policy agency may visit the other country in the course of conducting investigations.

—Either party may request that the other initiate an investigation in its territory on anticompetitive practices that adversely affect the interests of the requesting country.

—The parties must provide mutual assistance in locating and securing evidence and witnesses in the territory of the other country.

—The parties must hold regular meetings to discuss policy changes and exchange information on economic sectors of common interest.

As table 11-1 indicates, some trade agreements such as the CACM and the recent bilateral agreements signed by Mexico with Bolivia, Costa Rica, and Nicaragua do not have antitrust provisions. However, all other cases listed in the bottom tier of the table can be described as modified versions of the NAFTA approach, whose characteristics were also embodied in the mandate of the FTAA Negotiating Group on Competition Policy. Two explicit mandates of this group are to "advance towards the establishment of juridical and institutional coverage at the national, sub-regional or regional level, that proscribes the carrying out of anticompetitive business practices" and to "develop mechanisms to promote cooperation and exchange of information between competition authorities."

The Controversy on Antitrust versus Antidumping

A frequent obstacle to economic integration originates from contradictory domestic policies, whereby governments promote competition through certain channels such as trade liberalization, regulatory reform, and antitrust while creating market distortions through other channels such as state aids, unnecessary regulations, and antidumping actions. In contrast, one common characteristic among successful integration processes, such as the European Union, the European Economic Area, and the Closer Economic Relations Agreement (CER) between Australia and New Zealand, has been the abolition of antidumping measures among the member countries. This evidence is often used to support the argument that substituting antitrust for antidumping should be a mandatory step in every trade agreement.

This argument, however, overlooks the fact that the elimination of antidumping in the European agreements and CER was part of a deep integration process fostered by the convergence—at both the macroeconomic and microeconomic levels—of the competition conditions in the domestic markets of the member countries. The models of macroeconomic convergence varied from the search for exchange rate stability and the harmonization of monetary and fiscal policies, as in the CER case, to the creation of a single currency, as in the EU case. At the microeconomic level the process included the use of similar policies in all areas that affect the functioning of domestic markets, such as antitrust, subsidies and fiscal incentives, labor and capital mobility, and regulation of monopolies. Because CER has not established supranational institutions, its integration process has been based essentially on policy harmonization and cooperation between national authorities.

Therefore, both in the European agreements and in CER, despite their different approaches to economic integration, the elimination of antidumping was followed by the application of common competition policies at the regional level. However, this does not imply that one policy has replaced the other. Indeed, the political conditions that made the elimination of antidumping possible have resulted from the complete elimination of other trade barriers and the advanced stage of the convergence process among the members of those trade agreements. Not by chance have the EU and the Australian government remained leading users of antidumping against the rest of the world.[3]

The Canada-Chile free trade agreement, which entered into force on July 5, 1997, also abolished antidumping, but that agreement does not fit into the above pattern. First, in contrast to the EU and CER, trade flows between Canada and Chile are quite small. During the second half of the 1990s, the share of intraregional trade in the EU was about 44 percent, while bilateral trade within the CER represented 25 percent of New Zealand's foreign trade and 6 percent of Australia's figures. However, in the case of Canada-Chile their bilateral flows represented 1.5 percent for the latter and less than 0.1 percent for the former. Second, because Canada and Chile are not engaged in a policy harmonization process, chapter F of their

3. Miranda, Torres, and Ruiz (1998).

agreement provides special rules for safeguard actions (bilateral measures) during the transition period and states that "each Party retains its rights and obligations under Article XIX of the GATT 1994 and the Agreement on Safeguards of the WTO Agreement except those regarding compensation or retaliation and exclusion from an action to the extent that such rights or obligations are inconsistent with this Article" (global measures).

Thus, one interesting innovation made by the Canada-Chile agreement was to begin the trade liberalization process by substituting safeguards for antidumping. This may imply an important shift on the negotiating agenda during the transition period, particularly in regard to those industries that are not prepared to face international competition. Instead of blaming exporters from the trading partner for the increased quantities of imported goods and provoking unnecessary trade disputes, each government is led to address the domestic factors that may be hindering the competitiveness of the local industry.

The Canada-Chile experience is an important precedent for the FTAA negotiations. Given the disparities in size, level of economic development, and state of antitrust institutions among the member countries, the convergence of competition conditions in the hemisphere is feasible only as a long-run objective. Consequently, to establish a free trade area under these circumstances, the relevant challenge is about substituting safeguards, not antitrust, for antidumping. Moreover, the FTAA is a forum that would be particularly appropriate for this discussion, as tables 11-2 and 11-3 indicate.

Table 11-2 shows the distribution of the investigations affecting countries of the Western Hemisphere between 1987 and 1997.[4] The United States and Brazil, the leading targets of these measures in the region, were included in 67.4 percent of the cases initiated against FTAA countries. In a second tier, Argentina, Canada, Mexico, and Venezuela were involved in about 26 percent of the investigations; in a third tier, ten countries received the remaining share of 6.6 percent. It also should be noted that eighteen FTAA countries were not affected by antidumping measures during that period and that the distribution by users has a similar profile: Argentina, Brazil, Canada, Mexico, and the United States were responsible for 94.2 percent of the investigations, while six countries—Chile, Colombia, Costa Rica, Guatemala, Peru, and Venezuela—accounted for the remaining 5.8 percent. The other twenty-three FTAA countries have never used this instrument.

4. The figures were selected from a comprehensive study made by Miranda, Torres, and Ruiz (1998), which covered all members of the World Trade Organization (WTO).

Table 11-2. *Antidumping Measures Affecting FTAA Countries, 1987–97*

Target	Argentina	Brazil	Canada	Chile	Colombia	Costa Rica	Guatemala	Mexico	Peru	United States	Venezuela	FTAA countries	Rest of world	Total
Argentina		1	1	1				1		8	1	13	7	20
Bolivia									1			1	0	1
Brazil	31		8	2				18	1	19		79	26	105
Canada		1						4	1	19		25	10	35
Chile	2	2						1	1	2		8	0	8
Colombia	2							3	1	1		7	1	8
Ecuador										1		1	0	1
Guatemala						1						1	0	1
Mexico	1	2	3	1	2	2	1		1	12	1	25	10	35
Nicaragua						1						1	0	1
Paraguay	2											2	0	2
Peru											1	1	0	1
Trinidad and Tobago					1					2		3	1	4
United States	9	18	42	1	5	1		53			1	130	58	188
Uruguay	1	1										2	0	2
Venezuela	1	1	1	1				6		10		20	3	23
FTAA countries	49	26	55	5	8	5	1	86	6	74	4	319	116	435
Rest of world	74	71	133	4	12	0	0	102	8	317	8	729	1,032	1,761
Total	123	97	188	9	20	5	1	188	14	391	12	1,048	1,148	2,196

Source: Miranda, Torres, and Ruiz (1998).

Table 11-3. *Exports to the Western Hemisphere in 1997,*
Selected Countries and Industries

Billions of dollars

Industry	Argentina	Brazil	Canada	Mexico	United States	Venezuela	Total
Chemicals	0.9	1.8	6.9	2.8	19.0	0.5	31.9
Plastics	0.4	1.3	7.1	2.6	16.5	0.3	28.2
Pulp and paper	0.3	0.8	12.2	1.0	9.5	0.1	23.9
Textiles	0.6	1.0	2.8	7.4	13.3	n.a.	25.1
Base metals	0.8	3.2	13.2	5.6	17.4	1.4	41.6
Machinery, electrical equipment	1.0	4.9	24.6	39.5	100.5	0.1	170.6
Total	4.0	13.0	66.8	58.9	176.2	2.4	321.3
Percent of total exports to the Western Hemisphere	27.0	53.5	39.5	57.8	62.2	12.7	52.5

Sources: Inter-American Development Bank database, available at (www.iadb.org); WTO (www.wto.org); and Industry Canada (www.strategis.gc.ca).

Table 11-2 also highlights the intensity of antidumping actions among FTAA countries: 319 of the 435 cases affecting these economies originated in the region; yet, the main users of this trade remedy normally direct their actions against the rest of the world. For instance, 317 of the 391 cases opened by the United States have targeted countries outside the Western Hemisphere; Argentina, Brazil, Canada, and Mexico followed a similar pattern. The rest of the world, however, did not reciprocate with the same strength; in contrast with the 729 actions started from the Western Hemisphere toward other regions, the opposite flow was restricted to 116 cases.

About 80 percent of cases are concentrated in six industries: base metals (mostly steel products), capital goods (machinery and electrical equipment), chemicals, plastics, pulp and paper, and textiles.[5] Because the investigations are always focused on very specific products, the amounts of trade directly affected also tend to be very small, even among the leading antidumping users: less than 1 percent of total imports in the case of the

5. Miranda, Torres, and Ruiz (1998).

European Union, and 0.5 percent in the United States.[6] From the point of view of the exporting industries, however, as the investigations are continually focused on the same type of goods, this creates uncertain market conditions for the whole industry and therefore constitutes an obstacle to economic integration. As table 11-3 illustrates, for some countries such as Brazil, Mexico, and the United States, more than 50 percent of their exports to the Western Hemisphere are hampered by this kind of instability.

Competition Policy in the FTAA Negotiations

In 1998 the FTAA Trade Negotiations Committee (TNC) defined a work program for the Negotiating Group on Competition Policy (NGCP) that includes four mandates: identify the main principles and criteria of competition; establish instruments to ensure that the benefits of trade liberalization are not undermined by anticompetitive practices; develop mechanisms to promote cooperation and the exchange of information between competition authorities; and study issues relating to the interaction between trade and competition policy, including antidumping measures, in order to identify any areas that may merit further consideration and report to the Trade Negotiations Committee by December 2000.

During the first phase of the negotiations, the Negotating Group on Competition Policy discussed the possible issues to be included in the competition chapter of the FTAA agreement. These issues included anticompetitive practices with cross-border effects; exclusions and exceptions; the fundamental principles of competition; broad criteria concerning law enforcement; characteristics of the competition authority; cooperation mechanisms; technical assistance; regulatory policies, official monopolies, and state aids; dispute settlement; and a policy review mechanism. During the second phase of the FTAA negotiations in 2000, the NGCP began the preparation of a chapter on these issues, as instructed by the Toronto Ministerial Meeting in November 1999. At the end of the year 2000, the NGCP finalized a draft text.

The Tripartite Committee prepared several studies upon request from the NGCP, including an "Inventory of Domestic Laws and Regulations Relating to Competition Policy in the Western Hemisphere"; an "Inventory of Competition Policy Agreements, Treaties and Other Arrangements Existing in the Western Hemisphere"; and a "Report on Developments

---

6. Hindley and Messerlin (1996).

and Enforcement of Competition Policy in the Western Hemisphere." These reports are regularly updated and are available on the official FTAA web site.[7]

Challenges for the Future

The main challenge is related to the domestic character of competition policy. Despite the growing importance of this subject in many Latin American countries, since 1996 the number of countries without antitrust institutions has not changed. As this chapter has argued, international cooperation is feasible only as a complement to, not a substitute for, domestic enforcement. The mandates of the NGCP include a possible solution for this problem, which is to create policy instruments at the subregional or regional level. To become effective, this innovation would imply additional and differentiated adjustments to the existing trade agreements, according to the role assigned to supranational institutions and the number of members with competition laws in each region.

Another challenge is to clarify the relation between antitrust and antidumping. Both topics are crucial to the establishment of the FTAA and may lead to inconsistent policies, but they address different issues. In the near future, given the absence of a deep process of convergence in the competition conditions of the member countries, it seems more appropriate to inquire about the potential role of safeguards than to consider competition policy as a substitute for antidumping.

References

International Competition Policy Advisory Committee. 2000. *Final Report*. Washington, D.C.: U.S. Department of Justice, Antitrust Division.

Hindley, Brian, and Messerlin, Patrick. 1996. *Antidumping Industrial Policy*. Washington, D.C.: AEI Press.

Miranda, Jorge, Raúl Torres, and Mario Ruiz 1998. "The International Use of Antidumping: 1987–1997." *Journal of World Trade* 32 (5): 5–71.

World Trade Organization. 1997. *Annual Report*. Geneva.

7. www.ftaa-alca.org.

DONALD R. MACKAY
MARYSE ROBERT

12 | *Government Procurement*

G overnments around the world have always expended vast amounts of resources in acquiring
material goods and tangible and intangible services for use in the discharge
of their sovereign and civic responsibilities.[1] Governments, however, are
unique actors whose characteristics and purchasing motivations are not
identical to such familiar economic agents as firms and individuals. The
interaction between firms, and between firms and individuals, has created
markets whose operation, while not fully known, has at least the minimum
elements of transparency that allow for a wide and reliable exchange of
information. In contrast, procurement of goods and services by governments has resulted, in almost all cases, in a market within a market that is
not well, or at least not widely, understood.

Theories leading to the modern liberalization of markets, internal and
external, are increasingly being applied to questions of government procurement. Governments, particularly in the Americas, have come to acknowledge the growing existence of demands for overhaul and reform in
this sector. Firms and citizens who participate in the "normal" marketplace

---

1. For example, minimum estimates of 10 to 15 percent of the value of world trade are not uncom-
mon. See Sahaydachny and Wallace (1999, p. 462).

are increasingly concerned that their taxed contributions to the common good are expended and managed in a prudent and uncorrupted manner.[2] Pressure has also come from outside actors, in the form of foreign governments or competing foreign firms, who are interested in the opening of such protected markets.

Procurement of products and services by government agencies for their own purposes represents an important share of total government expenditure and of a country's gross domestic product (typically 10–15 percent of GDP). As a result, government procurement plays a significant role in domestic economies, and restrictions imposed on government procurement can have a notable impact on international trade in goods and services. Yet, despite its importance, government procurement has been effectively omitted from the scope of the "single undertaking" multilateral trade rules under the World Trade Organization (WTO) in the areas of both goods and services.

Approaches to Liberalization of Government Procurement

The original U.S. draft of the International Trade Organization charter would have provided for national treatment and most-favored-nation (MFN) treatment "in respect of governmental purchases of supplies for government use." This simple approach, however, fell victim to the realization that such a broad commitment would have been subject to "exceptions almost as broad as the commitment itself."[3]

The General Agreement on Tariffs and Trade (GATT) does not address government procurement issues per se. GATT Article XVII covers state trading enterprises but not their procurement activities, whereas GATT Article III:8 specifically excludes "laws, regulations or requirements governing the procurement by governmental agencies of products purchased for governmental purposes and not with a view to commercial resale or with a view to use in the production of goods for commercial sale." After years of failed attempts, GATT contracting parties settled for an approach

2. Pressure for reform has come from a wide range of sources. For example, an OECD (Organization for Economic Cooperation and Development) "Convention on Combating Bribery of Foreign Public Officials in International Business Transactions" came into force on February 15, 1999. In the Americas, Canada, Mexico, and the United States have all submitted their instruments of acceptance and ratification. Three other countries in the Hemisphere (Argentina, Brazil, and Chile) who are not OECD members have nevertheless also signed the convention.

3. WTO (1995, p. 190).

of *modified reciprocity* in government procurement.[4] The outcome was codified in the results of the Tokyo Round of GATT negotiations. The first agreement on government procurement was signed by a few GATT contracting parties in 1979 and came into effect in 1981. An amended version entered into force in 1988. Although the Uruguay Round did not tackle the issue as such, countries that were parties to the Tokyo Round Code negotiated the current Agreement on Government Procurement (GPA) in 1994; it includes procurement of both goods and services. The GPA is one of the plurilateral agreements set out in Annex 4 of the WTO agreement, which means that not all WTO members are bound by its obligations. Of the current 140 members (as of December 31, 2000) of the WTO, only twenty-seven are parties to the GPA.[5] In the Western Hemisphere, only the United States and Canada participate, while Panama continues the accession process, and Argentina, Chile, and Colombia are observer governments (in addition to Panama).

The cornerstone of the GPA is nondiscrimination, with respect both to domestic products, services, and suppliers (national treatment) and to goods, services, and suppliers of other parties (MFN treatment). The agreement applies to government procurement by entities selected by each party. Annexes 1, 2, and 3 respectively cover central government entities, subcentral government entities, and other entities. The obligations of the agreement apply to services and construction services listed in annexes 4 and 5. The GPA excludes purchases below a certain threshold and prohibits offsets, that is, measures that encourage local development or improve balance of payments problems by means of local content requirements, licensing of technology, investment requirements, countertrade, or similar requirements. The agreement also permits open, selective, and limited tendering procedures. It contains obligations on technical specifications to ensure that government entities do not discriminate among suppliers through the descriptive characteristics of products and services. The GPA sets out a requirement to publish laws, regulations, judicial decisions, administrative rulings of general application, and any procedures regarding government procurement. Another feature is that the GPA allows special and differen-

---

4. In the simplest of terms, Country A agreed to open to Country B the ability to compete for specified procurements made by government departments C, D, and E in return for modified reciprocal access in Country B. Such access is conditioned by a number of factors and regulations (such as national security exceptions and "carve outs" for specified sectors and levels of government).

5. Austria, Belgium, Canada, Denmark, European Communities, Finland, France, Germany, Greece, Hong Kong China, Ireland, Israel, Italy, Japan, Korea, Liechtenstein, Luxembourg, Netherlands, Netherlands with respect to Aruba, Norway, Portugal, Singapore, Spain, Sweden, Switzerland, United Kingdom, United States.

tial treatment to developing countries, least-developed countries in particular, in recognition of their specific development objectives. Finally, the agreement incorporates specific rules on enforcement and dispute settlement. Disputes between parties are covered by the WTO Understanding on Rules and Procedures Governing the Settlement of Disputes, but the suspension of concessions under the GPA as a result of a dispute under a WTO agreement is not allowed. The reverse is also true.

Within the WTO, efforts are being taken to negotiate an agreement on transparency in government procurement. A working group, launched at the Singapore Ministerial Meeting in 1996, is examining various approaches including current national practices.[6] The issue of transparency is also receiving more attention in the policies and programs pursued by various international financial institutions such as the World Bank, the International Monetary Fund, and the Inter-American Development Bank.

In the Western Hemisphere, the decade of the 1990s witnessed moderate progress in the conclusion of agreements relating to government procurement. A limited number of free trade agreements contain binding commitments, while others have sought to establish frameworks for further examination, study, and possible future negotiations. Customs unions in the Western Hemisphere have exhibited a more cautious approach to the acceptance of binding commitments but have established, within their respective frameworks, a number of committees and working groups that could well set the groundwork for negotiations.

The North American Free Trade Agreement (NAFTA) contains a fully developed and operational chapter on government procurement that has been largely implemented among its three members. NAFTA's chapter 10 essentially mirrors the GPA. It contains a detailed normative framework with associated schedules of covered entities and thresholds. NAFTA also contains provisions that ensure the continued evolution of government procurement as a negotiating issue, focusing on such possibilities as coverage of subcentral levels of government. To ensure effective market access for commercial entities, the three NAFTA governments have independently and cooperatively developed modern electronic means of publishing bid notices and submissions of proposals.

These developments have been followed by Mexico in its negotiation of various plurilateral and bilateral agreements, most notably with Colombia and Venezuela in the Group of Three and individually with Bolivia, Costa Rica, and Nicaragua. The bilateral free trade agreements signed by

6. Regular progress reports of the working group are published on the WTO's Internet site at (www.wto.org/english/tratop_e/gproc_e/gproc_e.htm).

Central American countries with the Dominican Republic and Chile also include a chapter on government procurement. The Canada-Chile agreement, the Chile-Mexico agreement, and the recently negotiated free trade agreement between Mexico and the Northern Triangle (El Salvador, Guatemala, and Honduras) do not cover government procurement. Eighteen months after the entry into force of the agreement between Mexico and the Northern Triangle, however, parties must start negotiating a chapter on government procurement, which will have a broad coverage and accord national treatment. In the case of the agreement between Chile and Mexico, parties agreed to start negotiations on government procurement one year after the agreement entered into force.

Within MERCOSUR (Common Market of the South) government procurement is being examined by at least two technical committees.[7] Those committees have had several meetings and are reported to have advanced in such areas as the exchange of information related to legislative and regulatory instruments pertinent to government procurement, but no binding market access commitments have yet entered into force. The Andean Community agreement does not cover government procurement, but the "New Strategic Design of the Andean Group," approved by the Andean Commission on August 31, 1995, establishes some guidelines on the subject. The document stresses the necessity of adopting legislation in the area of government procurement based on the parameters and taking as a reference the GPA. Within CARICOM (Caribbean Community and Common Market), much work has been done of late to update and revitalize that agreement and the framework of international trade relations of its members. Although progress has been achieved in a number of areas, the subject of government procurement has yet to be fully addressed. Central American countries have negotiated two free trade agreements that do contain provisions on government procurement, as do the free trade agreements signed by Costa Rica and Nicaragua with Mexico. There is, however, no regional agreement addressing this issue.

Convergence and Divergence

Any comparative examination of trade arrangements in the Western Hemisphere with respect to government procurement suffers from what

---

7. Technical Committee No. 4 on "Public Policies Which Distort Competitiveness." Government procurement issues are also being addressed by the ad hoc working group on services.

statistically would be called an insufficient sampling. Coverage of the sector is confined to the plurilateral Agreement on Government Procurement in the WTO (of which only Canada and the United States in the Western Hemisphere are currently members), NAFTA, and a number of the NAFTA-like agreements that were subsequently negotiated.

The GPA and NAFTA are structurally similar, although the latter has lower thresholds and is therefore more liberalizing in terms of coverage. One of the difficult elements to judge is the degree to which private commercial entities have used the agreements on government procurement in the hemisphere when penetrating external markets. Statistics that might indicate how the provisions have broadened access to these specialized markets are extremely difficult to obtain.

The Mexican bilateral free trade agreements that contain government procurement provisions are modeled on the NAFTA original and therefore their structure is almost identical. They differ from NAFTA in that the thresholds are in some cases different and can and do vary across partners. For example, in the Bolivia-Mexico agreement, Mexico was willing to accept higher thresholds for Bolivia during the transitional period than for itself.

The most notable area of divergence shows up in the two bilateral free trade agreements signed by Chile with two of NAFTA's founding members, Canada and Mexico. These agreements overall are strongly modeled on NAFTA. Yet government procurement does not appear as a covered discipline, albeit the agreement between Chile and Mexico calls for negotiations on this issue one year after the entry into force of the agreement. Chile has negotiated government procurement provisions in its free trade agreement with Central American countries.

Scope, Coverage, and Thresholds

NAFTA and the NAFTA-type agreements signed by Mexico with Bolivia, Costa Rica, the Group of Three, and Nicaragua apply to measures, adopted or maintained by a party, relating to government procurement by specific federal or central government entities and enterprises of covered goods, services, and construction services where the value of the contract exceeds specific thresholds. The higher the number of entities and enterprises covered by an agreement and the lower the threshold, the more liberalizing the agreement is. The thresholds negotiated in these agreements are $50,000 for procurement of goods or services or a combination of them by federal entities. The threshold is $250,000 for government enterprises. The threshold for procurement of construction services is $6.5 million for federal entities and $8 million for government enterprises. These thresholds are subject to indexation. A lower threshold of $25,000 inherited from the Canada-U.S. Free Trade Agreement applies to the procurement of goods by government entities of those two countries. These goods contracts may include incidental services such as delivery and transportation. It is worth noting that the two free trade agreements signed by Central American countries with Chile and the Dominican Republic do not contain any thresholds, which means that they are, in nature, more liberalizing.

NAFTA and the other agreements signed by Mexico do include transitional provisions allowing a party or a particular entity to set aside from the obligations of the chapter specified percentages of the total value of procurement contracts above the applicable thresholds for goods, services, and construction services.

National Treatment and Nondiscrimination

NAFTA as well as all the other regional free trade agreements signed among countries of the Western Hemisphere provide for national treatment, except for duties and other import charges. The MFN treatment clause applies only to goods and suppliers of other parties, which implies that a party is not obliged to accord to other parties any more favorable treatment granted to a nonparty.

Rules of Origin and Denial of Benefits

NAFTA and the Mexico-Nicaragua agreement provide that no party may apply rules of origin to goods imported from another party that are different from or inconsistent with the rules of origin that the importing party applies in the normal course of trade. This means that, in the case of NAFTA, a party may apply the NAFTA rule of origin to determine whether a good is entitled to preferential treatment and the party's own rule of origin when the same good is being used for government procurement purposes. The Bolivia-Mexico, Costa Rica-Mexico and Central America-Dominican Republic, and the Group of Three agreements refer to the agreement's rule of origin. The Central America-Chile agreement does not address this issue.

Subject to consultations and prior notification, all the agreements on government procurement in the hemisphere allow a party to deny the benefits of the government procurement chapter to a supplier owned or controlled by persons of a nonparty that has no substantial business activities in any party. NAFTA also permits a party to deny benefits to suppliers controlled by nationals of a nonparty if the party does not maintain diplomatic relations with the nonparty or if measures adopted by that party respecting the nonparty would be violated if the benefits were accorded to the supplier.

Offsets and Technical Specifications

All the agreements prohibit offsets, that is, conditions imposed in the process of granting a contract for government procurement purposes. They also require that parties ensure that their entities do not prepare, adopt, or apply any technical specification with the purpose or the effect of creating unnecessary obstacles to trade.

Tendering Procedures, Bid Challenges, and Provision of Information

Most agreements include provisions dealing with tendering and bid challenges procedures and obligate the parties to publish laws, regulations, precedential judicial decisions, administrative rulings, and procedures regarding government procurement covered by their respective chapter.

Exceptions

All the agreements with the exception of the Central America-Chile agreement set out general exceptions in their government procurement chapter. They provide that nothing in their chapter shall prevent a party from taking action or not disclosing information that it considers necessary for the protection of its essential security interests relating to military procurements or procurement necessary for national security or national defense. The second general exception establishes that nothing in the agreement is to be interpreted ("construed") as preventing any party from adopting measures that are necessary to protect public morals, public order, or the safety of human, animal, or plant life or health or that relate to goods or services for use by handicapped persons, philanthropic institutions, or prison labor.

Technical Cooperation

All the agreements except the Central America-Dominican Republic agreement require parties to provide other parties and suppliers information regarding training and orientation programs concerning their government procurement systems.

Rectification or Modification and Divestiture of Entities

All agreements allow a party to delete from its schedule a government entity that has been privatized. A few agreements such as NAFTA also permit a party to modify its coverage after notifying the other parties and proposing compensation.

Future Negotiations

Some agreements such as NAFTA and the Bolivia-Mexico agreement require parties to launch negotiations among themselves by a specific date to liberalize further this sector. Others, such as the Costa Rica-Mexico and the Central America-Dominican Republic agreements, note that a decision on this matter will be taken in the future.

Government Procurement in the FTAA Negotiations

In the context of the Free Trade Area of the Americas negotiations, government procurement as an area of governmental action began at the second FTAA ministerial meeting, held in Cartagena, Colombia, in March 1996. At that meeting trade ministers agreed to create a working group under the chairmanship of the United States; the United States continued to chair the group during the first phase of the FTAA negotiations, that is, until November 1999, when the chairmanship was passed to Canada.

The objectives established in the San José Ministerial Declaration for the Negotiating Group on Government Procurement (NGGP) directed it: to achieve a normative framework that ensures openness and transparency of government procurement processes without implying the establishment of identical systems in all countries, to ensure nondiscrimination in government procurement within a scope to be negotiated, and to ensure impartial and fair review for the resolution of procurement complaints and appeals by suppliers and the effective implementation of such resolutions. All these objectives are to be achieved within the broad negotiating objective of expanding access to the government procurement markets of the FTAA countries. This group has also been charged with studying national statistical systems to identify existing similarities and differences within the hemisphere and to seek a common understanding of statistical information systems on government procurement.

Like other negotiating groups, the procurement group has been charged with developing a draft chapter for presentation to trade ministers when they next meet in Buenos Aires in the early part of 2001.

The Negotiating Group on Government Procurement has been quite successful in moving forward on substantive negotiations. A press communiqué issued at the conclusion of the second meeting of the group noted that work was progressing "toward the formulation of a chapter . . . to ensure openness and transparency and address coverage."[8] The group has been addressing issues such as publication of laws and regulations, procurement procedures, publicity for inviting tenders, presentation of tenders, criteria for assessing bids and awarding contracts, and disclosure of bids received and contracts awarded.[9] Preliminary discussions also took place on the "principles/treatment granted to domestic and foreign goods, services, public works and their suppliers."

The Inter-American Development Bank, as part of the Tripartite Committee, is providing technical and analytical support to the negotiating group. The bank has prepared two studies: one on government procurement rules in the regional integration arrangements in the Americas and another on national legislation and regulations on government procurement in the Americas. Both are available on the official FTAA website.[10]

Challenges for the Future

In the Western Hemisphere governments in one form or another engage in the procurement of goods and services in excess of some $250 billion a year.[11] Of this amount, the United States accounts for approximately $180 billion. This is to be expected, given the dominant economic position of the United States within the hemisphere. Nevertheless, government

8. See FTAA.nggp/com/1 of February 10, 1999, on the official FTAA website (www.ftaa-alca.org).

9. See FTAA.nggp/com/07 of May 26, 2000, on the official FTAA website (www.ftaa-alca.org).

10. "Government Procurement Rules in Integration Arrangements in the Americas," and "National Legislation, Regulations and Procedures Regarding Government Procurement in the Americas," available at (alca-ftaa.iadb.org/eng/procuree.htm).

11. Statistical compilations from various sources, and for various years (thus diminishing exact comparability) indicate that total procurement of about $240 billion can be identified with a fairly high degree of confidence. Extrapolating from existing data, including where data do not exist, allows the authors to put forward an estimate of $250 billion for the region as a whole.

procurement opportunities in other countries are far from commercially insignificant. Procurement in Brazil exceeds $20 billion; Mexico, $11 billion. And the market in such countries as Chile ($4 billion) and Uruguay ($3 billion) is also attractive.

In the past this sector did not receive as much attention in regional or subregional trade negotiations as the size of the potential markets would warrant. But domestic or externally driven attempts at reform of government procurement practices is beginning to change this situation.

A solid agreement among FTAA countries on the issue of government procurement would be built on two fundamental pillars, each of which would support a myriad of policies and administrative procedures. The first pillar is that of transparency, broadly understood to mean that policies, government requirements, technical standards, and all administrative procedures and decisionmaking are subject to public scrutiny. The second pillar can be viewed as either administrative or judicial in nature; it essentially provides a place and a process for the lodging and adjudication of complaints. Competitors must have the opportunity to challenge procedures and outcomes in a fair and impartial forum that provides the essential counterbalance to ensure that public resources are efficiently used.

References

Sahaydachny, Simeon A., and Don Wallace. 1999. "Opening Government Procurement Markets. " In *Trade Rules in the Making: Challenges in Regional and Multilateral Negotiations*, edited by Miguel Rodríguez Mendoza, Patrick Low, and Barbara Kotschwar. Brookings/Organization of American States.

WTO (World Trade Organization). 1995. *Analytical Index: Guide to GATT Law and Practice*, 6th ed. Geneva.

ROSINE M. PLANK-BRUMBACK

13 | *Dispute Settlement*

The dispute settlement provisions within trade agreements serve as an important guarantor that the parties will fulfill the substantive commitments they have made and realize the benefits they expected to derive from these agreements. This can be seen when a party to a trade agreement withdraws a measure found to be inconsistent with that agreement by a formal mechanism designed to resolve legal differences. No less tangibly, it can also be seen when an effective dispute settlement system acts to deter a party from adopting an inconsistent measure in the first place; this is the "dispute avoidance" effect.

Unlike other subject matter treated in this volume, one cannot speak about "liberalization" of dispute settlement under hemispheric trade agreements. One can, however, observe the negotiation of increasingly detailed procedures for resolving differences as well as a trend in many agreements toward infusing the process with greater technical expertise, ethical codes, and default procedures to resolve impasses. One can also point to approaches that strike different balances between political control by the parties and institutional control over the process, with constant movement and evolution on this continuum.

255

Approaches to Dispute Settlement

At a certain level of generality, dispute settlement systems under hemi-spheric trade agreements can be divided between those that provide for a court or standing body (Andean Community), and those that provide for arbitral panels/tribunals or ad hoc bodies (the North American Free Trade Agreement and NAFTA-like agreements). One might have expected to draw a line easily in this respect between customs unions and free trade areas, or between agreements with several parties and those with only two or three. More elaborate institutional arrangements would seem to be required the deeper the economic integration and the more member states involved. But this expectation is not necessarily borne out.

The Andean Community is the premier example in the hemisphere of formalistic dispute settlement institutional arrangements. Since 1982 the Court of Justice of the Cartagena Agreement has existed to ensure that member countries comply with Andean Community law and that this law is uniformly interpreted throughout the community. The general secre-tariat also may issue an administrative ruling that a member country is violating community law and has standing to file claims in the court against members.

Another customs union, the Common Market of the South (MERCO-SUR), has not gone this route, however, but elected an ad hoc arbitral tribunal approach under the Protocol of Brasilia. Moreover, during its first thirty-seven years, the Central American Common Market (CACM) did not have an operational dispute resolution mechanism. It was not until October 2000 that the Council of Central American Integration Ministers adopted a NAFTA-like arbitral tribunal mechanism, to which the Central American Court of Justice is expected to delegate its responsibilities in trade disputes.

The Caribbean Community and Common Market's (CARICOM) Protocol IX and the Agreement Establishing the Caribbean Court of Jus-tice would grant to such a court exclusive original jurisdiction on disputes between the contracting parties arising under the Treaty of Chaguaramas and appellate jurisdiction over civil and criminal matters. In addition to adjudication, Protocol IX also provides for other modes of dispute settle-ment, including a conciliation commission and an arbitral tribunal. The protocol and the agreement establishing the court have not yet entered into force. As of October 2000 eleven countries had signed Protocol IX. The CARICOM dispute settlement mechanisms described later are therefore limited to the provisions of the Treaty of Chaguaramas as amended by Protocol I, under which disputes are settled primarily at the ministerial level.

The NAFTA model of dispute settlement prevails in the free trade agreements in the hemisphere. There are some differences among the NAFTA-like agreements, highlighted more fully later. The NAFTA model follows closely the multilateral model that has developed under the General Agreement on Tariffs and Trade (GATT) and the World Trade Organization (WTO) Dispute Settlement Understanding (DSU). Although the NAFTA model was negotiated contemporaneously with the DSU, the two differ in several important ways, including panel selection, appeal, retaliation, and special and differential treatment. The DSU is an integrated system for handling claims on any of the covered multilateral agreements, whereas NAFTA has distinct dispute settlement mechanisms depending on the subject area. The description of NAFTA-like dispute settlement mechanisms that follows is limited to general dispute settlement; special or additional dispute settlement, specific, for example, to investment, is dealt with in other chapters of this volume.

Virtually all the countries engaged in negotiating the Free Trade Area of the Americas (FTAA) participate in the GATT/WTO dispute settlement system. The continuing experiences with and perceived shortcomings of the DSU system influence hemispheric negotiators with each new trade negotiation. They often seek to draft new dispute settlement provisions in a way to avoid both problems that arose in a specific case and outcomes that they judged unfavorable to their interests.

Convergence and Divergence

All the dispute settlement provisions of the trade agreements covered in this volume apply to disputes between state parties arising under the application of the agreements. Most of the settlement mechanisms provide for a neutral body, whose members are selected by the parties to the agreement, to render a legal opinion on the merits of the case. The greatest divergences among the agreements concern the possibility of nonviolation complaints (that is, complaints against a measure that may not be inconsistent with the agreement, but that nullifies or impairs a benefit under the agreement); recourse by private persons for alleged noncompliance with the agreement by the state parties; the degree of control parties have over the selection of arbitrators for any individual case; the power of judges or arbitrators to order provisional measures and seek information and technical advice; the explicit binding nature of the decision rendered by a neutral body; the extent to which a neutral body may suggest or order the manner in which a party must comply with the decision; and the entitlement of the winning party to suspend benefits against a losing party that fails to comply with the decision. Some of these divergences are illustrated graphically in table 13-1.

Following is fuller detail on the principal features of the dispute settlement systems more or less in the order they would be covered under the agreements.

Scope, Cause of Action, Parties with Standing

In all the agreements, the scope of the dispute settlement provisions applies to disputes that arise between the parties in the "application" of the respective agreement. Except for the Andean Community, the scope of the settlement provisions also extends explicitly to disputes on the "interpretation" of the agreement. MERCOSUR's Protocol of Brasilia refers additionally to "noncompliance," and the CARICOM-Dominican Republic free trade agreement to "execution." NAFTA and NAFTA-like agreements speak not only about settling disputes, but also about avoiding them. Accordingly, a party may raise a "proposed" as well as an "actual measure of another party" that the former considers is or would be inconsistent with the agreement or causes "nullification or impairment." The Group of Three (Colombia, Mexico, and Venezuela) agreement does not explicitly mention "proposed" measures, but consultations may be requested on any matter that might affect the operation of the agreement.

"Nullification or impairment" is a term that comes from GATT Article XXIII:1, whereby a contracting party (now WTO member) may have a cause of action when it believes that any benefit accruing to it directly or indirectly is being nullified or impaired as the result of

(a) the failure of another party to carry out its obligations ("violation claim"); or

(b) the application by another party of any measure "whether or not it conflicts" ("nonviolation claim," used successfully in a few cases involving domestic subsidies that nullified or impaired the benefits expected from a tariff concession); or

(c) the existence of any other situation (this "situation claim" has never been made).

The CACM and Central America-Chile agreements refer the parties to case law under 1994 GATT Article XXIII:1(b) in interpreting nullification or impairment. NAFTA and NAFTA-like agreements provide for a "nonviolation" nullification or impairment cause of action. With the exception of the Central America-Dominican Republic agreement and the CACM, such actions are restricted, however, to benefits parties could expect to enjoy under specified chapters of the agreements.

State parties to the agreements have standing to have recourse to the government-to-government dispute settlement being described here. Under the Andean Community system, a member that considers that another member is not in compliance with its obligations must go to the general secretariat for an administrative ruling on the matter. If the secretariat concludes there is noncompliance, the secretariat has standing to file a cause of action before the Andean Court of Justice if the noncompliance persists. But if the secretariat does not take this action or does not issue a ruling within a certain time period, or makes a negative ruling, the complaining member may then have recourse directly to the court.

The Andean Community and MERCOSUR provide standing for private parties, namely, natural or legal persons, to file complaints in certain circumstances. Under the Andean system countries and individuals whose rights or legitimate interests are adversely affected may submit actions of nullity directly to the Court of Justice against commission decisions or general secretariat rulings that violate Andean Community law for reasons of deviation of power, or exceeding authority. The court and secretariat may also resolve private contractual disputes governed by community law.

Under MERCOSUR, natural or legal persons may complain to their national section of the MERCOSUR Trade Commission that administrative or legal measures of any party have a restrictive, discriminatory or unfairly competitive effect in violation of MERCOSUR law. The national section may consult directly with the national section of the party complained against or refer the complaint to the Common Market Group. The latter may reject the complaint or convene a group of experts to issue conclusions. If the legal basis of the complaint is sustained, any other state party can demand the withdrawal of the measure in dispute. If the withdrawal does not occur within a certain time period, the demanding party may resort directly to the arbitral tribunal procedure.

NAFTA and the bilateral agreements Chile has negotiated with Canada, Central America, and Mexico expressly prohibit a party from providing for a private right of action under its domestic law against another party on the ground that a measure of another party is inconsistent with the agreement.

Table 13-1. *Selected Areas of Divergence among Dispute Settlement Mechanisms under Hemispheric Trade Agreements*

Agreement	Non-violation complaint	Non-governmental parties[a]	Bilateral consultations	Neutral body (number of members)[b]	Binding nature of neutral body's decision	Retaliation by complaining party
WTO DSU	Yes	No	Yes	Ad hoc panel (3) and standing appellate body (7)	Yes, unless negative consensus in DSB[c]	Yes
Andean Community	No	Yes	No	Standing court (5)[d]	Yes	Yes if court finds noncompliance
MERCOSUR	No	Yes	Yes	Ad hoc arbitral tribunal (3)	Yes	Yes
CACM	Yes	No	Yes	Ad hoc arbitral tribunal (3)	Yes	Yes if panel finds noncompliance
NAFTA	Yes[e]	No	Yes	Ad hoc arbitral panel (5)[f]	No	Yes if parties fail to agree in thirty days
Bolivia-Mexico	Yes[e]	No	Yes	Ad hoc arbitral tribunal (5)	Yes	Yes if tribunal finds noncompliance
Canada-Chile	Yes[e]	No	Yes	Ad hoc arbitral panel (5)[f]	No	Yes if parties fail to agree in thirty days
Central America-Chile	Yes[e]	No	Yes	Ad hoc arbitral tribunal (3)	Yes	Yes if tribunal finds noncompliance
Central America-Dominican Republic	Yes	No	Yes	Ad hoc arbitral tribunal (3)	Yes	Yes if tribunal finds noncompliance

Chile-Mexico	Yes[e]	No	Yes	Ad hoc arbitral group (5) [f]	Yes	Yes if group finds noncompliance
Costa Rica-Mexico	Yes[e]	No	Yes	Ad hoc arbitral tribunal (5)	Yes	Yes if tribunal finds noncompliance
Group of Three	Yes[e]	No	Yes	Ad hoc arbitral tribunal (5)	Yes	Yes if tribunal finds noncompliance
Mexico-Nicaragua	Yes[e]	No	Yes	Ad hoc arbitral tribunal (5)	Yes	Yes if tribunal finds noncompliance
Mexico-Northern Triangle	Yes[e]	No	Yes	Ad hoc arbitral tribunal (3)	Yes	Yes if tribunal finds noncompliance
CARICOM	No	No	No	[g]	No	Yes with authorization of council by majority vote
CARICOM-Dominican Republic	No	No	Yes	[h]	No	No

a. Limited to general dispute settlement; not permitted, for example, for investor-state dispute settlement under the agreements.
b. Body composed of impartial experts who render factual and legal findings on the dispute, as opposed to a political body composed of representatives of the parties to the agreement, which may also engage in dispute settlement.
c. DSB stands for Dispute Settlement Body.
d. The general secretariat may also issue administrative rulings on whether a member is in compliance with its obligations.
e. For benefits in certain specified provisions of the agreements.
f. The ad hoc arbitral panel may also establish a scientific review board.
g. The annex to the Treaty of Chaguaramas provides for the possibility that the council may refer a dispute to an ad hoc tribunal. Protocol IX and the Agreement Establishing the Caribbean Court of Justice, which provide for ad hoc conciliation commissions and arbitral tribunals as well as a standing court, have not yet entered into force.
h. The council may exercise the option of arbitration to resolve any dispute.

In other words, a party cannot be sued in another party's domestic courts for violating the agreement.

Under the Andean Community, national judges may refer a question of interpretation of community law to the Court of Justice. Such a referral is obligatory when there is no appeal of the judge's decision under domestic law. Most of the decisions handed down by the Court of Justice are in this area of interpretation, as compared to nullity and noncompliance actions.

NAFTA and the NAFTA-like agreements, except the CACM, provide for a party to bring to the commission, or the political body of party representatives, any question of interpretation of the agreement that has arisen in domestic judicial or administrative proceedings. If the commission is unable to arrive at an agreed interpretation, any party may submit its own views to the court or administrative body in accordance with the rules of that body. Parties have seldom resorted to these procedures.

Choice of Forum

NAFTA and NAFTA-like agreements have choice of forum provisions whereby a complaining party may choose whether to pursue a claim under either the agreement or the WTO. Once a decision on forum has been made, a complaining party may not seek recourse in the other forum. The critical point of no return under the agreements is when a party requests a panel under the DSU.

NAFTA provides that before a party initiates a WTO proceeding against another party on "grounds that are substantially equivalent to those available" under NAFTA, the party should notify the third NAFTA party of its intention to go to the WTO. If the third NAFTA party also wants to initiate an action on the matter, the two should try to agree on the forum, but if they cannot, the dispute should normally be settled under NAFTA.

The Canada-Chile agreement provides that where the responding party claims that the matter is subject to environmental and conservation agreements under the agreement, the dispute must be resolved solely there.

The Group of Three free trade agreement stipulates that disputes between Colombia and Venezuela, which fall under both the agreement and the Cartagena Agreement, which established the Andean Community to which they also belong, must be submitted for resolution under the Cartagena Agreement. This is without prejudice to the rights Mexico may have under the Group of Three agreement. Disputes between the two Andean members in relation solely to their obligations under the Group of

Three are to be resolved under the free trade agreement, as are disputes that arise between Mexico and either of the other two parties or among all three parties.

Consultations

The two original GATT articles (XXII and XXIII) from which the GATT/WTO dispute settlement system evolved each require the complaining party to seek bilateral consultations before resorting to a multilateral track to resolve a matter. The party to whom the request for consultations is made must respond with "sympathetic consideration." Except for the Andean Community and CARICOM, hemispheric agreements similarly provide for direct negotiations or consultations upon written request, delivered according to the particular institutional arrangements worked out under the governing agreement.

Implicit in these provisions are the principles of cooperation and good faith; for example, many agreements state that the parties "shall attempt to resolve" the dispute. NAFTA and the NAFTA-like agreements require the parties to "provide sufficient information to enable a full examination of how the actual or proposed measure or other matter might affect the operation" of the agreement. These agreements also provide for protection of confidential information exchanged during the consultations.

NAFTA, the Group of Three, the CACM, Central America-Chile, and Mexico-Northern Triangle (all agreements with three or more parties) allow other parties to the agreement to join the bilateral consultations upon request. In this connection, NAFTA and the Group of Three refer expressly to third parties with a "substantial interest" in the matter. Like the DSU, the Central America-Chile agreement refers expressly to third parties with a "substantial trade interest" in the matter. (Unlike the DSU, however, the NAFTA, Group of Three, and Central America-Chile agreements do not permit the party to whom the request for consultations is made to veto the "claim of substantial interest" as not "well-founded.") MERCOSUR provides that the results of the consultations should be reported to the Common Market Group. The NAFTA, Group of Three, Central America-Dominican Republic, and Mexico-Northern Triangle agreements stipulate that the consulting parties should "seek to avoid any resolution that unfavorably affects the interests of a third Party."

All agreements that provide for consultations stipulate that if a matter is not resolved within a specified period of time, the complaining party may take the dispute to the next settlement stage, such as a commission or arbitral group. CARICOM-Dominican Republic, NAFTA, and all the NAFTA-like agreements, except Bolivia-Mexico and the Group of Three, provide for shorter time periods when perishable products are involved.

The agreements are silent as to the linkage between the subject matter discussed during the consultations and the specific measures and legal basis identified in any eventual complaint to which the terms of reference of a panel or arbitral group refer, and which set forth that body's jurisdiction. This has been a controversial question under the WTO. In some cases defending parties have objected to a panel's exploring issues or arguments that the panel deems relevant but that were not the subject of the original bilateral consultations.

Assisted Settlement

Assisted settlement encompasses good offices, mediation, and conciliation. Traditionally the term refers to the efforts of a neutral third party that helps the parties arrive at their own resolution, as opposed to an arbitral tribunal that issues a binding ruling. As the DSU states (and the 1979 GATT Understanding Regarding Notification, Consultation, Dispute Settlement and Surveillance before that), "the aim of the dispute settlement mechanism is to secure a positive solution to a dispute. A solution mutually acceptable to the parties to the dispute and consistent with the covered agreements is clearly to be preferred." Except for the Andean Community and CARICOM, all the other agreements in the Western Hemisphere provide for a dispute that was not resolved through bilateral negotiations or consultations to be referred to a commission or council or common market group, composed of representatives of the parties to the respective agreement. This commission or council may have recourse to good offices, mediation, or conciliation. Some countries consider that the efforts made at this level by the parties to the agreement constitute assisted settlement. All these agreements stipulate that if assisted settlement efforts do not resolve the dispute within a specified time period, the matter can proceed to arbitration.

Neutral Body (Court, Arbitral Panel/Tribunal)

MERCOSUR, NAFTA, and NAFTA-like agreements that provide for bilateral consultations, assisted settlement, or both also provide that if these efforts do not result in a mutually satisfactory solution within a fixed period, the complaining party may have recourse to an arbitral panel or tribunal to resolve the matter. Under NAFTA and NAFTA-like agreements, the party requests that the commission or council of party representatives convene and establish the dispute resolution panel or tribunal. The Mexico agreements with Bolivia, Chile, Costa Rica, Nicaragua, and Northern Triangle; the Central American agreements with Chile and the Dominican Republic; and the CACM stipulate that the request should identify the measure or other matter and the relevant provisions of the agreement at issue. MERCOSUR allows the complaining party to inform the administrative secretariat of its intention to resort to arbitration.

In the case of the Andean Community, the matter is referred to the Court of Justice by the general secretariat, a member country, or an individual for resolution, as explained earlier in the section on scope. The CARICOM Ministerial Council may refer a matter to an arbitral tribunal.

Composition, Selection, Qualifications

Perhaps the greatest number of articles in the dispute settlement chapters of hemispheric trade agreements are concerned with the composition, qualifications, ethical standards, and selection process for members of the court or arbitral panel/tribunal that will render a decision on the legal merits of a dispute. This is to be expected because confidence in the impartiality and competence of the judges is at the heart of a fair and effective dispute settlement mechanism. Agreements that contain less elaborate institutional arrangements must necessarily agree in advance on a list of preselected qualified arbitrators from whom the parties may eventually select and on a detailed selection process including default procedures.

The Andean Community Court of Justice is composed of five judges, who are nationals of the member countries and are appointed for six-year terms, with the possibility of one renewal. The judges, who are to have high moral reputation and legal expertise, are named from short lists of candidates submitted by each member country and elected by unanimous vote of all countries. The judges are independent and may not engage in other professional activities except teaching. Each judge has a first and second alternate. Judges may be removed at the request of a member country for serious failure in the exercise of duties.

The CARICOM Council may refer a matter to an ad hoc tribunal of three arbitrators. Each party appoints one arbitrator from a list of qualified jurists drawn up and maintained by the secretary general. The two arbitrators in turn appoint a chair, who, as far as practical, is not a national of a party to the dispute. If they fail to do so, the secretary general shall appoint the chair.

Arbitral panels or tribunals are composed of five members under NAFTA and NAFTA-like agreements, three under CACM and the Central America-Chile, Central America-Dominican Republic, and Mexico-Northern Triangle agreements. The parties each nominate to an agreed roster of candidates a certain number of candidates who must have specified qualifications in law or trade agreements, be independent of the parties, and have integrity. Except under the Group of Three, NAFTA, Bolivia-Mexico, and Mexico-Nicaragua agreements, a certain number of roster members must not be nationals of the parties. Roster members serve for a fixed number of years, subject to renewal. Arbitral members are normally or preferably to be chosen from the roster.

Under NAFTA and NAFTA-like agreements, the panel or tribunal is established according to similar provisions for cross-list selection. The parties first seek to agree on a chair. If they are unable to do so within a certain time period, one party, chosen by lot, may select the chair. (The Mexico-Nicaragua agreement goes further to provide that if that party fails to select the chair, the other party chooses.) The chair must not be a national of the naming party. Each party then chooses two arbitrators (or one in case of a three-member tribunal) from the list of the other party. If a party fails to choose an arbitrator(s), then the arbitrator is chosen by lot from the other party's list. Under agreements with the possibility of more than two parties to a dispute, if the parties fail to agree on a chair, one side to the dispute, chosen by lot, selects the chair. The two complaining parties each choose one arbitrator from the list of the party complained against, who in turn chooses two arbitrators, one from each complaining party's list. A party may exercise a peremptory challenge against another's choice of an arbitrator if that individual is not on the roster. In a significant difference with the WTO, this selection process guarantees that at least the majority of the arbitrators or panelists will be nationals of the parties. It also gives the parties a great amount of control in the process and thus depends on cooperation by the parties in the absence of a neutral referee to resolve impasses.

MERCOSUR also has a list selection process. An arbitral tribunal is composed of three arbitrators drawn from a roster of ten designees nominated by each state party to the dispute, half of whom are to be nationals of state parties and the other from third countries. Unlike NAFTA and the NAFTA-like agreements, arbitrators must be chosen from the roster. Moreover, the MERCOSUR administrative secretariat intervenes to break deadlocks whenever the parties cannot agree on a third arbitrator, who may not be a national of either party, or whenever a party fails to appoint an arbitrator within a fixed time period. Parties must also choose an alternate arbitrator. By mutual agreement each party may choose an arbitrator from the list of the other.

The parties to the dispute pay equally for the fees and expenses of the arbitrator tribunals under NAFTA and NAFTA-like agreements. CACM provides that the losing party bears these costs. MERCOSUR provides that the parties must split the costs unless the tribunal decides otherwise.

Terms of Reference, Powers, Basis for Decisionmaking

The Andean Court of Justice may nullify decisions taken by the commission and rulings made by the general secretariat. Before handing down a final ruling, this court, at the request of the claimant, may also order the provisional suspension of a measure if it causes or could cause irreparable harm. It is the court's responsibility to give a pre-judicial interpretation of Andean Community law to ensure that it is uniformly applied in the member countries. The court as well as the general secretariat may use arbitration to settle disputes of a private contractual nature governed by Andean Community law. The court may deal directly with authorities in the member countries whenever it considers such dealings necessary for carrying out its functions.

The Andean Court of Justice is to base its decision on the existing technical documentation, the history of the case, and explanations given by the body that is subject to the recourse. The court may base its ruling on law or equity. The general secretariat may also rule on the basis of equity.

Under the Protocol of Brasilia, MERCOSUR state parties have recognized as "obligatory, *ipso facto* and without need of special agreement the jurisdiction of the arbitral tribunal" established to hear and resolve a case. A tribunal may order provisional measures at the request of a party, if there exist well-founded presumptions that the continuation of the situation could result in irreparable and serious harm. An arbitral tribunal also adopts its own rules of procedures.

The MERCOSUR arbitral tribunal is directed to decide the case on the basis of the provisions of the MERCOSUR treaties, the decisions of the Common Market Council, and the resolutions of the Common Market Group as well as on the principles and provisions of international law relevant to the matter. If the parties agree, the tribunal may also decide on the basis of equity.

The terms of reference of arbitral panels or tribunals under NAFTA or NAFTA-like agreements are to examine in the light of the relevant provisions of the trade agreement the matter referred to the commission/council (as set out in the request for a meeting of that body) and to make findings, determinations, and recommendations as provided in the agreement. Except for the Group of Three, these agreements also stipulate that a complaining party that wishes to argue nonviolation nullification or impairment must so indicate in the panel's mandate. Further, a disputing party may ask that the terms of reference also direct the panel to make a finding "as to the degree of adverse trade effects on any Party of any measure found not to conform with the obligations of the Agreement or to have caused nullification or impairment." Under the WTO, compliance panels make such determinations, but not dispute resolution panels.

NAFTA and the NAFTA-like agreements (with the exception of the Group of Three) allow panels to seek information and technical advice from any person or body that it deems appropriate. NAFTA and the Canada-Chile agreement, however, require the parties to agree to this. Unless the disputing parties disapprove, and subject to such terms and conditions as they may agree, NAFTA and the Canada-Chile and Chile-Mexico agreements also provide that panels may request a written report of a scientific review board on any factual issue concerning environmental, health, safety, or other scientific matters raised by a party in a proceeding.

NAFTA and the Canada-Chile and Central America-Chile free trade agreements provide that unless the disputing parties otherwise agree, the panel shall base its report on the submissions and arguments of the parties and on any information from scientific review boards. The Mexico-Northern Triangle and CACM agreements also provide that the tribunal's report shall be based on the parties' submissions and arguments but do not specify that the parties could prevent the arbitral tribunal from taking into consideration any information or technical advice that it has received. NAFTA also states that the parties shall interpret and apply the provisions in the light of the objectives of the agreement and in accordance with applicable rules of international law.

Rules of Procedures, Public Access, and Ethical Codes

The Andean Court of Justice, which sits in Quito, has extensive by-laws and internal rules of procedure that, among other things, regulate the calculation of time periods and the process for submitting claims and evidence, issuing rulings, and requesting review. Judges are required to take an oath of office, swearing to carry out their job conscientiously and completely impartially, to keep court discussions secret, and to fulfill all the duties inherent in their role. Hearings are public, unless the court decides otherwise. Its deliberations are secret. There are procedures for removing a judge for enumerated serious offenses.

Upon being appointed to a specific case, experts on the MERCOSUR roster of arbitrators must sign a statement committing themselves to fulfill their duties with technical independence, honesty, and impartiality; declaring that they have no personal interest in the matter; and promising to respect the privileged nature of any information made available in the proceedings, of conclusions, and of the opinion. The Protocol of Brasilia provides that the arbitral tribunal should adopt its own rules of procedure guaranteeing a full hearing to each party and expeditious proceedings. The tribunal's seat is to be located in one of the state parties. A tribunal is required to render its decision within sixty days, a period that can be extended for an additional thirty days from the time the chair was appointed. Decisions are adopted by majority vote. State parties may choose the person or persons who will represent them before the tribunal and can designate advisors to defend their rights. An administrative secretariat provides support for the arbitration procedure.

Under NAFTA and NAFTA-like agreements, the panel's hearings, deliberations, initial report, and all written submissions to and communications with the panel are confidential. Parties must be given at least one hearing before the panel as well as the opportunity to provide initial and rebuttal written submissions. The agreements also provide for establishing model rules of procedures. The NAFTA Commission approved very detailed model rules of procedures regulating all aspects of the conduct of arbitral proceedings. Unless the parties agree otherwise, the panel is to conduct its proceedings in accordance with these rules. The panel's hearings are held in the capital of the defending party. Panelists, their assistants, representatives and advisers to the parties, and the secretariat may attend hearings. Advisers may not address the panel and may not have a financial or personal interest in the proceeding. The panel may not engage in ex parte communications with the parties. NAFTA also has a very elaborate code of conduct for panelists and staff with disclosure obligations. Similar detailed rules of procedures and ethical rules are contained in the Mexico-Northern Triangle agreement.

Third Parties

Under the Andean Court's by-laws, a member country or the general secretariat who are not parties to a suit may provide information or arguments to the court at any stage of its proceedings before it passes judgment.

Under NAFTA and the Group of Three, a third party that considers it has a substantial interest in the matter is entitled to join as a complaining party on delivery of written notice no later than seven days after the establishment of a panel. If a third party does not join as a complaining party, it is still entitled to attend all hearings, to make written and oral submissions to the panel, and to receive the written submissions of the disputing parties. Moreover, the third party "normally" shall refrain from initiating or continuing a dispute settlement procedure under the free trade agreement or the WTO "on grounds that are substantially equivalent to those available to that party under [the free trade agreement] regarding the same matter in the absence of a significant change in economic or commercial circumstances."

Under the Central America-Chile, Mexico-Northern Triangle and CACM agreements, a third party, upon written notification, has a right to attend hearings, to be heard, and to make and receive written submissions. Central America-Chile and CACM further provide that third party submissions should be reflected in the final report of the arbitral group. Under CACM, if a party decides not to participate as a third party, it shall abstain from initiating any other dispute settlement proceeding on the same matter, in the absence of a significant change in economic or commercial circumstances.

Preliminary Report

NAFTA and all the NAFTA-like agreements except CACM provide for the arbitral tribunal to issue a preliminary report with findings of fact, a decision as to whether the measure is inconsistent or causes (nonviolation) nullification or impairment, and a draft conclusion. The parties may make written comments on this report within two weeks, and the arbitral group may reconsider its preliminary findings in the light of the written comments.

Final Determination and Implementation

Under the by-laws of the Andean Court, a judgment of the court must contain certain specified elements, including the facts, a summary of arguments by both parties, the legal grounds on which the judgement was based, and the ruling. In a nullity judgment regarding a disputed commission decision, secretariat ruling, or convention, the court must indicate the effects of the ruling over time and allocate payment of costs by the parties. The body whose action has been nullified by the court must adopt the necessary provisions to comply with the judgment. In a judgment of noncompliance, the court will dictate the measures that the member country must adopt to execute the judgment. The member country is obligated to comply within ninety days. The court may also amend or expand its judgment within five days after it is read at a public hearing. A party may request clarification of points in the judgment that it considers to be ambiguous. The Andean Court may review rulings made in a noncompliance action at a party's request, on the basis of some fact that could have had a decisive influence on the results, provided that the fact was unknown by the party at the time the ruling was issued.

Under CARICOM, when the council or an arbitral tribunal finds that any benefit conferred on a member state is being frustrated, the council, by majority vote, may make recommendations to the member state concerned. The council may also authorize a member state to suspend its obligations as appropriate.

Under MERCOSUR rules, the decision by an arbitral tribunal must contain certain specified elements, such as a summary of the proceedings and arguments by the parties, findings of fact and law, and the proportion of costs to be covered by each party. The decisions of the arbitral tribunal cannot be appealed and are binding on the parties to the dispute upon notification and will be deemed by the parties to have the effect of *res judicata*. A party may seek clarification of the decision or of the manner of compliance within fifteen days of notification. The tribunal may suspend compliance with its decision while it deliberates on the request.

Under NAFTA and the NAFTA-like agreements, a panel shall issue its final report within thirty days of presenting its initial report. The CACM does not provide for an interim report; the final report must be issued within thirty days of the establishment of the tribunal. NAFTA and the Canada-Chile agreement allow the parties to agree to a different time period. Additionally under NAFTA, the parties have a reasonable period of time to transmit the final report to the commission along with any views that a party desires to add. Under NAFTA and the NAFTA-like agreements, the report is published within fifteen days, unless the commission decides otherwise. On receiving the final report, the disputing parties under NAFTA and the Canada-Chile agreement must agree on how to resolve the dispute "which normally shall conform with the determination and recommendations of the panel" and inform the secretariat of any agreement. "Wherever possible, the resolution shall be non-implementation or removal" of an inconsistent measure or measure causing nullification or impairment. In other words, the decision of the panel essentially empowers the winning party to negotiate a resolution with the losing party. Under the other NAFTA-like agreements, however, the final resolution of the tribunal is explicitly binding. These agreements require the parties to comply with the terms and time periods specified in the final report. Chile-Mexico provides that the parties may agree to different terms and time periods than those set out in the final report. The CACM and Central America-Chile agreements, moreover, state that there must be compliance with the final report within six months after it is notified. The NAFTA-like agreements allow the panel to suggest adjustments that the parties to the dispute may deem mutually satisfactory.

Suspension and Retaliation

The Andean Court may authorize a complaining country or other member country to suspend benefits under the Cartagena Agreement against a member country that the court rules has failed to comply with its judgment. Affected natural or legal persons may have recourse to local courts in case of noncompliance by member countries.

If a CARICOM member state fails or is unable to comply with a council recommendation, the council, by majority vote, may authorize any member state to suspend the application of obligations against the noncomplying member state.

Under NAFTA and the Canada-Chile agreement, when a panel determines that a measure is inconsistent, and the parties have not reached agreement on a satisfactory resolution within thirty days of receiving the final report, the complaining party is automatically authorized to suspend benefits of equivalent effect until such time as the parties have resolved the dispute. In the other NAFTA-like agreements, the complaining party may suspend benefits only when the arbitral tribunal determines that the party complained against has not complied with all of the terms of the final ruling. Under NAFTA and the NAFTA-like agreements, the complaining party may suspend benefits in the same sector as that affected by the measure or "when this is not practicable or effective" in another sector (this provision is similar to the DSU). The party complained against may request a panel to determine whether the level of benefits suspended is "manifestly excessive." The panel must present its determination within sixty days after the last panelist is selected or such other period as the parties agree. The suspension may continue while the panel deliberates.

Dispute Settlement in the FTAA Negotiations

Ministers responsible for trade established the following objectives for the FTAA negotiations on dispute settlement:

—to establish fair, transparent, and effective mechanisms for dispute settlement among FTAA countries, taking into account, among other things, the WTO Understanding on Rules and Procedures Governing the Settlement of Disputes; and

—to design ways to facilitate and promote the use of arbitration and other alternative dispute settlement mechanisms to solve private trade controversies within the framework of the FTAA.

The Negotiating Group on Dispute Settlement (NGDS) has concentrated its work on defining the procedures to govern the settlement of disputes between and among parties arising under the FTAA agreement, specifically on general procedures for settling government-to-government disputes. Pursuant to the Toronto Ministerial Declaration (paragraph 9), the group finalized its draft report, including a draft chapter on dispute settlement, in November 2000.

The NGDS completed the work begun by an earlier working group on an inventory on dispute settlement mechanisms. That inventory has been posted on the FTAA home page on the Internet.[1]

Pursuant to its objectives set out under the San José Declaration, the NGDS approved a document prepared on its behalf by the OAS Trade

1. "Inventory of Dispute Settlement Mechanisms, Procedures and Legal Texts Established in Existing Trade and Integration Agreements, Treaties and Arrangements in the Hemisphere and in the WTO," available at (www.ftaa-alca.oas.org/cp_disp/English/dsm_toc.asp).

Unit which contains the text of various international conventions on arbitration and the legal status of the conventions in each of the countries in the hemisphere (signature, ratification, reservations).[2] Also posted on the FTAA web page is information provided by individual FTAA countries on their respective laws and rules governing private commercial arbitration and other alternative dispute resolution methods, including the institutions that provide commercial arbitration services.

Challenges for the Future

Countries come to the FTAA negotiating table armed with their experiences under the dispute settlement systems described earlier. Yet designing a dispute settlement mechanism for the FTAA will require more than copying and pasting provisions from familiar trade agreements. A mechanism suitable for thirty-four countries of diverse levels of development will necessarily be more complex, including institutionally, than a model suited for two or three or even four countries. It will also be different from the model used by one hundred and forty countries, which are less integrated economically with one another than is the ambition for the FTAA countries.

Some of the specific issues that the drafters of the FTAA dispute settlement chapter must address are

—the interrelationship between the FTAA agreement and the regional trade agreements, with the particular implications this has for choice of forum, applicable law, selection of defendants—all members of a customs union or free trade area or only some at choice of complainant—and third party rights;

—the extent a national of an FTAA country may have direct recourse against another FTAA country (investment or other matters);

—the extent of public access to submissions and hearings and of nongovernmental participation in dispute settlement proceedings (by submitting *amicus curiae* briefs, for example, or acting as private advisors to governments or as technical experts);

—in making its determination, the value that the neutral body should accord to precedents, the principles of international law, or equity (*ex aequo et bono*);

---

2. "International Conventions Governing Private Commercial Arbitration: Panama, New York, Montevideo, and ISCID Conventions," available at ⟨www.ftaa-alca.org/busfac/canale.asp⟩.

—the precedent value that should be accorded the final determination of the neutral body; and

—the explicit binding nature of the final determination of the neutral body or the consequences or effects that will result from the determination.

It is beyond the scope of this article to elaborate on the many, complex issues listed here. Suffice it to mention one aspect of particular significance in the construction of an FTAA dispute settlement system; namely, the treatment of third parties. Should the drafters of the FTAA dispute settlement chapter accord a complaining party the exclusive right to choose its defendant(s), what procedural rights should drafters accord to third parties having an interest in the matter? This question will be especially critical when the measure at issue was taken pursuant to another free trade area or customs union agreement. Other members of that agreement that are not named as parties complained against in the FTAA case would want procedural rights equivalent to those enjoyed by the parties to the dispute. In such circumstances, should the line dividing the parties to the dispute from the third parties be maintained regarding issues such as attendance at all hearings, access to all submissions, receipt of the preliminary and final report, right to seek clarification, or right of retaliation? Also if in the interest of judicial economy, a party to the dispute should be prevented from having recourse to FTAA dispute settlement if the party has already pursued the same matter in another forum, should a similar ban be imposed on a participating third party? Should the ban cover the same cause of action but not extend to different legal grounds involving the same matter? What about a nonparticipating third party? Moreover, what kind of institutional and administrative support should be established if every FTAA dispute settlement proceeding potentially involves thirty-four parties?

In a Free Trade Area of the Americas superimposed over a mosaic of subregional free trade areas and customs unions, one can readily appreciate the complexity of fully taking into account the reality of hemispheric economic integration in crafting procedural mechanisms to solve trade disputes.

PART IV

The Road Ahead:
The Free Trade Area
of the Americas

JOSÉ MANUEL SALAZAR-XIRINACHS

14 | *The FTAA Process: From Miami 1994 to Quebec 2001*

A torch for the creation of a hemispheric-wide free trade area stretching from the Yukon to Patagonia was lit at the First Summit of the Americas, held in Miami in December, 1994. There, the leaders of thirty-four of the thirty-five nations in the Western Hemisphere—all except Cuba—agreed on the following: *except Cuba*

> Our continued economic progress depends on sound economic policies, sustainable development, and dynamic private sectors. A key to prosperity is trade without barriers, without subsidies, without unfair trade practices, and with an increasing stream of productive investments. Eliminating impediments to market access for goods and services among our countries will foster our economic growth. A growing world economy will also enhance our domestic prosperity. Free trade and increased economic integration are key factors for raising standards of living, improving the working conditions of people in the Americas and better protecting the environment. We, therefore, resolve to begin immediately to construct the "Free Trade Area of the Americas" [FTAA]. . . . We further resolve to conclude the negotiation of the "Free Trade Area of the Americas" no later than 2005, and agree that concrete progress toward the attainment of this objective will be made by the end of this century.[1]

1. Miami Summit of the Americas, Declaration of Principles.

279

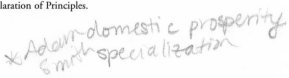
Adam domestic prosperity Smith specialization

The next three years served as a preparatory period, and in April 1998, at the Second Summit of the Americas in Santiago, Chile, the leaders decided to initiate formal negotiations leading toward the creation of the FTAA:

> Today, we direct our Ministers Responsible for Trade to begin negotiations for the FTAA, in accordance with the March 1998 Ministerial Declaration of San José. We reaffirm our determination to conclude the negotiation of the FTAA no later than 2005, and to make concrete progress by the end of the century. The FTAA agreement will be balanced, comprehensive, WTO-consistent and constitute a single undertaking.[2]

Since then, negotiations have proceeded actively. As leaders prepare for the Third Summit of the Americas, to be held in Quebec in April 2001, the torch is burning brightly, and despite the ambitious nature of this undertaking and the important obstacles that must be overcome, there are reasons to be optimistic that the FTAA agreement will be concluded on schedule. With a combined population of 800 million and a gross domestic product of $9 trillion, the FTAA would be the largest free trade area in the world and one of the most ambitious integration schemes in modern history.

When negotiations were launched in 1998, multiple factors converged to make the idea of creating an FTAA highly compelling. In addition to geopolitical, strategic, and collective security considerations, these included global business and technological realities, the new brand of "open regionalism" in trade and integration policies adopted by Latin American and Caribbean countries, and the advantages that these countries perceive in a rules-based world trading system. Additionally, the countries of the region had come a long way toward putting their economic fundamentals and macroeconomic houses in order.

Since mid-1998 the FTAA negotiators have achieved impressive concrete and detailed progress, and it could be argued that the negotiations are precisely where they should be at this stage. In this respect, it is quite extraordinary that in the face of the 1998–99 economic crisis, the Latin American and Caribbean countries did not resort to protectionist measures but instead continued to work on revitalizing their subregional integration arrangements, proactively negotiating bilateral free trade agreements, and remaining fully engaged in the FTAA negotiations. The FTAA process

---

2. Santiago Summit of the Americas, Declaration of Principles.

is also remarkable in that it has engaged in modern trade talks some of the richest industrialized economies with some of the smallest and, in some cases, least-developed countries in the world.

This chapter reviews the FTAA negotiations to date and attempts to shed light on progress realized so far in the hemispheric integration process. It summarizes the background to the FTAA process, underlines its achievements as well as main benefits, and analyzes the outstanding challenges that must be dealt with to bring the negotiations to a successful conclusion.

FTAA Process

At the Summit of the Americas in Miami, the thirty-four democratically elected heads of state and government in the Western Hemisphere signed both a declaration of principles, entitled "Partnership for the Development and Prosperity of the Americas," and a plan of action. The objectives of this new partnership are to preserve and strengthen the community of democracies of the Americas, to promote prosperity through economic integration and free trade, to eradicate poverty and discrimination in the hemisphere, and to guarantee sustainable development and conserve the natural environment for future generations. To achieve these four basic objectives, the leaders approved twenty-three initiatives in the plan of action, one of which is the creation of the Free Trade Area of the Americas.

The leaders acknowledged the asymmetries in the levels of development and size of economies existing in the hemisphere and stated their support for full and rapid implementation of multilateral trade rules and disciplines resulting from the Uruguay Round. They agreed that the FTAA agreement should be balanced, comprehensive, and consistent with World Trade Organization (WTO) agreements and that it constitute a single undertaking.

During the preparatory phase (from December 1994 to April 1998), the FTAA had clearly defined mechanisms of implementation—ministerial meetings, vice-ministerial meetings, hemispheric working groups, and the Tripartite Committee (consisting of the Organization of American States, the Inter-American Development Bank, and the Economic Commission for Latin America and the Caribbean). As instructed in the plan of action, trade ministers defined the technical work program to be undertaken in preparation for the negotiations. As of December 2000 the ministers had met five times. During the first meeting, held in Denver in June 1995, the

ministers set up seven working groups on the following subjects; market
access; customs procedures and rules of origin; investment; standards and
technical barriers to trade; sanitary and phytosanitary measures; subsidies,
antidumping and countervailing duties; and smaller economies.

In the second ministerial meeting, held in Cartagena, Colombia, in
March 1996, the trade ministers assessed the work done by the seven working groups and launched four additional groups: government procurement;
intellectual property rights; services; and competition policy. At the third
ministerial meeting in Belo Horizonte, Brazil, in May 1997, the ministers
took note of the reports and documents presented by the working groups
and created a working group on dispute settlement. At this meeting, ministers agreed that they would determine at the Fourth Ministerial Meeting
how the negotiations would proceed, including such features as their objectives, approaches, structure, and venue.

At the fourth ministerial meeting in San José, Costa Rica, in March
1998, the thirty-four ministers agreed on the Declaration of San José, which
defined the general objectives and principles of the FTAA, the specific objectives by issue area, and the structure, organization, and other substantive
and managerial aspects that would guide the negotiations.[3] Ministers also
agreed to recommend to the heads of state and government that they initiate the formal negotiations of the FTAA during the second Summit of the
Americas, to be held in Santiago, Chile, in April 1998. The recommendation was reflected in the Declaration of the Second Summit of the Americas, where the negotiations were officially launched.

The agreed structure for the negotiations consists of a predetermined
rotation of the chairmanship of the negotiating process as well as dates and
venues for ministerial meetings all the way to 2005, a Trade Negotiations
Committee at the vice-ministerial level, and nine negotiating groups (table
14-1). It was also agreed that the meetings of the negotiating groups would
be held in a single venue, which would rotate as follows: Miami (from May
1, 1998, to February 28, 2001), Panama City (March 1, 2001, to February
28, 2003), Mexico City (March 1, 2003, to December 31, 2004).

An administrative secretariat was created to provide logistical and administrative support to the negotiations, to provide translation services for
documents and interpretation during the deliberations, to keep the official
documents of the negotiations, and to publish and distribute documents.

---

3. The San José Ministerial Declaration of 1998 may be compared with the Punta Del Este Declaration of 1986, which launched the Uruguay Round of Multilateral Trade Negotiations.

Table 14-1. *Rotation of Chairs, Dates, and Venue of*
FTAA Ministerial Meetings

Position	5/1/98–10/31/99	11/1/99–4/30/01	5/1/01–10/31/02	11/1/02–12/31/04[a]
Chair	Canada	Argentina	Ecuador	Brazil, United States
Vice-chair	Argentina	Ecuador	Chile	Brazil, United States

a. Brazil and the United States will jointly hold both the chairmanship and the vice-chairmanship.

The administrative secretariat is to be located in the same venue as the meetings of the negotiating groups.

Trade Negotiations Committee and the Negotiating Groups

The Trade Negotiations Committee plays the central role in managing the FTAA negotiations. This role was recently reaffirmed in the Toronto Declaration of Trade Ministers (November 1999), which stated that the committee should guide the work of the negotiating groups and the three other groups and committees created by the San José Declaration, ensure transparency in the negotiations, oversee the administrative secretariat, oversee the implementation of approved business facilitation measures and identify new business facilitation measures, address issues that the negotiating groups could not resolve after due diligence, and ensure that progress is made in all of the negotiating groups and areas of negotiation. The committee is to meet at least three times between ministerial meetings—more often if required.

The initial nine negotiating groups included market access (covering tariffs, nontariff measures, customs procedures, safeguards, rules of origin, and standards and technical barriers to trade); investment; services; government procurement; dispute settlement; agriculture; intellectual property rights; subsidies, antidumping, and countervailing duties; and competition policy. Three nonnegotiating special committees were created as well: a Consultative Group on Smaller Economies; a Committee of Government Representatives on the Participation of Civil Society; and a Joint Government-Private Sector Committee of Experts on Electronic Commerce.

The three special nonnegotiating groups and committees were added to meet the concerns and interests felt by many participants in their respective area of the FTAA process. As spelled out by the San José Declaration, the role of the Consultative Group on Smaller Economies is to "follow the

FTAA process, keeping under review the concerns and interests of the smaller economies" and "to bring to the attention of the [Trade Negotiations Committee] the issues of concern to the smaller economies and make recommendations to address these issues."

In recognition of the interests and concerns of different sectors of society in the FTAA, ministers established the Committee of Government Representatives on Civil Society and asked it to receive the inputs of civil society, analyze them, and present the range of views to ministers for their consideration. The mission of the Joint Government-Private Sector Committee of Experts on Electronic Commerce is to examine a number of issues relevant to electronic commerce, including an examination of the Internet readiness of the FTAA nations and ways to deal with electronic commerce in the context of the negotiations (box 14-1).

Duties of the Tripartite Committee

The Tripartite Committee was asked to contribute technical, analytical, and logistical assistance to the FTAA process. In practice, this support has included assisting governments in compiling country and region-specific inventories of laws and regulations as well as trade and tariff data, analyzing existing trade-related rules and regulations, and preparing studies and background papers in the negotiating areas. The Tripartite Committee's functions have also involved supporting the chairs of the different groups according to their requests; working with the FTAA administrative secretariat to coordinate the translation, timing, and distribution of documents for meetings; managing the official FTAA web site on behalf of the countries; providing financial support to the administrative secretariat, and conducting training and educational activities for countries.[4]

Progress in the First Phases

Under Canada's chairmanship FTAA negotiators achieved significant progress during the first phase of the negotiations—the eighteen months from May 1998 to November 1999, the date of the fifth ministerial meet-

---

4. In the Toronto Declaration trade ministers recognized the analytical, technical, and financial support provided by the institutions composing the Tripartite Committee and acknowledged this support as being essential to the conduct of the negotiations. They requested the Tripartite Committee to continue providing such assistance for FTAA-related matters.

ing in Toronto. At this meeting the trade ministers lauded the "considerable progress" negotiators had made in this first phase.

Starting in September 1998, each of the nine negotiating groups has been convening regularly in Miami. Each round of negotiating group meetings brings together more than nine hundred trade negotiators from the thirty-four participating countries and constitutes an extraordinary effort of political will, technical talent, and strategic positioning of the participating nations. The process has generated comprehensive databases, compendiums of relevant laws and regulations, and other background information necessary for the negotiations. This process has greatly enhanced the transparency regarding existing trade and market rules in the hemisphere.

Finally, in terms of process it is important to note that several subgroups of countries speak with one voice at the negotiating table. These include the Andean Community, CARICOM (the Caribbean Community and Common Market), and MERCOSUR (the Common Market of the South). Each one of these subregional groups presents its positions jointly and following intense consultations among its members. The Caribbean has recently created a new structure to formulate and represent the views of CARICOM countries in international trade negotiations, and this Caribbean Regional Negotiating Machinery speaks on its members' behalf in the FTAA.

Accomplishments of the FTAA Negotiations

As of early 2001 the most important achievement of the FTAA process has been the development of an initial draft text for the FTAA agreement. The drafting happened in two stages. During the first stage, the nine negotiating groups developed annotated outlines for each of their respective subject areas. This work was guided by the specific objectives set out in the San José Declaration and the work program that vice ministers drew up in Buenos Aires in June 1998.

Based on the progress reported in these annotated outlines, the trade ministers, at their November 1999 Toronto meeting, instructed the negotiating groups "to prepare a draft text of their respective chapters . . . a text that is comprehensive in scope and that contains the texts on which consensus was reached and places the texts on which consensus could not be reached between brackets."

In addition, the trade ministers instructed the Trade Negotiations Committee to assemble the texts provided by the negotiating groups, to prepare

Box 14-1. *Electronic Commerce in the Process of Hemispheric Integration*

Following a relatively late start, the growth of the Internet in Latin America has recently gained momentum, to the extent that Internet access is growing faster in the region than anywhere else in the world. Today some 8.5 million people in the region use the Internet. The Latin American Internet population is expected to number between 27 million and 34 million users by 2003 and 66 million users by 2005. This figure still represents only 12 percent of Latin America's population of more than 400 million and compares with a current connectivity rate above 40 percent in North America.

After the United States and Canada, Brazil has achieved the highest connectivity rate to date in the hemisphere, with 45 percent of Latin America's total Internet population and around 88 percent of all electronic commerce transactions in Latin America. Mexico is the second-largest market, with almost 11 percent of the region's users. Other countries, such as Argentina, Chile, and Uruguay, are adding users at a fast pace. Recent studies estimate that the total value of the electronic commerce in Latin America will be between $8.5 billion and $16 billion by 2003.

The region has yet to overcome some barriers that would allow it to achieve the kind of Internet penetration levels that now prevail in North America and Europe and to ensure that the "digital divide" between and within countries does not continue to grow. The telecommunications infrastructure in much of Latin America is ill equipped to handle the high demand for data transmission services. The cost of Internet access remains high in most of the region, although competition and deregulation in the telecommunications sector are helping to lower costs of access. The basic equipment needed to access the Internet, such as computers and modems,

a report for the ministers' consideration at their April 2001 meeting in Buenos Aires, and to begin discussions of the overall architecture of an FTAA agreement (that is, general and institutional aspects). During the year 2000 each negotiating group focused on developing a draft text. This ambitious goal resulted in considerable forward progress for the FTAA. All negotiating groups were able to comply with the mandate, and the Trade Negotiations Committee is expected to present the first consolidated draft text of the agreement to ministers in April 2001.

The second most significant accomplishment of the FTAA negotiations, in line with the objective of achieving concrete progress in the nego-

must be within the reach of the majority of the population, yet individual ownership of personal computers is out of the reach of many people in the region.

Recognizing the potential benefits of electronic commerce, as well as the hurdles that remain to be overcome, trade ministers meeting in San José in 1998 agreed to create a Joint Government–Private Sector Committee of Experts on Electronic Commerce ("the Joint Committee") as part of the FTAA process. The committee was asked to make recommendations on how to increase and broaden the benefits to be derived from the electronic marketplace at the next ministerial meeting. In Toronto in November 1999, following a year of meetings in which private sector representatives worked alongside government representatives from participating countries, the Joint Committee presented its recommendations.[1] The report reflects the consensus reached in the Joint Committee on the principles to guide the development of a regulatory framework to support the growth of electronic commerce in the Western Hemisphere.

In Toronto, trade ministers extended the mandate of the Joint Committee, asking it to deliver a set of recommendations to ministers at the next FTAA ministerial meeting in Argentina in April 2001. The Joint Committee carried out its work under the chairmanship of Barbados during the first phase of meetings, and under the chairmanship of Uruguay in the second phase.

1. The report is available on the Internet at www.ftaa-alca.org/spcomm/commec_e.asp#mandate.

tiations by 2000, is an agreement on specific business facilitation measures. At their 1999 meeting, the thirty-four trade ministers agreed to implement, by the target date of the next ministerial meeting, eighteen business facilitation measures. Eight of these are customs-related measures, set out in annex II of the Toronto Ministerial Declaration. They involve temporary importation or admission of certain goods related to business travelers; express shipments; simplified procedures for low-value shipments; compatible electronic data interchange systems and common data elements; harmonized commodity description and coding systems; the elaboration of a hemispheric information guide on customs procedures; codes of conduct for customs officials; and methodology for risk analysis and targeting. These business facilitation measures are likely to generate more confidence among business communities in the hemisphere and further promote their active involvement in the negotiating process (box 14-2). To support the implementation of these measures, particularly in smaller economies, the Inter-American Development Bank/Multilateral Investment Fund approved a $5 million technical cooperation project in August 2000.

With respect to transparency-related measures, the Toronto Ministerial Declaration instructed that several important inventories and databases be published, disseminated, and periodically updated.[5] It also directed that information "on government regulations, procedures, and competent authorities" be made "more accessible, including via the use of Internet links to the FTAA home page." As a result, the Tripartite Committee developed a new section in the official FTAA home page that contains hyperlinks to nearly eight hundred websites, in all countries of the hemisphere, where detailed country information can be found on each one of the relevant negotiating areas.

Third, the FTAA process has also achieved a great deal in the area of technical assistance.[6] It has generated an increase in the demand for and supply of technical cooperation. There has been an explosive growth in a large variety of training activities, conferences, seminars, and forums organized by governments, think tanks, private sector organizations, and international organizations. The Tripartite Committee and members of the national negotiating teams have organized or participated in many of these programs, which have ranged in scope from increased awareness about globalization, free trade, and trade negotiations in general to specialized training and capacity-building programs on specific issues relevant for trade negotiations and implementation of trade commitments. Moreover, the negotiating sessions themselves have proven to be valuable training grounds. As Sidney Weintraub has pointed out, "The best way to learn about the dynamics of a trade negotiation is from actual experience and many small countries have not given their officials much opportunity for this learning-by-negotiating. The general assessment of persons connected with the ongoing FTAA exercise is that the process itself has been the most valuable teacher."[7]

5. See Annex III of the Toronto Ministerial Declaration.
6. Weintraub (1999); Salicrup and Vergara (2000).
7. Weintraub (1999, p. 2).

Box 14-2. *Importance of Business Facilitation Measures*

Despite the enormous progress made by Latin American countries in liberal-izing their economies and improving their economic fundamentals, there remains a tremendous scope for reducing the costs of doing business in the hemisphere. The business environment in the hemisphere is characterized by very large transactions costs including imperfect information; very un-even distribution of access to information; lack of transparency; diversity and inconsistencies in regulatory frameworks; costly and protracted proce-dures in the areas of customs, new investment undertakings, and the estab-lishment of new enterprises; and inconsistent certification procedures. These realities affect the everyday operation of businesses by, at best, producing inefficiencies and costs for business and, at worst, functioning as real disin-centives and insurmountable barriers to entrepreneurship.

These costs and disincentives often introduce a bias particularly against small and medium-size enterprises that do not have the resources to finance the information and transactions costs of doing business across a diversity of national conditions. Therefore, business facilitation measures have not only an economic, but also a strong social and equity rationale. The realization of these potential benefits is one of the major reasons why trade ministers at their Toronto ministerial meeting not only agreed to an initial package of business facilitation measures, but also agreed to make business facilitation a permanent exercise side by side with the formal negotiating process.

Significant steps have also been taken within the Consultative Group on Smaller Economies to assess needs for technical assistance, to build da-tabases on the demand and supply of trade-related technical assistance and training opportunities, and to develop a framework to increase transpar-ency and facilitate technical assistance flows among the countries of the hemisphere. One of the databases generated by the process was an inven-tory of training opportunities available in the FTAA-relevant areas of trade policy and negotiation for both government officials and the private sector in the region. This "Trade Education Database" contains information on more than two hundred and fifty trade-related education programs in eigh-teen countries of the Americas and is now available on the FTAA website under the Technical Assistance section.[8]

8. (www.ftaa-alca.org/trt/searchted.asp).

In Toronto ministers directly requested the Tripartite Committee to
—explore opportunities for providing technical assistance to facilitate
the organization of an inventory of measures that affect trade in services
and to establish a work program to improve statistics on trade in services;
—explore opportunities for providing technical assistance to help countries, where necessary, establish national contact points that could provide
information on national legislation and other measures affecting trade in
services in the hemisphere; and
—assist FTAA governments through the mechanism of the Consultative Group on Smaller Economies to identify possible sources of technical
assistance based on the existing database prepared by the Tripartite Committee and the needs as identified by countries.

No doubt, technical cooperation efforts will continue to grow in the
future as the additional demands stemming from active participation in
the multilateral as well as regional negotiations become apparent.

In summary, the main substantive achievements of the FTAA process
so far are the development of an initial draft text for the FTAA agreement,
the adoption of a significant group of business facilitation measures, and
an increase in trade-related technical cooperation initiatives and capacity
building. Although much remains to be done in these three areas, these
developments constitute significant and concrete results from the negotiating process.

Benefits of the FTAA

The major benefits of the FTAA process will accrue to countries when
this agreement comes into effect in 2005. Among other things, these advantages will include "dynamic" benefits associated with increased investment and trade flows, technology transfer, learning effects, and other
externalities, as well as reduced uncertainty concerning market access and
macroeconomic stability.[9]

Too much emphasis on the 2005 deadline and the final benefits runs
the risk, however, of overlooking several important benefits or positive externalities that the FTAA negotiating process has already generated. These
benefits include the strategic direction given to economic reform, with at-

9. For overviews of the costs and benefits of regional integration, as well as of the economic and
political rationale for the FTAA from the perspective of different actors, see Salazar-Xirinachs and
Lizano (1992); Devlin and Ffrench-Davis (1999); Dominguez (1999); Devlin, Estevadeordal, and
Garay (1999); and Hufbauer, Schott, and Kotschwar (1999).

tendant "lock-in" effects; positive signaling to investors; improved compliance with WTO obligations, renewed vigor in subregional integration efforts, positive effects on private sector behavior, competitive strategies, and networking; increased mutual knowledge and trust among negotiators; and, as discussed above, stepped-up technical assistance for trade reform.

Economic Reform, "Lock-in" Effects, and Signaling

Regional integration is not new in Latin America and the Caribbean, but the FTAA has helped to revitalize the region's engagement in trade negotiations and in respective national policy discussions under modern principles and commitments. This engagement, which has involved both the public and private sectors, helps give both a sense of direction and a sense of urgency to economic policy reform. From the trade regime to domestic regulations, from business facilitation to transparency in rules and procedures, the FTAA process reinforces the strategic orientation of economic policies and provides a positive feedback effect on national policy dialogue and priorities. Economic policy "learning effects" should not be underestimated either. A large amount of information sharing and benchmarking of economic policies and regulatory frameworks takes place naturally as part of the FTAA negotiations and related technical assistance and training activities.

Modern regional and bilateral agreements throughout Latin America and the Caribbean have a "lock-in" effect on domestic market-oriented economic reforms. This reinforcing effect can be expected to grow even larger after the 2005 FTAA commitments come into effect. Full engagement in multilateral and regional trade talks helps explain why countries in the region did not resort to protectionist measures in the face of the 1998–99 economic downturn and crisis but rather stayed the course of economic reform and in some cases benefited from a surprisingly rapid economic recovery.

Finally, active engagement in the FTAA talks has an important signaling effect for foreign investors and financial markets about the intentions of governments and the future prospects for the investment climate and business opportunities in specific countries.

Energizing the Building Blocks

The FTAA talks have reinforced the political determination of countries to deepen and widen their regional agreements. Some countries see greater subregional integration as a way of strengthening their hand at the negotiating table with larger economies. Others see negotiations with economies not too dissimilar in size or degree of development as a training ground for the more ambitious FTAA undertaking. Yet others have aggressively pursued bilateral agreements to maximize the benefits of being the hub in a hub-and-spoke architecture while waiting for the more generic arrangements to come into place.

The five ministerial meetings and the more than fifteen vice-ministerial meetings held to date under the FTAA process have produced an abundance of collateral negotiations among countries and regions. By creating a web of modern trade liberalizing agreements under codes consistent with the principles and rules of the WTO, deeper and wider subregional agreements are an effective way of advancing hemispheric integration. In fact, it is in this subregional-cum-bilateral track where the most tangible and impressive economic integration results in recent years are to be found, not just in terms of agreements on paper, but in terms of actual intraregional growth in trade and investment flows.

WTO Commitments

The FTAA process has also helped focus attention on timely implementation of WTO commitments. For many countries in the Western Hemisphere, the WTO commitments constitute the first set of demanding external trade obligations in their history. As a result of the FTAA experience and associated technical assistance efforts, officials in many countries are now better placed to implement their existing WTO obligations. In turn, the Uruguay Round implementation experience has also led to an increased understanding of the political, economic, and institutional requirements to implement the even stronger disciplines that will be entailed by the FTAA. From this point of view, multilateral and regional negotiations can be seen as synergetic and complementary efforts.

The "Trust Factor" and Other Intangibles

The involvement of more than nine hundred trade officials from thirty-four countries in a continuous dialogue, both in the negotiations and in numerous technical assistance activities, has led to improved communication, mutual knowledge, trust, and good will among a critical mass of trade officials.[10] The phenomenon has been particularly strong at the level of the Trade Negotiations Committee. The process has generated a tremendous amount of familiarity among participants, a much better knowledge of the personalities involved and of the fundamental reasons and nuances that characterize the official positions of each country. As a result each negotiator has a better understanding of the practices, cultural differences, and national technical and political sensitivities that he or she must deal with.

Private Sector Behavior, Competitive Strategies, and Networking

Just as there has been a process of formation and strengthening of a true hemispheric community of trade negotiators, the FTAA process has also generated more confidence and mutual knowledge among the business communities of the hemisphere. Business leaders organized in the multilayered system of chambers of commerce, industry, and services have been participating actively in the annual meetings of the Americas Business Forum and in innumerable business and academic activities to talk about integration, trade, and national policy priorities.

The FTAA process has prompted more business people to think and act globally and hemispherically. It has also increased support and provided a new rationale for economic reform. Most important, it has strengthened the trend toward a new paradigm in the policy dialogue between the business communities and governments in Latin America. The local business sectors have been changing from the old rent-seeking behavior to a new approach focused more on the elimination of economic distortions, improvement of national competitiveness and infrastructure, and investment in education.[11]

The engagement of important segments of the business communities of all countries through the Americas Business Forum and a myriad of other activities generated by the FTAA is also improving business networking and helping to identify and exploit new investment and trade opportunities.

---

10. This phenomenon has been stressed by a number of participants. The previous chair of the Trade Negotiations Committee, Canada's Vice Minister Kathryn McCallion, often pointed to this intangible benefit of the FTAA process in her public speeches.

11. See also Norton (2000).

FTAA, the Summit Process, and Strategic Interdependence

Free trade and economic integration in the Western Hemisphere are propelled not only by an economic rationale; strategic and collective security rationales also motivate trade negotiations. Regional trade negotiations in the Americas take place in a political context that includes collective security definitions, systemic interdependencies embodied in the OAS Inter-American system, and cooperation initiatives with specific institutional architectures at the hemispheric level.[12]

The trade issue is but one initiative, although perhaps the core one, in what is becoming an increasingly institutionalized process of summitry. This process includes twenty-three hemispheric cooperation initiatives; among these are efforts to promote democracy, improve education, eliminate poverty and discrimination, protect human rights, end illegal drug trafficking, combat corruption, and cooperate on environmental and labor issues (box 14-3).

These initiatives are the expression of a strategic agenda for cooperation and interdependence among the countries in the Americas. It is the strategic linkage between components and their simultaneous advance that makes the Summit of the Americas process so attractive and dynamic as a framework for a common hemispheric enterprise in the twenty-first century.

The role of the trade initiative in this broader context is threefold. First, the FTAA process has become a major venue for economic policy engagement between countries in the hemisphere. Second, this engagement for economic integration has become a catalyst for the broader dialogue on democracy, security, and other issues. Third, the FTAA serves as a fundamental piece in the relationship between market development and democratic development that was postulated by the heads of state and government as central to the Summit of the Americas vision. In effect, the FTAA strengthens the mutually reinforcing effects between markets and democracy by promoting economic interdependence, strengthening transparency and accountability principles, harmonizing domestic market regulations in key sectors, and promoting competition in the marketplace. From this point of view, it could be argued that the most important and beneficial "externality" of the FTAA process, beyond the trade area, is precisely the positive influence this rulemaking exercise provides for democratic development and good governance throughout the hemisphere.

12. For more insights into this point, see Dominguez (1999); Franko (2000); Salazar-Xirinachs (2000); and Gaviria (chapter 15 in this volume).

Box 14-3. *Miami Summit of the Americas Plan of Action, 1994*

Following is a listing of the twenty-three cooperative initiatives set out by the thirty-four heads of state and government. Together they form a strategic agenda for cooperation and interdependence among the countries in the Americas.

**Preserving and Strengthening the Community
of Democracies of the Americas**

1. Strengthening democracy
2. Promoting and protecting human rights
3. Invigorating society/community participation
4. Promoting cultural values
5. Combating corruption
6. Combating the problem of illegal drugs and related crimes
7. Eliminating the threat of national and international terrorism
8. Building mutual confidence

**Promoting Prosperity through Economic Integration
and Free Trade**

9. Free trade in the Americas
10. Capital markets development and liberalization
11. Hemispheric infrastructure
12. Energy cooperation
13. Telecommunications and information infrastructure
14. Cooperation in science and technology
15. Tourism

Eradicating Poverty and Discrimination in Our Hemisphere

16. Universal access to education
17. Equitable access to basic health services
18. Strengthening the role of women in society
19. Encouraging microenterprises and small businesses
20. White Helmets—emergency and development corps

**Guaranteeing Sustainable Development and Conserving
Our Natural Environment for Future Generations**

21. Partnership for sustainable energy use
22. Partnership for biodiversity
23. Partnership for pollution prevention.

Outlook for the FTAA Negotiations

Three years after the decision to initiate negotiations, there are grounds to be reasonably optimistic that the FTAA negotiations will conclude successfully by its deadline of 2005. These factors, both internal and external to the negotiations, include the impressive, concrete, and detailed progress achieved so far; the political determination trade ministers expressed in Toronto when they requested that a draft agreement be prepared for the Buenos Aires meeting, and the ability of all the negotiating groups to provide a draft text of their respective chapters in response to this request. The dedication and broad-based participation of the negotiators from all of the participating countries in the FTAA process has ensured that the two initial negotiating phases have gone forward successfully.

Some external developments that could have exercised a dampening influence on the FTAA negotiations have instead turned largely positive and bode well for the immediate future. These developments are the macroeconomic outlook of participating countries; the relationship between a WTO round of new trade negotiations and the FTAA; the ongoing unilateral liberalization and subregional integration efforts by Latin American and Caribbean countries; and the impact of the European Union in the hemisphere.

Macroeconomic instability (exchange rate instability, fiscal imbalances, inflation) and poor economic performance of participating countries are classical obstacles to economic integration projects.[13] Factors causing macroeconomic instability are further complicated by economic downturns. After the economic downturn and instability of 1998–99, which dampened optimism about the FTAA and also strained regional integration arrangements such as MERCOSUR, the majority of Latin American and Caribbean countries have managed to escape the worst of the contagion effects of the Asian and Russian crises and have entered into an economic recovery. Although average rates of growth for the region were only 2.1 percent in 1998 and 0.4 percent in 1999, in 2000 growth rebounded strongly, to 4.0 percent, and the International Monetary Fund predicts that in 2001 the region will grow at an average rate of 4.7 percent.[14] In addition, price stability was one of the main achievements of the 1990s; since 1997 the average inflation rate for the region has been fluctuating

13. Salazar-Xirinachs and Tavares de Araujo (1999).
14. ECLAC (1999, 2000b); International Monetary Fund (2000).

around a historically unprecedented low of 10 percent a year and is expected to remain at this level during 2001.

What is remarkable in all of this is not that the countries of the region were affected by financial contagion, but that they were able to weather the storm, implement effective policy responses, and overcome this economic adversity. Brazil's recovery has been particularly rapid and impressive, with most estimates predicting a period of fast growth and low inflation for 2001. This forecast improves the economic prospects for MERCOSUR in general and is a positive development for the FTAA process given Brazil's critical role as by far the largest economy in the Latin American group. Also remarkable is the continued growth to record levels of foreign direct investment toward the region.[15]

From a longer-term perspective, the economic record of Latin America and the Caribbean during the 1990s has been mixed, and the outcomes of the so-called "first generation" of reforms have fallen short of expectations. Although great strides were achieved in taming inflation, the rate of economic growth has been sluggish in comparison to world patterns. Social indicators on unemployment, income distribution, and poverty did not improve during the 1990s but with some exceptions, actually grew worse. There is a growing consensus that the next generation of reforms must focus more on growth and the poor, with investment in education, health care, and improved governance occupying center stage in the new concerns. This realization and the application of new policy mixes to deliver better social conditions are positive developments for trade negotiations, to the extent that they improve the capacity of the region's economies to deliver improved living standards during the next decade.

The failure of the third WTO Ministerial Meeting in Seattle in December 1999, although undesirable, had positive implications for the FTAA negotiations, confirming the wisdom of pursuing a double-track trade policy at both the multilateral and regional levels.[16] Although agriculture and services negotiations began in 2000 under the WTO, the multilateral negotiating agenda at present is still very limited, particularly compared with that of the FTAA, where participants are negotiating WTO-plus disciplines across the board, including investment, government procurement, and competition policy. Hemispheric negotiations should reflect regional interests more effectively than negotiations could do at the multilateral level, permitting

15. ECLAC (2000a); UNCTAD (2000).
16. Bergsten (2000); Hart (2000).

the realization of deeper hemispheric integration under the FTAA. This will be the case particularly if a global trade round is to be several years in the launching.

Perhaps the strongest and most positive force toward free trade in the Americas and the completion of the FTAA lies in the steady progress countries in the hemisphere have made toward unilateral trade liberalization and deepening of subregional arrangements. Several countries, including Argentina, Bolivia, Chile, Colombia, El Salvador, Guatemala, Peru, and Trinidad and Tobago, have been opening up their economies through unilateral measures, pursuing export-led development and regulatory reform.[17] Many countries have been liberalizing their banking and telecommunications sectors unilaterally or in conjunction with the completion of multilateral negotiations under the WTO. As previous chapters document, the main subregional arrangements (MERCOSUR, the Andean Community, the Central American Common Market, and CARICOM) have continued to deepen their preferential commitments and to expand them to new areas of discipline along the lines of modern "third generation" agreements, consistent with the proposed FTAA agreement. As a result of this growing tissue of modern trade agreements among Latin American and Caribbean countries, reciprocal market access has increased substantially, while trade rules and domestic regulations are converging toward the ultimate objectives of the FTAA.

Finally, the effects of the involvement and growing interest of the European Union (EU) in the Western Hemisphere should not be overlooked. The EU recently finalized a free trade agreement with Mexico and is engaged in negotiations with MERCOSUR and Chile. In addition foreign direct investment of European origin has increased significantly in several countries. As a result, the EU has been expanding its presence in the hemisphere, particularly in financial services, wireless telecommunications, automobiles, retail sales, and distribution.[18] This expansion will exert pressure on U.S. businesses that traditionally have had strong clients in the hemisphere, and it should put additional pressure on the U.S. government to

17. Devlin and Ffrench-Davis (1999, p. 9).

18. The free trade agreement between Mexico and the European Union was signed in Lisbon on March 23, 2000, and entered into force on July 1, 2000 (www.secofi-snci.gob.mx/noticias/lisboa.htm). The text of the agreement is available at (www.secofi-snci.gob.mx/Negociaci_n/Uni_n_Europea/Texto_TLCUE/texto_tlcue.htm). According to the Mexican Ministry of Economy (formerly SECOFI) statistics, foreign direct investment (FDI) from the EU represented 15 percent of Mexico's total FDI in 1999, and total trade between Mexico and the EU has grown by 86 percent since 1991.

increase the priority it gives to concluding the FTAA negotiations and re-storing the president's fast-track negotiating authority.[19]

While the previous four factors seem to play in a favorable direction for the progress of FTAA talks, the influence of other factors, mostly political in nature, is still highly uncertain. A key factor in the course of trade talks in the next few years, both multilateral and regional in the FTAA, is the leadership that the new administration in the United States will be able to provide. This in turn depends on the possibilities of securing fast-track negotiating authority and on the conditions of such authority, particularly regarding the controversial subject of whether to link trade with labor and environmental issues, and if so, how. Securing fast-track authority will send a key signal to all FTAA participants on the seriousness of U.S. intentions to negotiate the free trade agreement in the hemisphere.[20] The lack of fast track has already had repercussions on the U.S. ability to exercise trade leadership in the region, with the inability of the U.S. government to bring Chile into NAFTA as promised. The Clinton administration's two-time failure to obtain fast-track trade negotiating authority from the U.S. Congress has not so far slowed down the FTAA process nor diminished the enthusiasm of other participants in the region, but it has injected a note of caution in the form of "wait and see."[21] MERCOSUR members, in particular, have stated that they will be prepared to negotiate sensitive issues only when the U.S. president has secured fast-track authority.[22] A move forward in this direction in 2001 will most likely deepen the engagement of all the participating countries in the FTAA and will facilitate the completion of the free trade agreement according to planned dates.

Another key reason for caution lies in political developments in Latin America. Several countries in the region are going through difficult times economically and politically. There are major collective efforts in the inter-American system and the summit process to promote and protect democracy in all participating countries, but it is not difficult to imagine scenarios where certain political developments could exert a negative influence on the progress of the FTAA talks.

19. Latin America and the Caribbean account for more than one-fifth of total U.S. exports and thus represent strong clients for U.S. firms.

20. Weintraub (2000).

21. In November 1997 the Clinton administration withdrew the fast track bill from consideration in the House of Representatives, which was almost certain to defeat it. In September 1998, the fast track bill failed in the House vote.

22. See also Weintraub (2000, p.18).

Last is the issue of public opinion. Large and important sectors of civil society have enthusiastically embraced the objectives and vision of the FTAA and have benefited from the increased networking promoted by the FTAA process. Other groups have expressed qualified support, and yet others have expressed strong opposition and concerns. These groups have different visions about globalization and about the role of trade within the general picture of the development challenges and priorities of countries. In recognition of the interests and concerns of civil society, the trade ministers established a formal mechanism to receive and discuss the input of civil society in the FTAA process. The balance of public opinion and the positioning by different groups is another political factor that will influence the capacity of governments to lead and to move ahead in trade.

In conclusion, the FTAA talks have made impressive and detailed progress since they were launched in early 1998. There is still, however, a long distance to traverse between where the negotiations stand now and where they need to be by 2005. The challenge of the next four years will be to maintain the momentum driving the negotiations forward and to continue to narrow the various negotiating positions so that common ground is reached and a clean text is achieved in all areas. Equally important is the need to address the institutional issues that will necessarily accompany the conclusion of an FTAA agreement so that the agreement can become operational. A major change of gear in the process will be the moment countries decide to initiate market access negotiations, for both goods and services.[23]

Provided that the U.S. government obtains fast-track negotiating authority and remains a leader in the process, the existing strong underlying policy consensus in Latin America and the Caribbean should serve to reinforce the momentum and commitment to hemispheric-wide trade liberalization and help to propel the FTAA negotiations toward a successful conclusion in the year 2005 or earlier.

---

23. As of December 2000 countries are engaged in consultations regarding a possible acceleration of the deadline for finalizing negotiations. If the FTAA agreement is to enter into force on January 1, 2005, at least a year will be required for national legislatures to ratify it. This means that the negotiations would need to be finalized in late 2003. This is a "refinement" of the chronology building up to 2005 that has not been specified yet in this degree of detail by ministerial meetings nor summit meetings. If agreed, its effect will be to advance the target date to finalize negotiations to December, 2003.

References

Bergsten, Fred. 2000. "Towards a Tripartite World." *The Economist,* July 15, p. 23.

Devlin, Robert, and Ricardo Ffrench-Davis. 1999. "Towards an Evaluation of Regional Integration in Latin America in the 1990s." *The World Economy* 22 (2): 261.

Devlin, Robert, A. Estevadeordal, and Luis Jorge Garay. 1999. "The FTAA: Some Longer Term Issues." Occasional Paper 5. Inter-American Development Bank, Institute for the Integration of Latin America, Buenos Aires.

Dominguez, Jorge. 1999. *The Future of Inter-American Relations.* Washington, D.C.: Inter-American Dialogue.

ECLAC (Economic Commission for Latin America and the Caribbean). 1999. *Estudio Económico de América Latina y el Caribe 1999-2000.* Santiago.

———. 2000a. *Foreign Investment in Latin America and the Caribbean.* Santiago.

———. 2000b. *Latin America: Summary.* Santiago: ECLAC Economic Projections Center. May.

Franko, Patrice M. 2000. *Toward a New Security Architecture in the Americas: The Strategic Implications of the FTAA.* Washington, D.C.: Center for Strategic and International Studies.

Hart, Michael. 2000. "Reviving Regionalism? Canada, the United States, and the Next Steps to Deeper Economic Integration." In *Seattle, the WTO and the Future of the Multilateral Trading System,* edited by Roger Porter and Pierre Sauvé. Harvard University Press.

Hufbauer, Gary, Jeffrey Schott, and Barbara R. Kotschwar. 1999. "U.S. Interests in Free Trade in the Americas." In *The United States and the Americas: A Twenty-First Century View,* edited by Albert Fishlow and James Jones. Norton.

International Monetary Fund. 2000. *World Economic Outlook, May 2000. Asset Prices and Business Cycle.* Washington D.C.

Norton, Joseph J. 2000. "Doing Business under the FTAA: Reflections of a U.S. Business Lawyer." Prepared for a March 25 conference on the "United States and the Future of Free Trade in the Americas," Edwin L. Cox School of Business, Southern Methodist University, Dallas, Texas.

Salazar-Xirinachs, José M. 2000. *The Trade Agenda in the Context of the Inter-American System.* OAS Trade Unit Studies. Washington, D.C.

Salazar-Xirinachs, José Manuel, and Eduardo Lizano. 1992. "Free Trade in the Americas: A Latin American Perspective." In *The Premise and the Promise: Free Trade in the Americas,* edited by Sylvia Saborio and contributors. New Brunswick, N.J.: Transactions Publishers.

Salazar-Xirinachs, José Manuel, and José Tavares de Araujo. 1999. "The Free Trade Area of the Americas: A Latin American Perspective." In *The World Economy: Global Trade Policy 1999,* edited by Peter Lloyd and Chris Milner. Oxford, U.K.: Blackwell Publishers.

Salicrup, Luis, and Gisela Vergara. 2000. *Trade Policy Education in the Western Hemisphere: An Assessment of Demand and Supply.* Washington, D.C.: OAS Trade Unit/U.S. Agency for International Development.

UNCTAD (United Nations Conference on Trade and Development). 2000. *World Investment Report.* Geneva.

Weintraub, Sidney. 1999. *Technical Cooperation Needs for Hemispheric Trade Negotiations.* Washington, D.C.: Organization of American States and Inter-American Council for Integral Development.

————. 2000. "The Meaning of NAFTA and Its Implication for the FTAA." Prepared for a March 25 conference on "The United States and the Future of Free Trade in the Americas," Edwin L. Cox School of Business, Southern Methodist University, Dallas, Texas.

CÉSAR GAVIRIA

15 Integration and Interdependence in the Americas

A s the twenty-first century begins, economic and political relations among countries of the American hemisphere are marked by a complex web of interdependencies much more profound and sophisticated than any that existed in the past.

The phenomenon of interdependence has many facets. With the new technological and productive trends brought about by globalization, including the growing mobility of goods, services, capital, technology, and even people, relying solely on macroeconomic and quantitative indicators to assess interdependence would be a mistake. Although it might at first glance appear paradoxical, the rationale for economic integration is not strictly economic. When leaders of the hemisphere met at the Summit of the Americas in Miami in December 1994 and launched the initiative to create the Free Trade Area of the Americas, they situated this initiative in the context of a broad, strategic vision, as part of the collective effort to improve and strengthen democracy, to reduce poverty and discrimination in the hemisphere, and to promote sustainable development. When governments commit themselves to negotiating clear, transparent, binding, and predictable rules in the area of trade or finance, they do so for economic reasons, of course, but also for a series of domestic political, strategic, and developmental reasons and interests. Striking a balance among these different objectives is one of the greatest challenges facing the inter-American system, and a key ingredient in the creation of the Free Trade Area of the Americas.

This chapter offers an overview of this broader context in which the trade negotiations are taking place. By simplifying this complex reality somewhat for analytical purposes, we may distinguish three dimensions to the structures and activities that promote interdependence among countries of the Americas: the economic dimension, the legal and regulatory dimension, and the diplomatic and strategic dimension. This chapter examines the new hemispheric realities that pertain to each of these three dimensions and argues that the creation of the Free Trade Area of the Americas is a natural and positive step toward consolidating the economic, political, and strategic interdependence of the American hemisphere.

Economic Interdependence

Since the 1980s, and especially during the 1990s, the countries of Latin America and the Caribbean have made a fundamental shift in their development policies, revising the roles of the state and the market and adopting an ever greater degree of integration into the regional and world economy as the route for pursuing economic growth. The first steps taken in this new direction by most countries included unilateral trade liberalization and the reorientation of subregional trade agreements toward what the Economic Commission for Latin America and the Caribbean has very appropriately called "open regionalism." Between 1985 and 1997 the average tariff level in this region declined from 35 percent to 12 percent. Other important steps have been active participation in the multilateral trading system by countries of the hemisphere, all but one of which have become members of the World Trade Organization, and the proactive negotiation of a "new generation" of free trade agreements that cover new areas of discipline, such as competition policies, investment, intellectual property rights, and dispute settlement mechanisms, and new sectors, such as services.

To these new policies one must add the impact of new business strategies made possible by the revolution in information and communication technologies and in transportation. With telecommunications and transport costs falling, productive processes and "value chains" have been broken up and portions relocated around the world, foreign direct investment has taken on new impetus, and new opportunities and niches for exploiting comparative advantage have opened up for many countries.

The mutual reinforcement between technological trends and economic policy has accelerated the processes of economic change and interdependence in the Americas. This has meant, for all countries of Latin America and the Caribbean, a steady increase in the weight of exports relative to their gross domestic product: exports represented 12.4 percent of Latin America's gross domestic product in 1990, but they accounted for 18.9 percent only eight years later.[1] This overall Latin American trend is reflected in the indexes that relate aggregate trade in goods to the GDP of each country (exports + imports/GDP). In all countries of the hemisphere, including the United States and Canada, this ratio has increased, indicating the growing importance of international trade as a stimulus to economic growth in all countries.[2]

Which export markets have been most important to the growing export dynamism of Latin America and the Caribbean?

Figure 15-1 provides an answer. During the ten years between 1988 and 1998, the highest growth rate in Latin American and Caribbean exports overall was for shipments to the United States (14 percent), followed by those to other partners within Latin America and the Caribbean (13 percent). In other words, increasing international trade has implied ever closer relationships and interdependence among the countries of the American hemisphere. Although important in absolute terms, especially for the countries of MERCOSUR (Common Market of the South), trade with Europe did not perform as dynamically in this decade as did trade with the United States and within Latin America.

This growing hemispheric interdependence finds itself accentuated in each of the subregional integration processes. Here again, the importance of intraregional trade as a proportion of total trade has generally been increasing (see chapter 2). The value of intraregional exports within countries of the Latin American Integration Association (ALADI) has grown steadily to the point where such exports account for 19 percent of the region's total exports. For the three parties to the North American Free Trade Agreement (NAFTA), intraregional exports represent more than 50 percent of total exports, and for MERCOSUR (the Common Market of the South), this figure stands at 25 percent.

One fundamental structural change relates to the makeup of countries' "export portfolio." Figure 15-2 shows that the importance of primary

1. ECLAC (1999, p. 74).
2. World Bank (2000).

Figure 15-1. *Growth of Latin America and Caribbean Exports to the Region's Main Trading Partners, 1988–98*

Percent

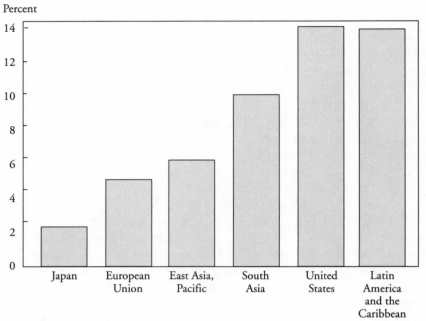

Source: World Bank, 2000.

products, which accounted for more than 80 percent of Latin American and Caribbean exports in 1980, had declined to less than 40 percent by 1998, whereas manufactured products increased their share from less than 20 percent to more than 60 percent during the same period. Given the economic vulnerability associated with dependence on primary product exports (for the well-known reasons of price volatility and deteriorating terms of trade), this diversification into industrial products must be interpreted as an improvement in the quality of the export portfolio and, hence, in the international presence of Latin American and Caribbean countries. Clearly, this aggregate trend conceals great discrepancies in the status of individual countries, and for most countries, in particular the smaller economies, the vulnerability and lack of diversification of their exports continues to be a severe problem, and one of their major challenges.

At the same time, services have been of increasing importance to economies of the Western Hemisphere. This sector is of enormous weight

Figure 15-2. *Latin America and the Caribbean: Exports by Sector*
(as percent of total FOB export value)

Percent

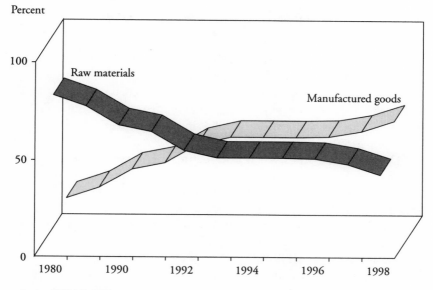

Source: ECLAC, 1999.

in the GDP of small island economies of the Caribbean and exceeds 75
percent of GDP in the United States and Canada. For all countries of
Latin America and the Caribbean, the output of services as a percentage
of GDP has increased during the 1990s, and although service exports as
a proportion of total exports have grown more slowly than those of goods,
they have increased steadily since 1985 and are particularly important
for a few countries where exports of services now exceed 50 percent of
total exports.[3]

   In conclusion, as economies have become more open to trade and globalization, there has been a simultaneous trend toward greater interdependence and reciprocal importance as trading partners among the economies
of the hemisphere. Moreover, for Latin America and the Caribbean as a
whole, the quality of the export portfolio has improved, with a highly significant increase in the relative weight of industrial products and services
as a share of total exports, a factor that is essential for reducing external

   3. Prieto and Stephenson (1999).

vulnerability, developing sustainable competitive advantages, and, in general, improving the quality of growth.

The Legal and Regulatory Dimension

A second sphere where there is growing interdependence among the countries of the Americas can be appreciated in the multiplicity of new trade and integration agreements that have been signed during the 1990s and in the revival and strengthening of some that existed earlier. The integration map has changed profoundly since the pioneering efforts of the 1960s and 1970s.

During the early postwar period, Latin American countries sought to reduce their dependence on commodity exports and the import of manufactured goods. Their economic policies were designed to promote a home-grown industrial base, through a model of import substitution. Tariff and nontariff barriers were set up to protect infant industries against international competition. In such a setting efforts to encourage economic integration among countries of the region were based on preferential trade liberalization schemes as an instrument for sustaining the industrial development so eagerly sought by Latin American countries. It was hoped that regional integration, by broadening markets and taking advantage of economies of scale and specialization, would help to offset the inefficiencies inherent in highly protected and restricted markets. This was the path followed with the Central American Common Market in 1960, the Andean Pact (today the Andean Community of Nations) in 1969, and the Caribbean Community and Common Market (CARICOM) in 1973.

In the mid-1980s and early 1990s Latin American countries were compelled to abandon the old economic model as they struggled to cope with the financial constraints sparked by the severe external debt crisis. During this time several reforms were launched to liberalize trade, to ease restrictions on foreign investment, to rationalize state enterprises, to liberalize and privatize financial systems, and to deregulate certain economic activities.

The recognition that it was essential to adopt a more dynamic pattern of integration into the increasingly globalized international marketplace led Latin American countries to reduce their trade barriers unilaterally, to revive existing trade and integration agreements, and to negotiate new agreements that would go beyond reducing tariffs in selected sectors. The preferential trade liberalization approach began to evolve into a context of open regionalism. What was now at stake was to ensure that policies for promoting regional integration were compatible with and complementary to policies for fostering international competitiveness.[4]

Thus, during the 1990s countries in the Americas have signed fourteen trade and integration agreements, including the two association agreements that MERCOSUR signed with Bolivia and Chile. Ten of these agreements are already in force; the remaining four are in the process of ratification by legislatures. In addition, negotiations are under way on eight other agreements (see table 1-1 in chapter 1).

These new agreements are compatible with the disciplines of the WTO. The objectives are to expand trade among the signatories without raising barriers to third countries and to serve, in fact, as a stimulus to a more open world market. The tariff-cutting programs that these agreements call for address the very essence of commercial exchanges and are consistent with the requirements of multilateral trading rules, including their time-bound implementation schedules.

Yet these agreements go well beyond the traditional model of a free trade agreement. They include provisions for liberalizing trade in services and the treatment of investments and, in many cases, the protection of intellectual property rights. All of these are issues that less than a decade ago were inconceivable as items for trade negotiations and for which no multilateral trading rules existed.

The new trade agreements hold important implications for the integration process in this hemisphere. In the first place, there is now a greater degree of legal and regulatory interdependence among the countries of the Americas. Not only do they share the disciplines of the multilateral trading system, they are also bound by a growing network of agreements, as we have seen in detail in earlier chapters, that include common rules in such areas as services, investment, technical standards, intellectual property, and competition policy—all areas that are key to development prospects of each country in the hemisphere. In the second place, the commitments assumed under the regional agreements have generated a liberalizing momentum that will result in more open markets even if no new agreements are negotiated (however improbable that appears). In fact, the tariff-cutting schedules already in place have set the stage for automatic tariff reductions that will have a major impact on liberalizing and stimulating regional trade during this first decade of the twenty-first century. All of this will lead to deeper integration among the countries of the Americas. The project

4. ECLAC (1994, p. 12).

to establish an FTAA should be seen, therefore, as a natural consequence of this process, and one that will at the same time reinforce it.

The Diplomatic and Strategic Dimension

Economic integration in the Western Hemisphere has not only an economic justification, but also a collective security rationale and a political and strategic purpose. Regional trade negotiations take place in political contexts of systemic interdependence, collective approaches to security, and cooperative initiatives among potential partners, where there are institutional instruments at the service of member states.

The new reality in which hemispheric relations are unfolding is characterized by, among other elements, the end of the cold war, the predominance of representative democracy, and the opening of national economies. In effect, the place that was once occupied by the cold war has today been taken by a new political agenda focused on consolidating democracy, respect for human rights, sustainable development, integration, and cooperation.

The fact that representative democracies exist in virtually the entire hemisphere, having replaced the authoritarian regimes of earlier times, has created a close link between the promotion of open political systems and the drive for open economies. From this perspective, the signature of trade agreements with clear, stable, transparent, and binding rules, accompanied by negotiated mechanisms for dispute settlement, may be seen as an important component of the new concepts of national and hemispheric security based on the rule of law and on an international society where legality is respected.

The FTAA was conceived from the beginning as part of a broader effort at rapprochement, one that was not limited to exclusively commercial aspects. This broader vision can be found in the Declaration of Principles and Plan of Action of the Summit of the Americas. The summit process has laid down the guiding principles for hemispheric relations and FTAA negotiations:

—Preserving and strengthening the community of democracies in the Americas.

—Promoting prosperity through economic integration and free trade.

—Eradicating poverty and discrimination from the hemisphere.

—Guaranteeing sustainable development and preserving the environment for future generations.

The corresponding agenda for cooperation was initially structured into twenty-three specific initiatives that were launched at the Miami Summit of the Americas in December 1994 and were reinforced by the Santiago Summit in 1998. The agenda also has specific institutional mechanisms relating to policy, administration, and implementation. These mechanisms include a presidential summit to be held every three years; country coordinators responsible for each of the twenty-three initiatives; a horizontal ministerial system of cooperation and coordination in each of the key areas; and a summit follow-up process in which the Summit Implementation Review Group and the Organization of American States (OAS) have an essential role. The summit process, moreover, has an institutional support structure involving a series of inter-American bodies, such as the OAS, the Inter-American Development Bank, the Economic Commission for Latin America and the Caribbean, the Pan-American Health Organization, the Inter-American Institute for Agricultural Cooperation, and others, depending on the specific area.

A further and no less important element of the diplomatic and strategic interdependence in which the creation of the FTAA is being approached is that its future members are already parties to a set of principles, rules, and legal and diplomatic instruments within the inter-American system, including practical measures of cooperation for the protection, defense, and promotion of democracy and human rights. In fact, as specifically mentioned in the summit declarations, the creation of the FTAA is based on the existence of a community of democracies in the Americas and on a convergence of political, economic, and social values. In light of the existing rules and mechanisms for collective action, this is more than a mere rhetorical point. Specifically, within the inter-American system, and in the context of the Organization of American States, countries have adopted multilateral procedures and instruments for collective action to deal with problems that arise when the democratic constitutional order breaks down.[5]

These procedures include OAS Resolution 1080, adopted in 1991 and known as the "Representative Democracy" resolution, which establishes a procedure for collective, immediate, and multilateral action to protect democracy in any member state where the regular institutional and political process has been interrupted. They also include a new article in the Statutes of the OAS (Article 9, in force since September 1997), which allows for suspension or exclusion from OAS activities of any government of a

5. For a full review and analysis of these mechanisms see Perina (2000).

member state that did not take office through a democratic process or that seized power through the use of force. It is also interesting to note that MERCOSUR contains a "democratic clause" according to which only democratic regimes are eligible for association. The inter-American system thus already has a number of multilateral mechanisms for exerting positive influence in the cause of protecting, defending, and promoting democracy and human rights, and the creation of the FTAA is expected to reinforce those mechanisms.

A further characteristic element of hemispheric relations is the coexistence of large and small economies. The challenge that the FTAA faces in the integration of small and relatively less-developed economies is a particularly important issue in hemispheric dialogue, one that goes well beyond the purely commercial sphere. Although, when looked at in strictly economic terms of market size, more than 90 percent of the combined FTAA market is accounted for by the three members of NAFTA and two members of MERCOSUR, the FTAA concept includes the other twenty-nine countries of the hemisphere as well. And just as the FTAA idea will never become reality without Brazil or Mexico, the same can be said with respect to the Caribbean or Central America or the countries of the Andean Community.

Facilitating the integration of small economies is not only an economic challenge, it is also an objective in which trade and other items on the hemispheric cooperation agenda interact closely in the search for integral and sustainable development. The creation of the FTAA is in fact part of a broader framework for hemispheric cooperation, in which parallel efforts are being undertaken in areas relating to integration and economic development. Thus, for example, under the heading of "Promoting Prosperity through Economic Integration and Free Trade," the Declaration of Principles and Plan of Action of Miami contains six initiatives that complement the FTAA in the economic area. These are

—development and liberalization of capital markets
—infrastructure
—energy cooperation
—telecommunications and information infrastructure
—science and technology cooperation
—tourism.

Thus, although from a conceptual viewpoint it is clear that development requires trade and financial flows alike, as well as nonreimbursable assistance flows, and although all these are components of the Summit

Plan of Action, in practice the trade and financial initiatives are organized in parallel tracks.

Nevertheless, there is a fundamental difference between trade and the other initiatives. Whereas the trade agreement will take the form of a legally binding contract, most of the other initiatives consist of efforts at cooperation and voluntary commitments to provide bilateral and multilateral funding and assistance. This fundamental difference serves to emphasize the importance of maintaining a political commitment to the overall strategic alliance that the summit process represents.

As a general point, the very fact of being part of the broader strategic agenda for hemispheric cooperation as defined in the summit process and of the legal architecture of the inter-American system offers in itself a basis for creating, justifying, or rationalizing the FTAA, and for generating support for it—something that is not available in the multilateral context.[6]

The FTAA: A Natural Step Forward

This chapter has argued that greater integration and economic interdependence among the countries of the American Hemisphere will emerge from a series of forces that, if current trends continue, will be mutually reinforcing. These include productive and entrepreneurial forces, government policies that not only have opened economies, but have bound them more closely into an ever-broader fabric of common rules and disciplines, as well as a strategic rationale based on shared values and new concepts of national and collective security.

In light of these trends and forces, the creation of the FTAA may be seen as a natural step toward the establishment of a common prescriptive framework based on strengthening and deepening market systems and consolidating democratic societies and the rule of law and as a means of supporting national development agendas. This is a highly ambitious undertaking, however, and many obstacles remain to be resolved before the current negotiations can reach their conclusion.

The process has advanced much further than is generally recognized and has done so in singularly difficult times. Despite the volatility of capital markets, financial contagion, low commodity prices, and recessions that

6. For a further examination of this argument and an exploration of these opportunities, see Salazar-Xirinachs (2000).

have affected Latin American and Caribbean countries, particularly during 1998 and 1999, the FTAA negotiating process has remained very active. In the past even lesser problems might have been enough to scuttle the process. It will be recalled that the traditional recipe for resolving an exchange crisis was to raise tariffs or ban imports, or both. Yet in the difficult circumstances of the 1998–99 crisis not one country reneged on its integration commitments.

On the contrary, those crises demonstrated the positive effects of interdependence and cooperation. Each of them in turn has shown how important external assistance can be in overcoming difficulties and restoring the confidence of nervous investors, while governments and business have recognized that integration commitments serve to maintain the rules of the game and to create a climate of institutional stability that is indispensable for overcoming a crisis swiftly and returning to a growth path.

Despite adverse macroeconomic developments during the first two years of negotiations, the FTAA process has moved ahead satisfactorily. The most important obstacles to progress in negotiations at this time are not so much technical as political. As the negotiations move toward the 2005 target date, their success will be determined by such factors as the ability of the U.S. president to obtain congressional "fast-track" authorization, the prospects for reaching consensus on the treatment of environmental and labor issues in hemispheric dialogue, and the positioning and activism of civil society for or against the FTAA idea. Moreover, some of the principal factors determining the course and speed of the negotiations will be related to what happens outside, not within, Latin America. One of those factors is the stability and growth of the world economy. Experience teaches that macroeconomic stability is a key ingredient of any integration process. The absence of any further crisis that might spill over into Latin America and a satisfactory growth performance on the part of its major trading partners would do much to sustain a climate conducive to successful negotiations.

References

ECLAC (UN Economic Commission for Latin America and the Caribbean). 1994. *Open Regionalism in Latin America and the Caribbean.* Santiago.
———. 1999. *Statistical Yearbook for Latin America and the Caribbean 1998.* Santiago.
Perina, Rubén. 2000. "The Inter-American Democratic System: The Role of the OAS." Unit for the Promotion of Democracy, OAS. Washington, D.C.

Prieto, Francisco Javier, and Stephenson, Sherry. 1999. "Liberalization of Trade in Services." In *Trade Rules in the Making: Challenges in Regional and Multilateral Negotiations,* edited by Miguel Rodríguez, Patrick Low, and Barbara Kotschwar. Brookings/Organization of American States.

Salazar-Xirinachs, José M. 2000. "The Trade Agenda in the Context of the Inter-American System." OAS Trade Unit Studies. Washington, D.C.

World Bank. 2000. *World Development Indicators.* Washington, D.C.

Index

Sanitary and Phytosanitary Measures, 141, 145; commitments by Western Hemisphere countries, 292, 298, 304; investment issues, 189–91; Seattle Ministerial Meeting (*1999*), 297; transparency in government procurement, 247. *See also* Agreement on Technical Barriers to Trade; Agreement on Trade-Related Aspects of Intellectual Property Rights; Agreement on Trade-Related Investment Measures; General Agreement on Trade in Services

World Trade Organization, Dispute Settlement Understanding (DSU): assisted settlement, 264; compared to subregional agreements, 257; consultations, 263, 264; government procurement disputes, 247; initiation of cases, 262; intellectual property rights disputes, 208; nullification or impairment complaints, 268; perceived shortcomings, 257; standards-related cases, 141, 144, 160

WPPT. *See* World Intellectual Property Organization

WTO. *See* World Trade Organization

YPF (petroleum company), 38